ROUNDED UP

ROUNDED UP

Artificial Terrorists and
Muslim Entrapment After 9/11

By

Shamshad Ahmad

Rounded Up: Artificial Terrorists and Muslim Entrapment After 9/11
Copyright © 2009 by Shamshad Ahmad

First edition of 1,000 copies printed in the United States of America

Book and cover design by Melissa Mykal Batalin

The Troy Book Makers • Troy, New York 12180 • www.thetroybookmakers.com

ISBN 978-1-9345534-174

*This book is dedicated to the members of the
Muslim Solidarity Committee (MSC) and its sister
organizations that promote freedom and justice:
essentially non-Muslim activists, intellectuals,
and peace-loving, justice-seeking humanitarians who
care for the freedom and liberty of all and who have come
forward openly to defend the rights of American Muslims
at a time when they are too frightened to defend themselves.
It is with their blessing that I wrote the following pages.*

Acknowledgements

A Muslim's thanks must always begin by thanking his Lord; I thank the Almighty with my fullest capacity.

My profound thanks are due to Mr. Steve Downs, Esq., who suggested that I write this book and then pushed me to do it. One day, after Aref and Hossain's conviction and sentencing, he told me, "You are uniquely qualified to write a book on this subject with a Muslim's perspective. Being a mosque leader, you are involved with the affairs of the Muslim community on a daily basis, and you have also witnessed this case first-hand, from beginning to middle to end." I had thought a few times about writing a book on this topic, but never took the initiative, thinking that since I was not a writer, I would not be able to do the job; Steve's suggestion gave me incentive and strength. During the writing of the book, he went through the whole manuscript and offered both suggestions and corrections.

Ms. Kathy Manley, Esq. offered me many tapes, documents, manuscripts, court recordings, etc., to facilitate my writing. She also went through the whole manuscript and corrected several legal and factual discrepancies.

Ms. Jeanne Finley did a painstaking editing of the manuscript, which included reorganization of some material, linguistic editing, and assembling the manuscript into its final book form.

I received help from other individuals and organizations as well. I wish to thank them all without mentioning them by name.

Table of Contents

Introduction

I am the founder and president of a small mosque, the Masjid As-Salam, in Albany, New York. In 2003–2004, the mosque was the scene of an FBI "sting" operation that targeted our imam (prayer leader), Yassin Aref, and another mosque member, Mohammed Hossain, and that ultimately led to their arrest, trial, and conviction on terror-related charges. These events also terrorized the Capital District's Muslim community and tore the larger community apart. How and why this political tragedy happened is the subject of this book; perhaps my perspective as the mosque's founder, as an immigrant and U.S. citizen, and as a Muslim will be valuable to you, the reader, for your understanding of not only the ramifications of this complicated series of events, but of the hundreds of other cases of Muslim persecution nationwide since September 11, 2001.

I was born on July 18, 1947 in northern India, in a Muslim village of approximately 200 families called Bandi Kalan in district Azamgarh in the state of Uttar Pradesh (U.P.) The village's public elementary school principal, who was a family friend, convinced my father to change my date of birth, and he entered it in the school register as March 12, 1951. So that became my "official" date of birth. I had spent a few years in a Qur'anic school, and the principal thought that my true age might be a hindrance for academic competition later on, since many benefits were denied to students who could not complete their grades by a certain age. Somehow I finished all the elementary school grades in two years, so perhaps the "moving forward" of my birth date was unnecessary. It helps me most of the time, though, as I usually feel four years younger than I really am.

Almost all the residents of Bandi Kalan were farmers or landowners. Between the villages there were vast areas of land divided into small farms that the villagers owned and cultivated. Bandi Kalan did not have electricity until 1986. Almost all of its 200 houses were close together, separated by narrow streets. The houses were not numbered; everyone knew everyone else. Once, long after I had left it for good, I visited Bandi Kalan with my son, Faisal, who was about seven years old at the time. I asked him, "What is the most surprising thing you see here?" His answer was another question: "Daddy, how come all these people know you personally?" Faisal had seen hundreds of people from Bandi Kalan, as well as from neighboring villages, come to meet and greet me. I was their "favorite boy" who had honored them by climbing the ladder of education all the way up to become the first in the village to obtain a Ph.D.

Only six families in my village were Hindus; three of them were grocers, and the other three were washermen who provided washing services to the whole village. All the other villages surrounding Bandi Kalan were Hindu, with no Muslim families in them. This is the case in some parts of India: very few villages have mixed populations, but towns and cities do, with Muslims in the minority in varying ratios. There are hardly any Christians in most of northern India; the first time I ever met a Christian was in my university hostel in Aligarh. On the other hand, my small village had four mosques. Unlike the custom in Western or some Middle Eastern countries, Muslim women in India never attend a mosque. But there were four *madrasas* (Muslim religious schools) in Bandi Kalan, two for girls and two for boys, which were supported by the community, in addition to the one public elementary school that I attended, which was financed by the state government.

After finishing my early education in the local schools, I attended Aligarh Muslim University in the city of Aligarh, about 500 miles from my hometown. This university with 28,000 students, founded in 1878 by a pro-English Islamic scholar and activist, Sir Syed Ahmad Khan, is a very special place for Indian Muslims. It is a modern residential university financed by the federal government of India. After obtaining a Bachelor of Science (Honors), a Master of Science, and a Master of Philosophy in physics there, I traveled to Australia in December 1975 to study for a Ph.D. The Australian National University of Canberra offered me a very attractive scholarship, a generous monthly stipend, a two-bedroom apartment, and return airfare, which included my family. I had married in 1968; my son Sajid was five, and my daughter Huma was only six months old at the time.

My three and a half years in Canberra were the best years of my life. Facilities at the university were vast. Libraries, computers, and lab equipment were the most modern and state-of-the-art. Australians claim that Canberra is the neatest city in the world—neat physically, as well as "neat" or free from any sort of crime. The city had been built to be the capital of Australia, and was constructed from scratch on a hilly area according to a sophisticated plan. The Australian Parliament House stands next to the waters of Lake Burley, a man-made lake.

However, a mosque built and managed by five foreign Muslim countries was an extra blessing. The Muslim community in Canberra at that time consisted only of staff members from some of the foreign embassies and of graduate students from the university, most of whom were from Southeast Asian countries (none from the Middle East). There were a few other Muslim residents either doing business or employed in the city. I could not find any Muslim undergraduate students. Despite this, I founded a chapter of the Muslim Students Association (MSA), but not many were interested in it.

Once I completed my Ph.D. in physics in May 1979, I made the important decision to accept a post-doctoral research position at the State University of New York (SUNY) at Albany, the capital of New York State. This meant that my family and I would have to relocate to the U.S. However, my youngest son, Faisal, was born on May 7, and we had to wait until June 6, when he and his mother were strong enough to travel, to depart. After spending a few weeks in India, we landed in Albany on July 2, 1979.

Compared with today, Albany was a small, sleepy town in 1979. I had expected it to be on a par with Canberra, but with many rundown houses and some dirty neighborhoods I found the city disappointing. The total Muslim population in the city was almost non-existent, only about forty families in the whole area; today there are at least 2,000 families, and the number of businesses—mostly small stores— owned by Muslims in Albany is about 100. The number of Muslim students at SUNY at that time was about two dozen, consisting of foreign graduate students from various Middle Eastern and Southeast Asian countries; today there are about 200 Muslim students, the majority of them American-born children of the parents (like me) who immigrated to the U.S. in the Seventies and Eighties.

Before I left Australia, I had obtained information that a new mosque just outside the Albany city limits, called the Islamic Center of the Capital District (ICCD), would be inaugurated soon. I participated in this event on July 4, 1979, two days after I arrived in the U.S. Only about thirty-five people, including TV and newspaper reporters, were present, although the opening was portrayed as a big news event in the media. The general public and the media had started taking an interest in Muslim affairs because of the Iranian Islamic revolution that dominated the news earlier in the year. The pro-American dictator, the Shah of Iran, had been deposed and exiled, Iran had become an Islamic theocratic republic, and it was something new to talk about.

I became a very active member of the ICCD from the day it opened. I organized the graduate students on the SUNY campus and laid the foundation for a SUNY chapter of the Muslim Students Association in September 1979, even though I was not a student. There were no undergraduate Muslim students at all. The purpose of establishing an MSA chapter was to cater to the social and religious needs of the students. For the next ten years, its role would be only to conduct Friday prayers on campus and have occasional social meetings. But by the late Eighties, children of the first generation of Muslims living in the U.S. were ready to attend college, and they began to establish MSA chapters on most U.S. campuses. In recent years, the MSA of SUNY Albany has been very active, and the majority of active members has been the female students.

However, many students from the Middle East have been hesitant to participate actively in MSA activities due to fear of their governments back home, since many tyrannical rulers and dictators of the Middle East see anything Islamic as dangerous. Usually it is the Islamists who have demanded the removal of these dictators, to change the countries into democracies or into Islamic republics. But the U.S. State Department has always helped these dictators keep themselves in power. The Bush-Cheney Administration has been a particularly big blessing to these tyrants, who deprive their people of every blessing the modern world enjoys, treat them with an iron hand, and tell the administration that they are doing these things to control "Islamic fundamentalism." Thus the ties and friendships between the Bush Administration and these tyrants grow exponentially. Hundreds of millions of people, myself included, cannot understand why Bush wants to sacrifice American blood and dollars to try and establish democracy in Iraq, for example, when at the same time the U.S. does not even offer lip service to democratize any of the countries ruled by other ruthless dictators. I sincerely pray to the Almighty for guidance for the people of America who, after seeing all this, are still singing in defense of Bush.

In peace,
Shamshad Ahmad
Albany, New York

Foreword

In the spring of 2006, I decided to become involved in the terrorism case of *United States of America* v. *Yassin Aref*. I had read about the case in the newspapers, and talked with the defense lawyers, and there seemed to be something wrong with the charges. The allegations of terrorism, coming out of a government sting operation that had swept up Aref and his co-defendant, Mohammed Hossain, simply did not make sense to me. So, as an attorney retired from a State of New York job with time on my hands, I volunteered to assist attorney Terry Kindlon, who was representing Aref, with the defense. One of my first assignments was to meet with Shamshad Ahmad, the president of the Masjid As-Salam mosque, where Aref had been the imam until his arrest.

Shamshad is a small, compact, bearded man with a luminous smile who teaches physics at the University at Albany/SUNY and devotes a great deal of his spare time to the mosque that he's helped establish for the small but growing Muslim community in Albany. Since I had spent two years in India in the Peace Corps during the 1960s, we had a common point of reference, and we quickly formed a bond of friendship. I have found Shamshad to be a wonderful blend of religion and science—a person who carefully analyzes data and speaks only when he is absolutely sure of his conclusions, yet is anchored by his faith against being blown about by every ill wind that sends others flying in all directions. His demeanor is extremely modest and simple, to such an extent that only after some months of knowing him did I realize the depth of his accomplishments and his influence in the community. In the tragedy of the criminal convictions that followed the trial of Aref and Hossain, I, like others, quickly came to recognize Shamshad as the one who best understood the motivations of those who had brought the charges, as well as the one who could best get at the truth of what had really occurred. His love of the United States was apparent in everything he did, but it was softened by a sadness that his adopted country would turn on his own religious community (and on him), abandon its firm commitment to justice and the rule of law, and substitute manipulations, lies, trickery, and deceit in order to convict two innocent Muslims and throw the whole Muslim community into turmoil—a pattern common to many Muslim communities nationwide. It is apparent that Shamshad, coming from a third world country and having very high regard for the stand of Western countries on freedom, fairness, and justice, feels very disturbed when he sees the blatant erosion of these values by the Bush Administration.

Eventually I came to understand that Aref was targeted by the government because he was "suspicious"—he might present a danger in the post-9/11 atmosphere. In the Bush Administration, which insisted that the FBI and the Justice Department follow a new paradigm of preventing terrorist attacks before they occurred, any Muslim who was "suspicious" needed to be targeted and incarcerated. It was a sort of "preventive conviction," in which the "suspicious" person would be convicted of a crime before he would have an opportunity to commit the crime. (The government justified this new paradigm by saying, in effect, "What would you have us do—sit on our hands until the next 9/11?" without explaining how, under American law, someone could legally be convicted without having committed a crime.) In Aref's case, the vehicle for the conviction was a sting operation ostensibly designed to entrap him in a fake terrorist plot run by the government—but in fact, so little information was given to Aref that it would have been impossible for him to understand that anything illegal was intended. It was a frame-up designed to eliminate a "suspicious" person while at the same time send a warning to the Muslim community—and a reassuring message to the rest of the country—that the government was hard at work rooting out terrorists.

In the months before the trial, I became immersed in trial preparation. I read through many hours of sting tape transcripts. I pored over translations (from languages that I did not know) of exotic documents (from places in the Middle East that I was only vaguely aware of). I interviewed dozens of immigrant members of the mosque, most of whom were going through the "immigrant experience" with a foot in two cultures. I helped draft legal papers to try and unseal the secret evidence that the government was showing to the judge on a regular basis. I spoke to Aref several times a week for months and sat through the presentation of evidence in court. And so, after Aref and Hossain were convicted and the appeal was filed, I would have said that I knew the case about as well as anyone—and yet, until I read this book, I did not realize how much of the case I had missed or misunderstood.

Rounded Up takes the same case that I believed I understood so well and tells it from Shamshad's point of view as a Muslim and as president of the mosque. During jury selection, the defense lawyers asked prospective jurors if they could view the evidence dispassionately—as though a Mr. Smith or a Mr. McDonald who lived next door were on trial, rather than two Muslim immigrants. The jurors, almost all white and none of them Muslims, said that they could. But in fact, looking at the grainy surveillance videos of Middle Eastern men discussing politics in foreign languages, referring repeatedly to Islamic religious ideas, and discussing their experiences in foreign countries before coming to America, it would have been almost impossible for the jury to see these defendants as McDonald or Smith, their next-door neighbors. The jurors, by their own admission on the jury questionnaires, knew almost nothing about Islam or the Middle East. Even I, a defense lawyer who had lived in India for two years, had difficulty following all the nuances of language and culture that permeated the trial. The government brilliantly exploited this perception gap by introducing mistranslations of conversations and documents taken out of context to create a highly inaccurate and prejudicial picture of the defendants and their culture. The prosecution even called in an "expert" on terrorism and the Middle East who had virtually no knowledge of his subject except what he had learned on the Internet, mostly from the government's own counterterrorism sites. The fact that no crime was ever committed was lost in the fear that strange men from foreign countries were actually talking about God and politics right here in America!

In this book, Shamshad, with a foot solidly in both cultures, is able to explain how this miscarriage of justice occurred. He *could* see the defendants as the Muslim equivalent of Smith and McDonald, they *were* his next-door neighbors, and so he can explain how their actions, their conversations, and their perceptions were perfectly natural and innocent to them while appearing suspicious and sinister to Westerners. Neither defendant ever said anything to indicate any interest or involvement in radical Islam or terrorism, nor had either defendant, both of whom were well known in the Muslim community, ever been involved in such activity. The only criminal activity was suggested by the government "instigator," who did so in such a way that the defendants were unlikely to understand that they were being involved in an illegal loan transaction.

The government instigator offered to make a substantial and badly needed loan to Hossain to fix up his rental properties, to be gratuitously witnessed by Aref as an imam in accordance with the practices of Islam. All of this was perfectly legal and normal in the Muslim community. Separately, in many long conversations scattered over more than ten months, the government instigator inserted a few sentences suggesting that he was acting as an arms merchant to a jihadist group trying to liberate Kashmir from India. It is common in Muslim countries for men to arrange loans between themselves, using an imam or equivalent as a witness in the same way as a notary public. It is also common for those men to discuss the politics of their countries of birth, and to be concerned that their actions conform to the requirements of Islam. If a Middle Eastern businessman wants to help a jihadist group in Pakistan liberate Kashmir—or if an American businessman wants to sell arms to the IRA in Ireland—how does that transform an otherwise perfectly legal loan from a businessman to a pizzeria owner looking to fix up his property, into a criminal act? And how does it make a witness (or the notary) to such a loan into a criminal? No American would be prosecuted for this, but it's an entirely different matter when all the government has to do is scare the jury into believing that the defendants are real Muslim terrorists. At this point, evidence that a person is a devout and practicing Muslim becomes proof of extremism, and therefore any activity by a Muslim religious "extremist" must further terrorism.

In this sense, the crime that Aref and Hossain were charged with and convicted for was entirely one of perception. The message to the American people was, "We, the government, are hard at work catching terrorists who live among us in the Muslim community. Be afraid," and the message to the Muslim community was, "You come from third world dictatorships where the government wiretaps, eavesdrops, and manufactures evidence and where every other acquaintance is a government informant. Do not expect anything different in America, because we can frame you here just as quickly. Be very afraid."

Rounded Up explores why the government went forward with a case in which no crime had been committed, and how, when the government realized that it had no case to present, it attempted to create one: by threatening Muslim witnesses who were vulnerable to coercion, and by presenting false material and lies in court. To cite just one example: a section of one of the sting tapes was largely inaudible, but the government argued that Aref had told the government instigator that he should "send [his money for] terrorists." The defense claimed that Aref actually said "send taxes." (The issue was eventually submitted to the jury, which apparently agreed with the defense, since they did not convict Aref on this particular count of the indictment.) Shamshad notes the absurdity of what the government was claiming: if someone like Aref were truly a terrorist urging that money be sent for radical violence, he would never call the recipients "terrorists." "Terrorist" is a pejorative term used by Westerners but never by committed Islamic radicals. Such a person would instead use terms like *mujahideen* or jihadists or "freedom fighters." Thus it is obvious that Aref did not tell the government instigator to "send terrorists" (which is grammatically absurd as well)—the government was just making this up. *Rounded Up* is full of such perceptions and insights. It makes clear the government's lack of good faith in bringing the charges in the first place, as well as its desperation to obtain a conviction by any means for political reasons.

Shamshad has also written a very readable account of the Aref-Hossain case that moves like a murder mystery and focuses on the question, "What did the defendants do wrong?" It's a useful exercise at the end, after reviewing all the evidence, to try to answer this question for each defendant. Where did each man step over the line into criminality? What act was actually criminal? I've studied this case for a very long time, and I cannot find such a criminal act or moment for either man, but that doesn't mean that someone else studying this "crime of perception" won't find such a line or moment, since the jury apparently did. Each chapter contains surprising twists in the case, unexpected cultural insights to explore, and bizarre characters who play their roles for the government on the witness stand. And Shamshad views all individuals—defense lawyers and mosque members included—with the same critical eye as they struggle with the implications of the government's prosecution. In the process, he has produced a narrative of extraordinary insight.

I believe this book will become a classic description of what happens to justice in a time of ethnic conflict. It's a case study of how an immigrant community was attacked by the very government that was supposed to protect it, and how many Americans who should have known better closed ranks to scapegoat this vulnerable population. But it's also a story of how some Americans fought back against this scapegoating and joined ranks with their Muslim neighbors to protest the cynical abuse of power by the FBI and the Justice Department. Similar bogus prosecutions against innocent Muslims have been brought all across America, and similar groups of Americans have formed to protest such targeting of their neighbors. In this sense, the Aref-Hossain case is also a case study of a larger phenomenon—the corruption of the Justice Department, and its abandonment of the Constitution and the rule of law, for political expediency. It is not the first time in our history that the rule of law has been abandoned in order to systematically abuse a vulnerable immigrant population, but it is surely the most recent example.

Shamshad's deep understanding of Islam, and his scientific respect for fact, combine to produce a thorough analysis of how this scapegoating, achieved in the Aref-Hossain case, is a way to understand how and why our government has proceeded against Muslim communities in many other localities across the U.S. No one who reads this book will ever view the government's obligation to do justice in the same way again. And the reader will come to appreciate the struggle of the Muslim community, like other immigrant communities before them, to fit into mainstream American life while still retaining the essential faith and culture that make it unique. That this story is told with both wisdom and humor by a religious man of science makes it an unusually rich experience.

Stephen Downs
Selkirk, New York

O mankind! We created you from a single pair of male and female, and made you in nations and tribes, that you may know each other (not that you may despise each other), indeed the most honorable among you in the sight of Allah is the one who is most pious.

— Qur'an, Chapter 49, "The Chambers," Verse 13

The highest form of jihad is to speak the truth in the face of an unjust ruler.

— Prophet Muhammad

CHAPTER 1

"The Mosque Is Being Raided and Searched"

I will never forget August 5, 2004. It was approximately 1:45 a.m. and I was sound asleep upstairs at 274 West Lawrence Street in Albany, New York, where my family and I had been living for the last twenty years. Somehow I heard a knock at my bedroom door and the voice of my eldest son, Sajid, calling to me coolly through the door.

"Two FBI agents are downstairs. They told me that the mosque is being raided and searched, and they want to talk to you."

Sajid was a thirty-two-year-old computer engineer who, in the manner common to Muslim families from third world countries, was living with his parents until he had his own family and could move out. Sajid does not go to bed until after the dawn prayer, at the first sign of morning in the eastern sky. He reads, contemplates, and prays during the night. In retrospect, this must have made the agents' job easier; otherwise it might have taken some effort on their part to wake someone in the family at such an early hour.

Sajid's words made me fully awake and alert. *The mosque raided and searched? Why?*

I had returned home from the Masjid As-Salam just two and half hours earlier, after finishing the night prayer. I had seen nothing out of the ordinary, and I knew very well that nothing objectionable or of a criminal nature existed inside it. It was an old building in the middle of the business district of Albany. Normally it was open from early morning to late at night, with people coming and offering their prayers all day long. It had a large prayer hall, a few rooms normally left unlocked, a few rooms under renovation, and a few rooms usually locked during the night but opened during the day so that they were accessible to everyone. Some rooms were used as classrooms and contained nothing but old chairs and tables. Others were used as storage rooms and contained several cardboard boxes filled with books, household items, building materials, repair tools—certainly nothing illegal. Had some criminals entered the mosque after I left? Had any criminal activity taken place there? Even if that were the case, the FBI would not be at my door; most likely the Albany police would be taking care of it at the mosque.

I walked downstairs with Sajid in my sleeping clothes and went to the front porch, where I saw two gentlemen waiting for me. I recognized one of them, Agent Tom Jensen. The other one seemed not to be an FBI agent in the usual sense. Rather, he was a bulging-bellied, tense-looking, security-guard type in a T-shirt and pants whose eyes were intensely fixed on me, as if gauging whether I was going to exhibit any resentment or irritation or violence. I am only 5'6" and 140 pounds, a gentle-looking guy in my late fifties; I thought to myself that he wouldn't have to do much to handle me if I misbehaved.

Agent Jensen addressed me politely, looking straight at me. "Hello, Mr. Ahmad. I'm the FBI agent who came here with a female agent about two weeks ago."

"Yes, I remember you," I said. And then a memory flashed through my mind like lightning.

Jensen and Special Agent Laura Youngblood had come to our house presumably to talk to our eldest daughter, Huma, about her website, www.Jannah.org. Huma maintains this world-famous website that is especially geared towards Muslim women. Essentially it is an encyclopedia dealing with the social, educational, cultural, and religious issues of Muslim women in the modern world, and it contains a series of articles, publications, and references.

Huma had posted a long article, written by a female graduate student at a university in Boston, regarding the effective display of tables and exhibitions by Islamic workers to promote their religious and cultural viewpoint. The author had provided a comprehensive roster of the literature, posters, and pamphlets that might be involved in such efforts. It was a simple academic guide, and had no overtones of anything political or anything that could be considered even remotely objectionable. Huma had downloaded the article from the national website of the MSA (the Muslim Students Association of the U.S. and Canada). MSA is an organization that caters to the social, cultural, and religious needs of Muslim students, and MSA chapters are present on most of the college campuses in the U.S. But according to Agents Jensen and Youngblood, the author of this article was a person of interest for them as a fugitive, and they wondered if Huma had any idea of her whereabouts.

Huma had just left for work that morning. I promised to discuss the matter with her as soon as she came home, and to tell them if she had any information about the whereabouts of the author. I asked Jensen if he had a copy of the article or a picture of the author. He said he did, but had left it in the car. He went to his car to retrieve it, and when he came back he showed me a grainy Xeroxed picture of the author.

At that point, skepticism about the reason for their visit started to develop in my mind. In my judgment, it was unprofessional for these two somewhat senior FBI agents to come to interview a subject and to leave their files in the car.

After they left, I asked my other children if they could guess the purpose of the agents' visit. Their response was, "What do you mean? Do you doubt them?"

"Definitely," I said. "I am trying to figure out why they were here." When Huma got home from work, she shared the same skepticism. She thought she had seen them waiting for her to leave the house in the morning before knocking at the door.

That same day, Huma called the FBI office, told the agents the source of the downloaded article, and said that she did not know anything about the author. She told them that she thought it was a nice and useful article, and that was the only reason she had downloaded it to her website. They seemed to be satisfied with that, since they did not follow it up. But in the back of my mind, I still felt something was odd about their visit.

Now, looking at Jensen standing on my porch at 1:45 a.m., I thought I knew the reason he and Youngblood had been here two weeks ago. Perhaps their intention was to assess my attitude and temper in connection with the planning of the event of this night, and to familiarize themselves with our residence and its surroundings.

"Please change your clothes. The mosque is being searched. I want to take you there," Jensen said.

I went back to my room, changed, and came back downstairs. Other than Sajid and my wife, Kishwar, the rest of the family was still sound asleep. Our house was very full that summer, since everyone had gathered to participate in the wedding of our youngest daughter, Shazia, which had taken place two weeks earlier. Our four children are specialists in computer fields by education and training, and graduated from local universities; three of them graduated from the State University of New York at Albany (SUNY). Our youngest son, Faisal, and his wife, Sana, had resigned from their IBM jobs a year before and moved to Damascus, Syria, where they were studying Arabic, Islamic culture, and Islamic law. They were planning to go back to Damascus shortly. All our children (and Sana) are very religious and use traditional Muslim dress.

I looked at Sajid and Kishwar and said, "They want to take me to the mosque." Then I closed the front door behind them, leaving them staring at me with many questions, but apparently with no fear. A thought came to me: *Maybe I will be taken to the mosque so I can be charged with something and arrested there, or maybe they'll find something during the search and I'll be arrested for that.*

On the porch I put on my sandals that I had left there. According to tradition, some Muslims take off their shoes before entering the living quarters of the house. This tradition is followed in some non-Muslim cultures of third world countries as well. I looked at Jensen to indicate that I was ready. I felt cool and composed. I thought the FBI must have a well-rehearsed plan in place, and there was no way I could interfere with or alter it. So why should I worry? I would just watch and see how things unfolded. I had enough confidence in myself that I had never said or done anything that would cause them to be interested in me. If they really suspected something, or had evidence of something and asked me about it, I would tell them the truth and cooperate with them without reservation. But I did not rule out the possibility of my arrest at the mosque, and I was already thinking of steps I should take in that situation.

As if he read my mind, Agent Jensen said, "You are not under arrest. You'll ride with us. We want to hand over the mosque to you after the search is completed, and we'll drive you back here."

"Fine," I said.

I followed Jensen to his jeep that was parked on the road, while the second "security guard" agent followed me, still looking at me very intently. I took the passenger seat and the security guard took the back seat. It was a pleasant, beautiful night. But it was certainly not going to be pleasant for the Muslim community, because the FBI raid that was underway would haunt them for months and years to come.

"THE NEWS IS EVERYWHERE"

After a five-minute drive through almost deserted streets, Jensen stopped the jeep in front of the mosque at 276-278 Central Avenue. The road was filled with about ten official cars with flashing red lights, but no individuals seemed to be in the area. We all remained seated. The security guard was still very attentive toward me.

Jensen called someone on his cell phone. "Should we bring him in?" he asked. But when he was finished, he told me that we had been instructed to wait.

Since we had left my porch, I had not spoken a single word. So I said to Jensen now, "What are you looking for? Maybe I can help you." But he did not look at me, nor did he say anything.

After about ten minutes he received a cell phone call. "Time to go in," he said. Looking at me straight on, he asked, "Are you armed?"

"No."

I thought the security guard would relax at that, but he did not.

Jensen started the car. He drove around the short block and parked behind the mosque next to the first back door. Cars with flashing lights were all around this block, too, but still no people. We remained seated in the car for the next five minutes.

"What are you looking for? You did not answer me," I finally said.

After a long pause, he said, "I won't tell you. You'll see it in the warrant." Then he asked, "Do you have computers inside?"

"Yes," I said. "There are two computers. One, someone donated to me to be used in the mosque, and the other I have seen lying on the floor in one of the rooms. Both are simply stored there, they are not being used."

"So they're not online?"

"That's right. We have no connections inside."

I saw a man in handcuffs being taken out of the second back door of the mosque toward a police car. I recognized him as Faheem, a young man whom I had first met about fifteen years before when he was a student at Rensselaer Polytechnic Institute in Troy, where I taught in the mid-Eighties. In the past, he had asked for my permission to stay overnight in the mosque because of his desperate situation of being unemployed and homeless. I had flatly refused permission and had advised him what

The banner above the front door of the Masjid As-Salam.

Photo by Steve Jacobs. Courtesy of Albany *Times Union*.

else to do. But it seemed that he would sneak into the mosque during the night and stay there, or hide somewhere until after the night prayer so he could remain in the mosque overnight. I came to know later that he was not charged for anything he did in the mosque on August 5, but was jailed for some violation of a previous probation. I was told that he was sick and in a terrible situation in the jail where he was being held. I paid $250 to bail him out. I have not heard from him since.

We got out of the jeep. I followed Jensen, with the security guard still alert behind me. We entered the mosque from the first back door. A cardboard box filled with some sort of white cloth was lying at the entrance inside the hallway. These proved to be shoe coverings. Jensen picked up a pair of them and fitted them over his shoes. I copied him, and so did the security guard.

I thought the FBI was well prepared and kind enough to make this arrangement for the respect of the mosque. Muslims do not enter the carpeted prayer area of a mosque in their shoes. This is considered to be disrespectful, since our shoes have collected the filth of the street and would make the prayer area impure.

Two years later, a journalist told me that the FBI had brought a dog inside the mosque first, to ensure the absence of any undesirable substances before entering in person. No one in the Muslim community knows about this, and I have never tried to verify the report. In the Islamic tradition, dogs are not allowed in places of worship. I hope I never find out whether the report is true or not. Even if I learn it is true, I will not inform the community, as they will really be upset about it.

Jensen, the security guard, and I walked through the mosque's hallway. I noticed a few FBI personnel moving swiftly from place to place and from room to room. All had their shoe coverings on. Jensen asked me to unlock the four-door filing cabinet located next to the eastern wall in the prayer area, which I did. This cabinet was for my use only, and only I had its key, and apparently Jensen knew this. I had some personal papers in the cabinet, as well as some bills and correspondence belonging to the mosque. Later I found out that all the papers pertaining to loan transactions to the imam, or arranged for others through him, as well as his salary records, were removed by the FBI during this search. Other papers, such as my personal letters and mosque bills, and the money that was in the cabinet, were not touched.

We stayed in the hallway close to the prayer area. I felt very calm and relaxed. I sensed that everyone in the mosque was somewhat surprised at my attitude. Perhaps they were expecting me to be irritated, tense, and angry. From time to time Jensen went to other areas to talk to someone or to answer the phone, but the security guard always remained next to me.

After half an hour or so, the security guard seemed to relax, and he sat down in a corner on a bench. It was the first time that his eyes were off me; he seemed to have lost all interest in me.

Suddenly Jensen came over to me and asked in a very relaxed and casual manner if my summer courses at the university were over. I told him that they had ended about two weeks ago. Then he asked me to show him the computers that were in the building. While walking with him, I noticed that all doors of all rooms were wide open, and that a number tag was affixed to each. Some doors had obviously been opened with keys and had no damage, while others had been kicked open, breaking them from one end to the other. Even today, mosque attendees wonder why the FBI assaulted and kicked these doors when they had all the keys to them before they entered the mosque. The front and back entrance doors had no damage.

I asked Jensen, "Who will be responsible for all this damage?" He made a few telephone calls and then informed me that the FBI would pay for it. He told me to contact someone named Lee Pugh at their office. We at the mosque decided not to overburden the FBI with this trouble. To date, some of the doors remain broken.

Jensen asked me to show him the room that the imam used as his office. I showed him the room, with a broken table and a defective chair, saying, "This is not really an office, but it is what the imam has for his office."

It was at this point that I realized the raid had something to do with the imam, either directly or indirectly.

During my time inside the mosque that night, the whole search team was very respectful to the premises, as well as to me. I did not notice any act by them that could be termed disrespectful to the mosque, and toward the end, everyone was very friendly to me. Surprisingly, the security guard had left before the search was over.

From the gestures and conversations of the members of the search team, I realized they wanted to conclude the search fast. About half a dozen people were running back and forth looking at everything, from the donation box to bookshelves to trash cans to cardboard boxes. One man seemed to be in big demand: everyone wanted "Lou" to come over and determine whether a particular paper was of some value or not. I quickly figured out that Lou, a South Asian-looking man in his fifties, was an Arabic translator, either working for the FBI or hired by them.

The agents told me around 4 a.m. that they would give me a copy of the inventory of the items they were taking with them, and that they would leave at any moment.

Around 5 a.m. I was told that Sajid and Faisal were at the back door and wanted to talk to me. I wanted to bring them in, but was told that no one other than myself was allowed inside. Sajid and Faisal both said that people were offering their morning prayer on the sidewalk because they were not allowed in the mosque.

Adult Muslims are required to pray five times each day. On average, a prayer takes less than ten minutes. Prayers can be offered at any clean and hygienic place, but men are encouraged to pray in mosques in congregation. Women may go to a mosque to pray if they wish, but in the majority of places around the world, women do not go to the mosque, but rather pray at home. The first prayer of the day, called morning prayer, is due after the break of dawn but prior to sunrise. In As-Salam mosque, about twenty devotees used to come for the morning prayer, and they were the ones who now had to do their prayer on the sidewalk.

Sajid said to me in one breath, "The news of the mosque raid is everywhere. It's become national news. The whole street is filled with media and spectators. We heard on the news that Imam Yassin Aref, Mohammed Mosharref Hossain, and Abdulbarr Shuaib were arrested. We're glad that you're OK, Dad. Hope to see you home soon." Then he and Faisal left, and I returned inside.

I could not come up with any clue as to why these men had been arrested, and what the raid of the mosque had to do with it.

Around 5:30 a.m. the FBI left. The last agent to leave brought the inventory sheet for me to sign. He thanked me, gave me a copy, wished me a good morning, and swiftly walked away. The inventory consisted of two computers, papers from the filing cabinet, printed booklets, pamphlets, cassettes, and diskettes. Some of these items had been left in the mosque for safekeeping by two neighbors of the mosque who had gone on an overseas trip.

As soon as the FBI left, some angry and dismayed mosque members entered the mosque, along with reporters. I knew it was time for me to leave. I decided not to talk to the reporters at that point because I had no information whatsoever about the background of the raid.

Then I noticed a stack of papers stapled together that had been left behind on a bench in one of the corners. It was a warrant by Albany FBI Special Agent Timothy Coll, signed by a federal magistrate, Honorable David Homer of Albany, the first page of which read: *United States of America v. Yassin Muhiddin Aref and Mohammed Mosharref Hossain*. I decided to bring this paper home with me to read.

I do not remember how I got home that morning. Either someone gave me a ride or I walked, a twenty-five-minute walk that I often do.

CHAPTER 2

Targets of the FBI

THE OPENING OF MASJID AS-SALAM

Masjid in Arabic literally means "place of prostration" or "place of worship." It is translated in English as "mosque," and is considered to be the counterpart of a church. In the majority of cases, it is actually an empty hall of some sort where Muslims pray on the carpeted floor by standing, bending, sitting, and prostrating themselves five separate times over the course of a day and night, without using any music, equipment, or furniture.

Muslims throughout the world desire to have both a mosque to worship in and a *madrasa* (in Arabic, literally a "place of learning," or a religious school) in every residential enclave. Sometimes *madrasas* are part of a mosque or are conducted inside a mosque. Wherever Muslims settle, they look for these facilities. If such facilities are not found, they strive to create them as part of their religious obligation. Building a mosque or establishing a *madrasa* is considered to be one of the noblest actions by a Muslim or a group of Muslims.

With respect to race, language, ethnicity, and nationality, a mosque in America is the most diverse entity one can ever imagine. However, since the fundamentals of Islam are the same throughout the world, these hold Muslims together. The format and language of Islamic prayers throughout the world are also the same: they are offered only in Arabic, in the same way Prophet Muhammad taught his followers fourteen centuries ago. Every Muslim child learns in the *madrasa* or at home how to say and do the daily prayers. Some differences based on various interpretations and opinions do exist, but they are not a significant factor in an American mosque. Sometimes divisions and conflicts are seen in mosques, but normally they occur not because of a difference in belief but because of personality clashes among the leaders, differences that are often based on ethnicity or other factors.

Once I invited a local labor leader who had never been to a mosque to attend Friday service at Masjid As-Salam. He was shocked to see people from at least thirty nationalities and ethnic groups greeting and hugging each other. "How are you able to hold these folks together?" he asked. I smiled at him. "You have to come here more often to understand this secret," I said.

Ever since I had arrived in Albany, I had been interested in opening a mosque. Albany is the capital of New York State, with a population of nearly 96,000 (in 2000). It is the seat of state government, and also has one of four State University centers, half a dozen good colleges, a similar number of hospitals, hundreds of churches, and many synagogues. So I felt it should also have a working mosque where Muslims could meet, pray, discuss their issues, and invite non-Muslims to interact with them. But finding a suitable and affordable place for a mosque was extremely difficult.

In October 1982 I bought a four-unit residential property at 169 North Lake Avenue and opened a mini-mosque in its basement. It functioned as such for about ten years. Then a group of local Muslims started a mosque in a rented room at 91 Lexington Avenue. Eventually the group split and started another mosque at 178 Washington Avenue in a small rented two-bedroom apartment. In 1998, Mohammed Hossain became president of this mosque. But with the increasing Muslim population, these places were too small and became unsuitable to function as mosques.

On behalf of and with the help of the local Muslim community, in December 1999 I bought a totally rundown property at 276-278 Central Avenue for $40,000 cash. Roughly half of the purchase price was paid by a friend and by my family. The space had formerly housed an appliance store. It was a large, street-to-street building, roughly 175 x 32 feet over two floors, with eleven finished or unfinished rooms in very bad condition and needing total rehabilitation. The title to the building was taken in the name of the North American Islamic Trust, a national Muslim parent organization that holds titles to roughly 400 other mosques and Islamic centers throughout the U.S. I preferred the title to be in the organization's name due to its legal and tax-exempt status, as well as to avoid any misuse of the building in case there was a dispute or split in the local membership.

On the day of the closing I encountered Ali Yaghi, a very funny, naughty, and humorous member of the Muslim community whom I had known for some time. Yaghi offered to drive me to the attorneys' office, John Maxwell and Paul VanRyn, to sign the final papers and to get the building's key. The payment had already been made. At the closing, John Maxwell pushed the title toward me to sign as representative. But Yaghi pulled the paper away from me. "I want to sign, I want to sign," he said laughingly. I looked at John. "No problem," he said, and Yaghi signed the paper, took the keys to the building, and left the office with great enthusiasm, leaving me to shake hands with John and say goodbye to him. Yaghi was not the only one to have this enthusiasm. It was the first time Muslims would have a mosque of their own in the City of Albany.

From the many proposed names that were suggested for the mosque, Masjid As-Salam (House of Peace) was adopted. My eldest daughter, Huma, who was working at a computer mapping company at the time, designed and prepared a sign for the mosque using some of the company's computer programs. It was installed against the glass atop the front door of the building.

Within hours of the closing, rehabilitation work began. In the beginning, for about a month four of us—Yassin Aref, Ali Yaghi, Paul Breslin, and myself—spent an average of ten hours a day working without a break. Paul Breslin was my employee-subcontractor who had worked on several of my other buildings for a number of years. An extremely talented builder who had experience in electrical, plumbing, roofing, carpentry, and everything else related to construction, he was the backbone of building the mosque. Occasionally a few volunteers showed up for an hour or two, but they were not of much help.

Despite the fact that Yassin Aref, a newly arrived UN refugee from Iraqi Kurdistan with a family of four, was in dire need of financial help, he refused to accept such help from anyone. I pressured him hard to accept compensation for working on the renovation of the mosque, but he refused and did not accept even a single penny, saying he wanted to be compensated by the Almighty in the hereafter. The mosque had just enough resources to pay for the construction material; the rest of the expenses I was able to manage somehow.

After a month, Yaghi had to leave us to take care of his children because of a domestic dispute. But Aref remained committed until the end. Because of his physical strength, zeal, and commitment, he was equal to at least two people, if not more. During this eight-month period, I had abandoned all my engagements except for teaching my classes. Many times I used to spend fourteen hours a day working on the mosque. My construction equipment, truck, contacts with other contractors, and prior experience with construction helped a great deal. The code enforcement and planning departments in Albany were considered to be unfriendly territories, but they were very helpful to me. In July 2000, we finished the building enough to open it as a mosque.

It is very difficult to get a qualified imam for a mosque in the U.S. There are no seminary schools where students can be trained, and very few colleges or universities offer Islamic theology courses. Since 9/11, the problem has become even more acute. Many imams left the country because of harassment or fear, and people from overseas do not want to come to the U.S. for the same reason. Even if someone is willing to come, it takes a lot of time and patience before all the security checks are completed and a temporary visa is issued.

Because of Aref's involvement in the mosque from the first day, his sincere commitment to serve the community, and his college education in Islamic theology, he was a natural choice to be appointed imam of this humble new inner-city mosque. He was appointed part time at first, and then upgraded to full time. He was extremely sincere, committed to serving the mosque and the community, and he soon became well liked by the worshippers. Within a few months, he learned enough English to be able to communicate on a basic level with people. The mosque could afford only $1,500 a month for his salary as a full-time imam, but he was happy with it. It was not sufficient to support his family, but he did not want to take more. He said, "It is enough for me; let the mosque money be spent for other useful purposes." Every year I wanted to increase his salary, but he refused to accept it.

A mosque is like an open or public place: it does not require membership to attend or pray in it. When it opened in 2000, the Masjid As-Salam had a maximum attendance during the Friday congregation of about 150, but the number grew to about 300 by 2004. The five daily prayers (morning, noon, afternoon, sunset, and night) were each attended by about twenty people. Business owners, deliverymen, shoppers, and pedestrians could walk in at will, offer a brief prayer, and go on their way. Almost all of its attendees were mainstream Sunni Muslims who resided in the downtown Albany area or who were employed in that vicinity.

Located in the heart of the city—in the middle of the city's original business district on one of Albany's main streets—the mosque was kept open from early morning until late at night. It served as a place of worship as well as a community center. It provided a weekend school for children, and classes and counseling for adults. It also catered to community needs such as weddings, dinners, and funerals. A small community grew up in the area surrounding the mosque, featuring several stores and many residences.

The mosque was independent of any affiliation with or influence from outside groups or organizations. It had no outside support or sponsorship and no connection with local, national, or international politics. Its only financial resource was the voluntary donations left in the donation box by the prayer attendees, just sufficient to meet operating expenses. There was no required contribution. It was open to all, and anyone attending was considered to be a member.

Over the years, a good number of attendees at the masjid have been ex-convicts who accepted Islam while serving time in prison. They are mostly African Americans, but include some whites and Hispanics as well. Common sense suggests that this factor must have added to the FBI's interest in our mosque; members believe that the FBI put the mosque (and them) under electronic and human surveillance immediately after 9/11. Frequently members would inform me that they saw suspicious people secretly focusing their cameras on the mosque from cars parked across the street, or looking at the mosque with binoculars, or noting down license plate numbers of cars parked around the mosque during Friday prayers. I always downplayed such concerns to avoid planting fear in their minds: "Let the government do its job. You have nothing to worry about since you are not doing anything wrong. Mind your own business, stay strong, and do whatever your religion requires you to do." Nevertheless, I very carefully took note of some strange and unknown people attending the mosque. I also noted that these individuals always avoided interacting with me, while interacting freely with the imam and some other regular members.

For awhile, I hoped to make the mosque security very tight, but there were difficulties. One of the difficulties was Imam Aref. He was extremely considerate of the people attending the mosque, including these suspicious individuals. His view was that many people in society had trouble because of their upbringing or domestic problems. Some of them were poor, jobless, and homeless. "If they come to the mosque," he said, "we must help them and try to accommodate them." Some of these people used to just hang around in the mosque most of the time. A few had even started spending part of the night there. Aref brought a coffee pot and a microwave to the mosque for them. Occasionally he would bring food from his home, and some Muslim pizza owners would send leftover pizzas.

Imam Aref was an extremely generous and caring person. Somehow he assumed that taking care of every Muslim was his personal obligation or responsibility. Several people started coming to him every week seeking financial help. It appeared that their rent, utility bills, and grocery shopping were Aref's or the mosque's problem. He never questioned whether the need was real or genuine. He would empty his pockets whenever possible, or he would ask others in the mosque to help these individuals, or ask me to give them money from the mosque donations.

My attitude was exactly the opposite. I wanted the mosque's role to be limited to catering to the spiritual, not the financial, needs of the people. I suggested to Aref that he should advise these people not to depend upon the mosque for their financial sustenance, because there might be no end to the need and the needy and it would create an unsound environment in the mosque. Aref and I used to argue about this, and it became one of the serious differences between us—so much so that at times we were not even speaking to each other. I used to repeat the old adage, "Rather than providing them with fish, teach them how to catch fish. Guide them to take care of their lives, to go and get a little training, to get a job and start living responsibly. They need to be empowered, not made dependent on others." When an able-bodied man came to the Prophet asking for help, He gave the man an ax and a rope and sent him to the forest to cut wood to sell. In this way, the Prophet gave him the message that even menial labor was more honorable than begging from people.

I was totally convinced that the mosque was under full surveillance, and that some of these individuals were part of it. Despite heavy pressure from the members, I did not allow long-distance telephone service in the mosque, nor did I allow any computers to be connected online. I had no doubt that if those services were available, someday a suspicious overseas call or a suspicious e-mail would become a source of serious problems for us.

Realizing the difficulty of making the mosque security tight, I reversed my previous strategy and disabled the locks on most of the rooms so that they could be accessible to anybody at any time. I thought that way there would be no suspicion that the mosque was hiding something, and that it would be very difficult for the government or anyone else to set up surveillance inside. I was confident that the FBI would not attempt to plant anything illegal inside the mosque to be used against us.

MUSLIMS AND MOSQUES UNDER SURVEILLANCE

The tragic events of September 11, 2001 brought many changes to this country. Some of those changes started the moment the towers were hit, and as a consequence were initiated in the minds of President George Bush and Vice President Dick Cheney. These two most powerful men on earth were being transported secretly from one hidden location to another in a very frightened atmosphere. Security forces were hiding them and trying to protect them from an unknown enemy. Naturally they felt utterly humiliated and disgraced. It was at this moment, I believe, that the two vowed to take revenge for their humiliation. But revenge on whom? On the enemy, obviously, but who was the enemy? The hijackers were dead, but bin Laden and al-Qaeda, which was supposedly behind the attacks, were very much alive. But how would America locate this shadowy organization? By making any supposed supporter of or sympathizer with al-Qaeda, in any shape or form, bear responsibility for 9/11. Mr. Cheney is once reported to have said that if law enforcement authorities suspected someone of having even a 1% chance of supporting terrorism, America would treat him as if he were 100% a terrorist—the so-called "One-Percent Cheney Doctrine."

But who were such suspects, and where to find them? *American Muslims* was the easy answer to both questions.

Even though the 9/11 attacks were planned and executed by people who entered this country from abroad expressly for that evil purpose, it was to the Muslims in America that the eye of suspicion turned. Muslims in the U.S. normally lack social, political, business, and sports organizations or clubs, although they have mosques in every city. Thus American Muslims, and their institutions and mosques, became the focus of investigation and the objects of extreme scrutiny.

However, analysis tells us that the terrorists succeeded on 9/11 primarily because of an intelligence failure on the government's part. In response, the government allocated tremendous amounts of resources, money, and manpower to the intelligence agencies, including the FBI in Albany and its Joint Terrorism Task Force (JTTF). This—coupled with previously unthinkable new legislation that permitted government surveillance of its own citizens without judicial oversight, and a so-called secret evidence law that allowed people to be tried without even knowing what was being used as proof of their guilt—empowered the authorities tremendously.

Our intelligence agencies felt an extra pressure, too—a pressure to produce visible results. This led to results across the nation, but often incorrect ones. Thousands of Muslims were detained and questioned, their property seized, and some were even charged with terrorism. But no real terrorists were found. Most cases were based on suspicion and hardly any actual evidence. Many innocent people fell victim to this aggressive policing, and many families, communities, mosques, and Islamic institutions suffered. Somehow, in this new age of suspicion, the Masjid As-Salam and its members became a special target of investigation by the Albany FBI.

Probably the first mosque member the FBI began to look at was Ali Mounnes Yaghi. He was born and raised in Jordan; his parents were Palestinian. He came to Albany in 1985 at the age of sixteen. He finished high school and attended college locally but could not complete his education, so he decided to go into the pizza business. As a young man he was very naughty, cunning, stubborn, and hyperactive. He had multiple personalities, one of them being very funny, childish, loose-tongued, big-mouthed, and jolly. To his black acquaintances he used to say, "You are my nigger, you must become my slave." To Iraqis he used to say, "I love Saddam, he is my friend, I wonder how he spared you?" To an older person he would say, "You must marry a young woman, otherwise you will die very soon. I know several, I can connect you with one of them." To his women customers he would say, "I hate women." And he made outrageous general statements, such as, "I hate America, I want to make it a Palestinian state." And so on. He did all of this with a big laugh. In his pocket he carried pictures of Hitler, Lenin, Arafat, Saddam, Qaddafi, and others and used to show them to his friends: "These are my heroes, I am going to be like one of them." He got a kick of this outrageous humor.

Yaghi was robbed in Albany a few times while delivering pizza. Once in 1992, as he was about to be robbed, someone called the police. They discovered a loaded, unregistered gun in Yaghi's car and the set of pictures of dictators in his pocket, and they could not figure out why he had those pictures. Yaghi did not cooperate with the police and used his loud mouth as usual, saying, "Keep your dirty hands off me, I hate Americans." He was charged with possession of an illegal weapon, convicted, sentenced to one year, and sent to the Albany County Jail.

After he was released from jail, Yaghi was a changed man. He became very religious, caring, interested in reading books and attending mosque, and showed signs of maturity and responsibility. He started talking about the futility of advancing the Palestinian cause through violence and began advocating a struggle through religious and peaceful means. But his naughtiness, his loud mouth, and his loose tongue never changed. He was married to an Afghan refugee and had three boys; inside the mosque I used to see him shaking and kicking his children laughingly and kissing their behinds. Sometimes they cried because of his excessively clownish activities.

One day in early September 2001, I was working alone in the basement of the mosque. Yaghi came down and started whispering in my ear, "They got hold of me and talked to me." I felt something was terribly wrong. Yaghi used to always enter the mosque with a loud mouth and naughty comments; we always knew he was coming. But I had never heard him whisper.

I told him that I couldn't hear him. He repeated his whisper again: "They got hold of me and talked to me."

"Who?" I asked.

"The police," he answered.

"Why, and what were they asking about?"

"About the mosque and its people."

"Well, what did you say?" I asked.

"I told them I did not know anybody here."

"Ali!" I exclaimed. "How could you say that? You are a regular member of the mosque, you know everybody here. You should have told them everything honestly. You have nothing to hide."

I had universally advised members of the Muslim community that if they were asked any questions by law enforcement, they should have an attorney at their side. "If you cannot afford one," I told them, "the mosque will arrange for one. Don't try to outsmart the authorities, they have a lot more experience and know a lot more about you than you think. Tell them everything honestly." And I had posted everywhere in the mosque a poster advising people what to do if they were contacted by the FBI for an interview.

Dozens of our community members were subsequently questioned by the FBI. I am not sure how many of them cared to follow my advice. Usually an FBI agent grabs a Muslim immigrant and shows him some mistake on his visa or citizenship application—unless the agent can find some other error in the records with which to accuse him. Then the agent threatens and intimidates the immigrant with arrest and imprisonment or deportation, after which the agent offers the shaking and frightened guy a deal: "We can spare you or help you, if you help us." What kind of help? "Spy on other Muslims. We have a list. We will teach you how to do that."

Unfortunately, Yaghi's loud mouth triggered a catastrophe for him and for the Muslim community. Just after 9/11, he stood in front of his pizza store on Delaware Avenue and in his usual laughing and joking style said loudly, "I am very happy with whatever is happening to America." A neighboring businessman, toward whom Yaghi had some animosity, called the police and informed them about Yaghi's seemingly anti-American remarks. That triggered an FBI investigation, because he had several ingredients that fit the FBI's profile of a "person of interest." He was a young Palestinian, religious, bearded; he wore long Arabic dress and a *koofi* on his head; he was talkative; and he was a businessman. More importantly, he had disposed of his house and business, sent his wife and children to Jordan, moved his money, relocated to Texas, and then came back to Albany—all this just prior to 9/11. Apparently some of these things, though coincidental in Yaghi's case, seemed to be common to the 9/11 hijackers, or were considered by the FBI to be part of a terrorist's method of operation.

Yaghi was arrested on suspicion of being a terrorist. He was handcuffed, shackled, and interrogated; he was given a polygraph test but no access to an attorney. He was sent to the Schenectady County Jail. After three days, he was allowed to make a telephone call to let his brother know about his arrest.

I had known Ali and his elder brother, Nizar, for many years. Prior to the purchase of the mosque building, I did not like Yaghi and kept a distance from him. But he contributed to building the mosque in many ways and developed a great respect for me, became my staunch supporter, and helped promote positive relationships with various people and groups in the community. So I decided to help him in his time of need.

I went to the Schenectady County Jail to inquire about him, but no one was willing to give me any information. Whenever I mentioned his name, the jail authorities looked at me as if I were another terrorist. I felt very frustrated and returned home utterly disappointed. I fell on my bed and cried. The America of my dreams had really changed.

But Yaghi was not alone. Over 1,000 other young Arabs or Muslims were arrested and imprisoned nationwide around the same time and treated in a similar way. On October 25, 2001, Yaghi was transferred to the Metropolitan Detention Center in Brooklyn, where he joined an unknown number of federal detainees like him. They were kept in windowless cells, had almost no contact with the outside world, and were allowed few, if any, telephone or attorney contacts. None of these detainees were terrorists, and they were never charged with anything, but each one was penalized and paid a price in one form or another. Everyone's American dream was shattered: heavy-handed injustice in broad daylight in front of the entire modern world!

Both Yassin Aref and Mohammed Hossain were questioned about Yaghi after his arrest. Yaghi had a very good relationship with Aref, who had worked in Yaghi's pizza business as a deliveryman for some time. Yaghi had also helped Aref in a variety of ways in Albany when he had first arrived here.

Unfortunately, Yaghi and Hossain did not like each other. Sometimes I thought that they actually hated each other for personal reasons. Hossain also told me that during his interview, the FBI had asked him about me as well. I told him, "If they ask about me again, please tell them everything you know about me." I was not curious to learn what they wanted to know about me; I didn't want to know, so I could keep myself from becoming biased.

Many other members of the mosque, as well as Yaghi's relatives, business associates, employees, and acquaintances, were questioned by the FBI. Several did not return home after finishing their questioning; they were sent to prison mostly for visa violations or other minor charges. Yaghi's brother, Nizar, was brought to Albany from Texas to be interrogated and was given a polygraph test. He told me that he had been shown some pictures, supposedly of terrorists from the Middle East, and was asked if he recognized any of them. He did not. Then they questioned him about "Yassin," starting with asking Nizar for his last name. Nizar did not know it. He was asked why Ali had relocated to Texas and then came back; Nizar told them that Ali had gone to Texas to start a pizza business with one of their brothers, and because of a family argument he became upset and decided to return to Albany. Nizar passed the polygraph test. He did have an attorney present during his interrogation.

Initially the FBI suspected that Yaghi knew some of the nineteen 9/11 hijackers, or that he had some idea if any of them had ever been in Albany or had contact with anyone here. "He was shown pictures of Middle Eastern men, including the nineteen hijackers, and given a polygraph test that he failed," his attorney Thomas O'Malley informed the media. "Federal authorities are not going to charge him, as they are convinced he has no terrorist connections."

Despite all of this, Yaghi was kept in his windowless cell for many more months. Finally in July 2002 he was deported to the Jordanian authorities who, according to him, treated him nicely and finally released him. He called me from Jordan, a free and happy man, and related to me some of his ordeal in the Metropolitan Detention Center. He said the guards would make fun of him and manhandle him and call him "Osama." Some of them apparently treated him as if they had found the real Osama and wanted to teach him a lesson. His attorney remarked, "Once they handcuffed and shackled him and put him in a cell, it was as if all his civil rights were thrown out the window."

Despite all this, Yaghi's stubbornness and naughtiness did not go away. He said that the last time he was brought into court in Manhattan, there was a female judge on the bench. "I hate women, I hate Americans," he said to her. Yaghi told me this, laughing.

He invited me to come to Jordan. "Come here, man, why are you rotting in America? I have already chosen some chicks for you."

The FBI Goes into High Gear

As evidenced by their questioning of Yaghi, the FBI had a suspicion that some of the 9/11 hijackers had something to do with the Albany area. According to one theory, the terrorists' alternate target was a tall building in Albany, such as the Corning Tower in the Empire State Plaza, or possibly they wanted to hijack another commercial plane from the Albany International Airport. So, the theory went, some of them must have made a visit to Albany to make an assessment, and someone in Albany must have some information about this.

Albany's FBI office contains a Joint Terrorism Task Force, whose jurisdiction extends over northeastern New York State as well as Vermont. But at one point the whole office was assigned to counterterrorism investigations only, abandoning any other kind of investigation like drug trafficking, corruption, murder, white collar crime, etc. The agents had their eyes fixed on every Muslim of status or visibility in Albany, and the number of agents in this action was huge. It was one of the most elaborate and costly counterterrorism investigations on record in upstate New York.

Muslims are wary of law enforcement, because most of the time agents approach Muslims not only to obtain information but also to demand information about other members of the community. This makes the situation worse. However, in public and in the press things were presented differently. The Albany FBI bureau chief at that time, Louie Allen, an African American, claimed that the bureau did not run after Muslims blindly, and was careful that Muslims' civil rights were not violated wholesale.

Yet these investigations discovered nothing—no plots, no terrorists, no connections with terrorism—because none were there. The same thing was true throughout the nation. Out of approximately six million Muslim residents of the country, not a single real terrorist has ever been found. Some cases were elaborately hyped in the media, but on closer scrutiny no connection to terrorism was found anywhere.

After Ali Yaghi was deported, it would have been nice of the FBI at this stage if they had left the Muslim community alone, or at least developed a good relationship with Muslims for the betterment of society, but it appears that they decided to create an artificial scenario for a case of terrorism. They needed this in order to claim success against terrorism, to assure the public that they were protecting them, to justify their large budgets and manpower, and to please the politicians by providing them with photo opportunities. So the FBI drew up plans to entrap or set up some individuals from the Muslim community for this purpose. In Albany, they zeroed in on the Masjid As-Salam to initiate a "sting operation."

THE DEFENDANTS

YASSIN MUHIDDIN AREF

Yassin Aref was born in 1970 to a religious family in the northern region of Iraq known as Kurdistan. This region is populated by Kurds who are primarily Sunni Muslims but consider themselves a separate people from Arabs, since they have a different language, Kurdish, and a different culture and tradition. Their struggle to achieve a separate state of their own, independent from Iraq, Iran, and Turkey, where Kurdish populations exist, is a very old and historical one.

Aref grew up as a religious Muslim but also as a nationalist Kurd. He became a staunch activist against the regime of Saddam Hussein during his youth, helping and participating in the struggle for Kurdish independence from the tyranny and atrocities of the dictator. Because of the various difficulties he was facing there, he left Iraq and moved to Damascus, Syria as a refugee. He attended an Islamic college in Damascus and graduated with a degree in Islamic theology. He applied to a United Nations refugee program to immigrate overseas, preferably to a European country. He succeeded in being approved, but was selected to move to the U.S.A. In October 1999, through the auspices of the UN refugee program and the help of St. Michael's Episcopal Church in Colonie, New York, he landed in Albany with his wife, Zuhur Jalal, whom he had married in 1994 in Kurdistan, and their three young children. He started his new life at 8 Leonard Place, a two-bedroom apartment leased for him for six months by the church.

When we opened the As-Salam mosque in July 2000, Aref became its first imam, which in Arabic literally means "in the front." Technically it means a prayer leader. A prayer leader always stands in front of the congregation to lead them in prayer. Practically, an imam in a mosque is more or less the counterpart of a priest in a church. Aref's duties were to conduct religious services, deliver sermons, offer religious classes for adults and children, perform counseling and marriage ceremonies, conduct burials, and so forth.

Aref was an energetic and hard-working man. Just after his arrival in Albany he worked as a janitor at Albany Medical Center Hospital for some time, and as a pizza deliveryman. In order to supplement his income, he also drove an ambulette for a company that transported patients receiving

Yassin Aref

Anonymous photographer

Mohammed Hossain

Photo by Michael T. Farrell. Courtesy of Albany *Times Union*.

medical treatment. Because of his devotion, commitment, and sincerity, Aref was very much liked by the people attending the mosque. In the beginning he had communication problems, since he did not speak English, but he learned the language fast and soon was proficient enough in English to communicate with his audience. He was commonly called "Brother Yassin" or "Imam Yassin" or simply "Yassin" by his peers and by his congregation (although in official papers and news reports he is referred to as Aref).

He was a law-abiding individual, not willing to get involved with anything that was not allowed according to the laws of Islam and the law of the land. He was also very independent, both as a person and as an imam. He did not belong to any groups or organizations, and he never tried to associate or affiliate himself or the mosque with any groups. He did not even want to associate with other area mosques or their imams. He was extremely opinionated and stubborn in his ideas and almost always rejected the ideas and opinions of others that did not coincide with his own.

I was of the opposite view: I wanted close cooperation and a good relationship with all the area mosques and their imams. Because of this difference in attitude, I often had serious difficulty dealing with him. On occasion, I was barely on speaking terms with him. Around the time of his arrest, this was the nature of our relationship.

On August 4, 2004, after finishing the night prayer at around 11 p.m., Imam Aref locked up the mosque and walked home to 44 West Street, just around the corner from the mosque, about a three-minute walk. Two FBI agents were waiting for him in a car parked in front of his house. They invited him to their car to answer a couple of questions.

They had done the same thing a few times in the past. Aref told me once that in total, he had been visited by agents five times. They had asked him simple questions about his finances, the purchase of his house, his immigration status, and the situation in the mosque, and had inquired if he needed any help from them. They had talked to him either in their cars or inside his house. The visits and the questionings were always brief, and seemed to be routine. They would leave their business cards, telling him to call them if there was any problem or if he needed any help.

This time, expecting a repeat of his previous experience with them, Aref entered their car and sat down in the back seat. But one of the agents showed him a pair of handcuffs and said, "This is not like the other times. This time you're under arrest." They asked him for the key to the mosque. He gave them a bunch of about eight keys, and he was then promptly handcuffed behind his back.

The agents drove him to the Albany FBI headquarters at 200 Mc-Carty Avenue, about a ten-minute drive away. The Joint Terrorism Task Force is also housed in this building. I am told that the entire building is made up of bulletproof walls and equipped with state-of-the-art bugging, listening, recording, and audio-visual devices and equipment. I think the law should require that these devices be used only against criminals and criminal activities.

Aref was taken inside the building and tied in a chair while his hands and feet were chained. For almost six hours he was interrogated by five agents and two translators, who sometimes shouted at him and other times threatened him. According to him, Special Agent Tim Coll, the head of the JTTF, became very angry at one point during the interrogation and rushed toward him with a closed fist and threatened to punch him in the face. Aref was told a few times that he would not see his children again. An agent speaking Aref's native language, Kurdish, was also present. Aref later told me some details about the questioning that sounded very much like "good cop-bad cop" stories. He also told me that after the hostile questioning was over in the morning, the whole atmosphere changed entirely. The same interrogators suddenly became very friendly. They smiled and even joked with him. They untied him and let him offer his morning prayer.

Aref had waived his right of attorney at the time of the interrogation, which was not recorded. I consider the waiver very naïve and foolish on Aref's part, and very smart and cunning on the FBI's part. I asked Aref why he waived his right to an attorney. "I had not committed any crime and I had nothing to hide, so what did I need an attorney for?" was his answer. The FBI's claim that they did not record the interrogation is very puzzling and disturbing. As we will soon see, the FBI's informant had been busy recording each of his many conversations with Aref and Hossain for nearly a year, and the FBI claimed to have fifty hours of recordings on tape. Consequently, almost all of their arguments in court were based on these recordings. Why, then, did not they record the most important conversation—the interrogation? I am told that the FBI does not record its interrogations so as not to reveal its interrogation methods.

In the morning, probably just as the search of the mosque was concluding and I was planning to return home, Aref was driven to the Rensselaer County Jail at 4000 Main Street in Troy, just a fifteen-minute drive across the Hudson River from Albany. Since there is no federal prison in the Albany area, the government has an arrangement with this jail to hold federal prisoners there prior to their trials or sentencing.

Around the same time that Aref was being arrested, FBI agents, including some Kurdish-speaking and female agents, raided his house. They removed his wife, Zuhur, and their three young children from the house and drove them to a hotel near the Albany Airport before they searched the house. After the search was over in the morning, they brought the family home from the hotel. I think it was very nice of the FBI. I have heard that in some towns in which Muslim houses were raided, during the search the family members were shoved into a corner, frightened and humiliated.

The FBI ransacked Aref's apartment mercilessly and hauled away diaries, magazines, newspapers, books, audio-video cassettes, documents, letters, and papers. According to Zuhur, they did not give her a list of the items they took from her apartment. A few days later, someone came and took away a large plastic toy car from the apartment. This toy had been given as a gift to Aref's children by the government's informant, Malik. We speculate that perhaps it was fitted with a bugging device that the agents forgot to remove during their raid. If this is true, it was the Trojan gift horse of the century! (Later in court, the government acknowledged that the case against Aref and Hossain was not the "case of the century," while one of the defense attorneys shot back that it was not even the "case of the weekend.")

Zuhur was interrogated by the FBI agents at the hotel. She had not much idea as to what was going on, nor what wrong her husband had done. She did not believe her husband had anything to hide. "Weapon? What weapon? Buying a weapon? For what?" were some of her answers when the agents asked her if her husband was involved with dangerous weapons. She told them that she did not believe anything they were talking about. According to her, her husband was open and friendly to everyone.

When I met her in the mosque later that day, the first thing she asked me was, "For what accusation is my husband arrested?" Our conversation was in Arabic.

"For witnessing a loan arrangement that the government says was a money-laundering scheme." I tried to explain to her about the charges with what little knowledge of the arrests I had been able to acquire.

"Is witnessing a loan a crime in this country?"

"No, but the government…" I realized I would not be able to explain. I asked my daughter-in-law, Sana, to take over.

MOHAMMED MOSHARREF HOSSAIN

Forty-nine-year-old Mohammed Mosharref Hossain, known in the Muslim community as Mosharref, became a naturalized U.S. citizen in the early Nineties. He had come to Albany around 1985 as a young man, poor and knowing very little English, from the Noakhali region of Bangladesh. Prior to that, he had spent some time in Bombay, India. Altough his mother tongue is Bengali, he was able to speak in broken Urdu.

The first time I met him, soon after he arrived here, he was working as a dishwasher in the Colonie Diner on Central Avenue. Then he drove a taxi and worked as a short-order cook. Because of his determination and hard work, he succeeded in starting a pizza business in partnership, and then in 1994 with his wife Fatima, he finally owned his own pizza shop, Little Italy, at 2 Central Avenue. Fatima (also known as Mosammat) came from his hometown in Bangladesh; the family, including their five young children who were all U.S.-born, lived upstairs in the same building. Hossain also learned how to manage rental properties, and he purchased several rundown residential properties in Albany that he renovated and rented for additional income.

When I first knew him, Hossain tended to be very argumentative and short-tempered. He used to engage in heated discussions and began feuds very easily. Even though I knew him well, I used to keep a distance from him because of this. But when he visited Bangladesh during the summer of 2000, he met some religious scholars who influenced him to moderate his attitude. He became somewhat humble and a lot more committed to helping others. My relationship with him improved after that. He was very religious and was present in the mosque for daily prayers most of the time, where he talked to others and invited them to be more committed to Islam. He was a very law-abiding citizen and had an extremely good relationship and friendship with Aref, for whom he had great respect as imam of the mosque.

On August 5, 2004, around 1:00 a.m., Hossain arrived home from a three-hour trip to New York City, where he had purchased airline tickets for his mother-in-law and two of his children who were planning to visit Bangladesh. FBI agents were spread around the block waiting for him. As soon as he stopped his car, he was surrounded by the agents. The block was cordoned off by dozens of cars with flashing lights.

Fatima, in shock and in tears, asked the officers, "What wrong did he do? Why is he being treated like this? What is going on?"

"You'll know later," they replied.

Hossain was arrested, handcuffed, and transferred to a waiting car. Fatima informed them that he suffered from diabetes and high blood pressure, and she wanted to make sure that his sugar level was OK. They were kind enough to let her test him. The number was around 400. She became terribly worried but did not know how to help him or what to do. They allowed her to give him his medication. He was promptly driven to FBI headquarters, where he faced a similar situation as Aref.

Hossain's car, parked in front of his house, was thoroughly searched and photographed and all of his papers and cash, as well as the tickets and his passport, were confiscated.

Fatima noticed from the sidewalk that about half a dozen agents with a dog were climbing the stairs and entering her apartment without asking her permission or showing her any papers. She rushed to the apartment. The agents proceeded to ask everyone in the apartment to go downstairs to the pizza shop. Fatima woke all of the children and brought them downstairs, where they were locked in and guarded until the search of the apartment was over, about 6 a.m. The FBI confiscated the Hossains' home computer, letters, books, notebooks, diaries, videotapes, and $6,848 in cash. Fatima signed the sheet for the inventory of the items. They gave her a copy and left.

"That was all the money I had collected to pay the rent, taxes, utilities and medical bills," she told me later in the morning, wiping away her tears.

At FBI headquarters, Hossain waived his right to an attorney. He was also chained in a chair and interrogated and then driven to the Rensselaer County Jail. Most likely he was interrogated under the same conditions as Aref was, but Hossain did not want to share this with me.

ABDULBARR SHUAIB

The third person from the mosque arrested that morning was Abdulbarr Shuaib, 53, an African American man born and raised locally. He had converted to Islam and changed his name many years ago. He was a regular and senior member of the mosque and had a good relationship with both Aref and Hossain. He had had some problems with the law in the past and had been in prison, where he had become very practiced in dealing with law enforcement authorities. The FBI came to his apartment in upper Albany in the early morning of August 5 and asked him to come out. They wanted to interview him about the alleged crimes of Aref and Hossain, who had already been arrested. According to Shuaib, they tried to implicate him in these alleged crimes so that they could make him plead guilty and use him to testify against Aref and Hossain. They told him that they had tape-recorded a meeting in which he had participated with the two men when they were discussing an illegal deal.

Shuaib told them, "I know that if I did anything wrong, or if you have something indicating that I did something wrong, I would be in handcuffs in your car rather than you guys discussing these things with me this way." After realizing that they were going nowhere because they were dealing with someone familiar with the law, the agents charged Shuaib with violating a child support order issued by the Rensselaer County Family Court and drove him to the Rensselaer County Jail, where Aref and Hossain had been taken.

They brought Shuaib to court later the same day. The judge found that the charge against him was bogus, dismissed the case, and set him free.

In the afternoon, Aref and Hossain were brought in handcuffs under very heavy security to the federal courthouse at 445 Broadway in Albany and presented to federal magistrate David Homer, who informed them of the charges against them: money laundering, conspiracy, and giving material support to a foreign terrorist organization.

Both Aref and Hossain sat in court totally confused, not understanding what was going on around them. They did not enter any plea, and were swiftly taken by U.S. marshals back to their jail cells.

Faisal Ahmad speaks to the media on the sidewalk in front of the Masjid
As-Salam after the arrests on August 5, 2004.

From a news video by WRGB CBS 6 Albany

CHAPTER 3

Media Frenzy

After the search of the mosque was over, I returned home and quickly went through the search warrant that I had picked up in the mosque. I saw the whole picture of Aref and Hossain's arrest immediately. I concluded that they had been tricked into participating in an elaborate "sting" operation devised by the FBI, which employed a Pakistani criminal as a confidential informant. I had some idea of the FBI's other sting operations around the country, which helped me quickly figure out the situation. From this warrant, I also concluded that Aref and Hossain would be charged with dealing with dangerous weapons while involved in some kind of terrorist plot. Many of the other FBI terrorist cases turned on a strategy of creating a fictional terrorist plot that involved dangerous weapons and then trying to involve unsuspecting Muslims in it.

I sat down in front of the TV with a radio on. My house was empty. Everyone had rushed to the mosque. I saw on the TV that the whole area around the mosque was packed with reporters and spectators. About a dozen cars belonging to various media groups and a dozen large mobile studio trucks had taken all the parking spots. I jumped from one channel to the other and from one radio station to the other. News flashes were short, sharp, and tense, but frequent and frightening. The following quotes are taken from personal recordings that I made from various media outlets:

"Two men were arrested and are suspected of providing material support for terrorism," reported one national TV outlet.

"Two men were caught in a sting operation and tried to buy shoulder-fired missiles from an undercover agent," reported another TV station.

"The men were selling shoulder-fired missiles like this…" (a picture of a turbaned, bearded Afghan man with a long missile on his shoulder flashed on the screen).

"They are accused of dealing with a man who they believed was plotting to kill a Pakistani diplomat in New York City."

"They were plotting to kill a Pakistani ambassador as payback for the jailing of Abdul Qadir Khan, a founder of Pakistan's nuclear program. The assassination was supposed to take place near United Nations headquarters."

"These men are members of a terrorist organization, Ansar al-Islam in Iraq, which is linked with the Jordanian terrorist Abu Musab al-Zarqawi, who is linked with al-Qaeda."

"…Aref's links to the radical Muslim group Ansar al-Islam give a chilling glimpse into the world of al-Qaeda operatives living in the United States."

"The arrested doughboy belongs to foreign terrorist organizations Jamaat-e-Islami and Jaish-e-Mohammad."

" …one of them recently bought a plane ticket which triggered the arrest."

"If convicted, the men could get up to seventy years in prison and up to $750,000 in fines."

After listening to these news flashes, I became extremely concerned. I had a sense of the immense power of the FBI, as well as the additional authority formally or informally offered to them by the Bush-Cheney Administration. I knew very well that in the current environment, the FBI could proceed based on racial or religious profiling, or in violation of human rights, or even in violation of the U.S. Constitution, and no one would dare take them to task. They would simply pass on their information to the administration, saying, "Whatever we do is only to track down Muslim terrorists and punish them." And there would be nothing but smiles!

But on the other hand, since I knew both Aref and Hossain very well and was familiar with their attitudes and capabilities, I thought the FBI in this case had taken a bigger bite than they could swallow. The two men were very simple, religious, family men. I had known them both for a number of years, and I knew that they were not even remotely like terrorists. They had neither the talent, resources, money, nor capabilities to do any of the things they were being accused of—buying and selling missiles, shooting down a plane near the United Nations. They were very considerate, law-abiding members of society, busy with their own lives, unconnected to any sort of crimes or illegal activities. I concluded that the FBI must have tricked them into some sort of trap.

Simultaneously, some of the regular members of the mosque were expressing the same feelings while talking to reporters in front of the mosque:

"We do not believe any bit of it," said Murtaza Hasan, a computer technologist, originally from India.

"Neither of those men are terrorists. They are 100% innocent," said Aref Khan, a young man of Pakistani descent who worked in a store near the mosque.

"I think it was a publicity stunt for the FBI to say they are closing in on terrorism," said Muta Ali, an African American in his late thirties who also worked in a store close to the mosque. "This is the election season, after all, and now they can say, 'See, we are making you safe.'"

"There must be some sort of big misunderstanding. These are very religious, nice people," my son Faisal commented. "Don't jump to conclusions, wait for more details."

"The two men are God-fearing people," my son Sajid explained. "They cannot do anything to harm others because they believe in the judgment in the hereafter."

"I'm upset. It's racial profiling," said Abdul Malik, an African American car mechanic. "They're honest men, good family men."

One of Hossain's tenants, Ruth Rivera, expressed herself thus to one reporter: "I don't believe it. I think he was set up. I'm Christian and he's Muslim, but I always felt comfortable talking to him. He's very respectful about my thoughts on religion."

I kept hearing these statements on the TV and the radio and occasionally read them on the computer.

A Photo Op for Politicians

The local TV news stations reported that George Pataki, New York's Republican governor, had organized a news conference in front of Albany's police headquarters, only a few blocks from the mosque. Flanked by Albany's Democratic mayor, Jerry Jennings, Police Chief James Turley, and representatives of fourteen law enforcement agencies, Pataki stated, "The fact is, there are terrorists among us who would do us harm. The government is taking this threat to our freedom very seriously."

Jennings said, "It's been an ongoing investigation, and obviously the results are good. This is something we've anticipated. People shouldn't be concerned because we've been on top of this for quite awhile."

A journalist described this gathering as "long on congratulations and reassurances but short on information. Not a lot of news at that conference." But Pataki's statement was sufficient to send a tremor through my spine and make me, a Muslim, tremble. No doubt the chief executive of New York State had made every Muslim a suspected terrorist, and had described the local sting operation as if it were an actual "statewide event" regarding terrorism.

It was a little past noon. I was sitting on the sofa with a heavy head and a pounding heart, thinking about what the whole episode was going to bring to us as mosque members or to the Muslim community at large. Suddenly I heard a news flash that there was going to be a press conference in the afternoon in Washington D.C., called by the U.S. Justice Department to address the Albany case. That's when I started praying: *O my God, save us! This is much heavier than I thought. It's an event of national importance now!*

The news coverage was still going on. I noticed that the sensational tone had died down a little, and the reporters were expressing curiosity about details of the case. I shut off the radio and waited for the televised press conference in Washington to begin.

Then the telephone rang. It was Al-Jazeera Arabic TV, which wanted to send a crew from Washington to interview me the next day. I agreed, but somehow they could not make it to Albany and the interview never took place.

The phone began to ring in earnest: back-to-back calls from England, Bombay, and Singapore, all friends of my children who wanted to know if the information they had just seen on TV and the Internet were true.

Mayor Jennings called. He asked if we needed any protection or security arrangements. Police Chief Turley also called and offered help. I asked both of them to send a patrol car past Aref's house and the back of the mosque now and then. The front of the mosque was still crowded with media people, and Hossain's pizzeria and apartment were on a busy corner, so I did not expect any danger or mischief there.

"What about the mosque demonstration at 6:30 p.m.?" Turley asked.

This surprised me. "I am not aware of any plans for a demonstration," I said, "and I do not want any demonstration to take place until the whole situation is clarified."

"Everyone has a right to demonstrate," Turley said.

"Well, I'll find out about it and let you know," I answered.

Faisal later told me that he had circulated a press release among the reporters and had arranged a press conference in front of the mosque at 6:30 p.m. Apparently Turley mistook it for a demonstration. In the press release, I, as president of the mosque, had pleaded with the media and the public not to rush to conclusions from the arrests, lest they lead to anti-Muslim backlash and hate crimes.

WASHINGTON PRESS CONFERENCE

At about 2:30 p.m., the promised Justice Department press conference began when James Comey, Deputy U.S. Attorney General, walked into a large room packed with anxious and tense reporters. He told them that he was there to report on the arrest of two Muslim men in Albany, New York who were involved in a terrorism plot. The two were being charged, he said, with providing material support to terrorism by participating in a conspiracy to help someone they believed was a terrorist purchase a shoulder-fired missile. "This case is a sting," he said. "It's a sting where two men were presented with the opportunity to assist someone who they believed was a terrorist facilitator, supplying weapons to be used in terrorist attacks. The informant, a Pakistani national, has a criminal record and was working with authorities to get a reduced sentence."

I saw that the reporters became very excited at this, and took Comey's elaboration about the success of law enforcement authorities in Albany and elsewhere with great seriousness.

Comey went on to emphasize that "it was a sting operation, not an interruption of an actual unfolding plot to use the missile."

I noticed that the enthusiasm of the reporters began to die down.

"Then isn't it a case of entrapment?" one reporter asked.

"That is something that would come up in court…" replied Comey.

"Is it not true that the government was picking on these two men because they're from a mosque?" another reporter dared to ask.

Comey said, "We have way too much to do to just spend our time on a case like that. It's a good case, a solid case. It's important to note that it is not the case of the century, and has nothing to do with the heightened security alert. Our purpose here is to lock up two guys who committed a crime."

Comey's phrase "not the case of the century" would later be repeated by reporters and defense attorneys inside and outside the courtroom.

"We hope this sends a message to those out there who might be plotting to harm people in this country or around the world," Comey continued. "Anyone engaging in terrorist planning would be very wise to consider whether their accomplice is not really one of our guys."

Describing some of the defendants' statements that had been recorded by the informant on tape, Comey stated, "Hossain, one of the arrested men, acknowledged there was both an inner jihad and an outer, violent jihad, and added that now was not the time for violent jihad."

I saw skepticism on the faces of some of the reporters, as if some doubt were developing in their minds. *Then how come a real terrorist would make a statement like this?* was the question I read on their faces.

At this point, my own skepticism changed to certainty that the so-called "government informant," who was also described as a criminal, was not really an informant. Rather, he was the real "player" of the scheme cunningly devised by the FBI. Aref and Hossain had somehow been entrapped in this scheme by deception, trick, or by simple association. The FBI's net is very wide! I had heard about several cases around the nation where the FBI and their agents had played tricky games against innocent individuals. I was not willing to express these conclusions, however, without consulting the men's attorneys.

MOSQUE PRESS CONFERENCE

My household gradually trickled back home, and around 6 p.m. we all freshened up and went to the mosque. About twenty mosque members were already there. Fear had kept others away. Most of them were very upset, tense, and confused. Everyone had heard the terrorism allegations and nobody believed a bit of it. The question was where to go from here.

I had come to the mosque prepared to talk to the media. My intention was to state the position of our religion, our community, and our mosque against terrorism and violence, to express skepticism about the case, and to challenge the motives of the government behind this sting operation, based on whatever I knew so far. But I considered it advisable to talk to the members of the mosque first, particularly when so many of them were there.

So we all sat down on the carpet in the back room. I gave them all the information I had and suggested that we should separate the interests of the mosque community from the charges against Aref and Hossain.

"Let the legal difficulties of the sting charges be confined to the two indi-viduals," I said, "because the mosque and the community have nothing to do with their alleged criminal dealings." But a suggestion was made that we should not divorce and abandon them, since they were targeted only because they were Muslims and belonged to the mosque. They were not targeted as individuals; rather, the whole scheme was to disgrace the Muslim community.

When it came to the question of who would be the official spokesper-son for the mosque, contrary to my expectation that everyone's eyes would turn to me, people suggested that Faisal should be the one to speak. The members argued that they had seen him talking to reporters and others all day and that he had been doing a fine and eloquent job.

Sana did not like the idea at all. I think she was fearful that her hus-band would become a very visible person and that the government might mark him for that, a fear that has become commonplace in every Muslim household in the post-9/11 atmosphere. And here we were, facing a real crisis. I reassured her, and asked Faisal to write something in the next ten minutes for the press conference.

A little after 6:30 p.m., we all came out and informed the media that we were ready to make a statement. The crowd of reporters and camera-men surged. Faisal stood up on a chair on the sidewalk so they could see him. The mosque sign just above his head read, in Arabic, "Masjid As-Salam," along with its translation, "House of Peace." He was flanked by mosque members on each side, though some members strategically stood behind the cameras, rather than faced them, because they did not want to go on record.

Faisal emphasized that we were religious people opposed to terrorism and violence in any shape or form. "The two arrested men are righteous Muslims and dedicated family men," he said. "Do not judge them, their place of worship, or their faith before all the facts are known. Look at our faces. If you see any evil in our faces, please talk to us. Our religion, Islam, is a religion that teaches peace, kindness, and charity." Pointing to the mosque's sign over the door, Faisal said, "We stand together to condemn this sort of violence. Must we fight for our innocence, or are we assumed to be innocent?"

The media received him and his statements well. But someone shout-ed, "If we lived under one God, we would not be here right now!" Faisal took this in stride and invited a cordial dialogue, without confrontation. After half an hour or so, the conference ended peacefully.

We went back inside the mosque to get ready for the evening prayer. The crowd of reporters thinned but did not vanish. More than a dozen media cars and satellite trucks would remain parked there for the next two days, and about eight of them stayed for the next five days.

SOME DETAILS START TO EMERGE

The evening news bulletins were less sensational. More concrete details were emerging. And reporters were not buying the story that the two men were interested in terrorism; a case of simple greed and money laundering was on everybody's mind instead. Some reporters started suggesting that it was entrapment by the government. But not everyone thought this way. In the morning, I heard a radio talk-show host blustering very loudly. "The FBI should be given credit," he said. "They've busted a case where these two guys were selling illegal licenses and running around with missiles shooting airplanes." A caller to the station, a very provoked elderly lady, demanded, "We should find out how many mosque members are state workers. They must be fired." I shivered. I was a state worker, teaching at a state university!

By arresting Muslims around the country in fictitious plots and by sensationalizing those cases, the FBI did a favor for many loudmouth radio talk-show hosts who had already been playing on the public's fear and planting false information in uninformed minds. "Many of these radio talk-show hosts belong in psychiatric wards, but they fly high on the airwaves," a psychology professor shared with me. "They're really very dangerous to society and should be kept away from microphones. Unfortunately, most of the radio stations are owned by companies that care about business, not the interests of the public. This is the cheapest way to make a station popular."

"But we live in a free society. What about freedom of speech?" I asked.

"Even hate-mongering is a form of freedom of speech," he said. "Besides, we all have the freedom to praise Bush, but as a Muslim you know that if you criticize him, you won't have to guess who will be knocking at your door." I could not have agreed with him more.

CHAPTER 4

The Law Proceeds

CHOOSING ATTORNEYS

Immediately after the raid on the mosque, I made and continued to make numerous inquiries about the legal aspects of the case. By August 6, I had a good idea about how the government was planning to move legally. My job was to find one or possibly two experienced, capable, and bold attorneys. My responsibility was mostly to arrange a defense for Aref, because he was the imam of the mosque that I had founded. I felt that if I did not take on this responsibility, I would be doing something morally wrong. Aref knew very little English, had no money, and had hardly any idea about the legal system in the U.S. Moreover, I had a suspicion that at some point I might be implicated or forced by the FBI to be a witness in the case, or I might be used in some other capacity, since my documents had also been seized during the mosque raid. But I could not think of a lawyer who would come to Aref's defense.

I was not sure about Hossain. Unlike Aref's wife, Fatima Hossain was capable of handling some of the responsibility for her husband's defense, plus Hossain was a citizen, had lived here long enough to have an understanding of the legal system, spoke English well, and could afford his defense financially.

I could not find a local attorney who had experience in terrorism-related cases. But through CAIR (Council on American-Islamic Relations), a Washington, D.C.-based Muslim civil rights advocacy group, I did find a New York City attorney, Khurrum Wahid, who had such experience. Wahid was willing to defend the case but advised me to get a local attorney right away. After some more inquiries, I decided to retain a criminal law attorney, and I called Terence Kindlon of Kindlon Shanks & Associates in

Albany. I had been told that he had thirty years of criminal law experience, and that he was a Vietnam veteran and a very bold lawyer who would never be intimidated by the government or the media. After discussing a few points with me, Kindlon said, "Hossain's wife also called me and left a message, and I was going to return her call and talk to her, but since you're the president of the mosque and represent the community, I'll be more comfortable with you. I will take the case and defend Aref."

"Please find another capable attorney of your choice to defend Hossain," I asked him. "I will talk with Fatima, and if she has not chosen one already, I will convince her to accept your choice. I am more than sure it will be fine with her."

I invited Kindlon to come to the mosque at 2 p.m. to talk to the congregation right after the Friday Prayer. "This way," I said, "people will have an assurance of your defense commitment and strategy, and at the same time you'll be able to sense the community support for the case." He agreed without any hesitation.

FRIDAY PRAYER

Friday is a special day of the week for Muslims. Friday Prayer, performed in the first hours of the afternoon, is an important event that should be attended by every capable adult male Muslim who can afford to take time off from other commitments. For women, attendance is optional; they may offer their prayer at home instead. At the mosque, a sermon is given by the imam, partly in Arabic and partly in the local language, lasting about twenty or thirty minutes. At the conclusion of the sermon, the prayer is conducted in Arabic; it normally lasts for ten minutes or less. Other daily prayers do not require sermons, only readings from the scripture in Arabic. This format and procedure are the same in every part of the globe. In our tradition, anyone with reasonable religious knowledge can act as an imam. There is no requirement for an official ordained "priesthood."

Since Aref, our imam, had been arrested, I had to arrange for another imam to give the Friday sermon on August 6. I did this, but the substitute called me in the morning and said, "Brother, I am sorry. I am a little scared, so I will not be able to do the job."

I told him, "No problem, take it easy." I contacted another person, who expressed his readiness to give the sermon, but half an hour before the service he called me and said that he was a little shaky this time but would be ready for next Friday. I thought that at least the two men had been frank and honest. I decided not to look for anyone else and to give the sermon myself. I had done this plenty of times in the past, often at a moment's notice, so it was not a challenge for me.

In my sermons, I normally begin the introduction by reciting three verses from the Qur'an, just as the Prophet used to do at the beginning of his sermons. The Qur'an (sometimes written as Koran or Quran) is the holy book of Islam. It is written in Arabic, but has been translated into all major languages of the world. It is roughly one-third as voluminous as the King James Bible. It has 114 uneven chapters: the shortest chapter contains only three short verses, while the longest one contains 286 long verses.

So I began my sermon this way, as the Prophet did: "Thanks and praise be to Allah, Whom we thank and from Whom we seek help and forgiveness. We believe in Him and we put our trust in Him. We seek His refuge from the wrongdoings of our souls and the evils of our bad deeds. Whomsoever Allah guides, will never be misled and whomsoever He lets to be misguided, will never find someone to guide them. I testify that none has the right to be worshipped, except Allah, alone without partners, and that Muhammad is Allah's slave and Messenger.

"Allah says in the Qur'an, 'O you who believe! Be conscious of Allah as He deserves to be conscious of Him and die not except in a state of believing in Him.' (Chapter 3, Verse 102). He the Almighty also says, 'O Mankind! be dutiful to your Lord Who created you from a single soul and from it He created its mate and from them both spread out a lot of men and women, and fear Allah through Whom you demand (your mutual rights), and do not cut the relations of the wombs (kinship). Surely, Allah is watching over you.' (Chapter 4, Verse 1). Allah also says, 'O you who believe! Keep your duty to Allah and fear Him, and speak the right things. He will direct you to do righteous deeds and will forgive your sins. And whosoever obeys Allah and His Messenger (Muhammad), he has indeed achieved a great achievement.' (Chapter 33, Verse 71–72)."

For my sermon, I decided to quote some additional text from the Qur'an and to use its translation and explanation to deliver my message to the congregation. I chose short portions from Verses 2 and 8 of Chapter 5 as appropriate for the occasion. I translated, "O you who believe! …help and cooperate with each other toward righteousness and piety, and do not help and cooperate with each other for the path of evil and transgression; be fearful of the Almighty…" After elaborating on and explaining various aspects of this divine message, I moved to the second one and translated, "O you who believe! be steadfast for the sake of Almighty, be witnesses to the justice; let your animosity toward another people not drive you that you do not do justice to them; do justice to them, this is closer to piety; be God-conscious; indeed Allah is all-aware of what you do."

After explaining these words with examples of history and other texts, I concluded by saying, "My dear brothers and sisters! Look at the miraculous beauty of the Qur'an that the text revealed 1,400 years ago, and that seems to be given to us now, on this occasion, to follow. Whatever message I want to give to you is not part of some sort of diplomacy. It is the word of God." I encouraged the attendees, as members of the Muslim community, to be bold, not to express their anger against any people or the government, not to fear anything, and not to do anything morally or legally wrong. This last sentence was necessary because people were really fearful, angry, and confused.

Normally on a Friday in our mosque, the number of attendees was about 250. That day, the number was no more than 150. Because of fear, many decided not to come.

After the prayer was over, I introduced Terence Kindlon to the audience. Those interested in staying to hear him numbered only about thirty. "This is a case of great injustice to your imam," Kindlon began. "I will defend him with full vigor and make sure that he receives justice and is proven innocent." He gave his credentials as a criminal law attorney, explained the jury process and trial procedures, and asked for the continuous support of the community. He left after promising that he would come to the mosque on a regular basis to brief the community firsthand about the progress of the case—unfortunately, a promise on which he could not deliver.

GRAND JURY INDICTMENT

Aref and Hossain were indicted by a grand jury at the U.S. Courthouse on August 6, with Honorable David Homer presiding.

Abdulbarr Shuaib was subpoenaed, along with several other witnesses. He told me later that the government's lead attorney, William Pericak, initially wanted to present him as a government witness, but circumstances had changed and he was treated as a hostile witness. Shuaib was peppered with harsh questions by Assistant U.S. Attorney Greg West, the anti-terrorism coordinator in New York's Northern District. Both prosecutors referred to a meeting that Shuaib had attended, during which Aref and Hossain and the government informant supposedly discussed some allegedly illegal transaction (see Appendix A, Sting Tapes 2003, December 10). Shuaib told the grand jurors in essence that Hossain had approached the informant for a loan because he needed money, and that Aref offered to be a witness to the loan according to Islamic tradition. He told them that he did not recall any discussion about weapons or about China at that meeting.

Along with a female translator, Zuhur, Aref's wife, was also taken to court at the same time by FBI agents. Whether Zuhur was questioned or presented to the jurors, we do not know. She was so distressed, paranoid, and confused that to this day she cannot recall what they said or did to her in court. Other witnesses were also called to give testimony, but their identities were not disclosed.

At the conclusion of this proceeding, the grand jury handed up a sealed nineteen-count indictment against Aref and Hossain. Both defendants were charged with carrying out an illegal money-laundering scheme to support terrorism; according to the FBI, the acts of money laundering they carried out in the sting implied support of Malik's weapons business of supplying SAMs to terrorists, thus providing material support to terrorism. Each count generally corresponded with each of their meetings with the government informant, during which time the loan transactions were conducted. (Aref would later be additionally charged for lying to FBI investigators during his post-arrest interrogation when he claimed that he did not personally know Mullah Krekar, a Kurdish terrorist leader; that he was not a member of the Islamic Movement of Kurdistan [IMK], a supposedly terror-related organization—which it was not; and for lying on his refugee and immigration applications when he claimed that he did not belong to any political organizations after his sixteenth birthday.) Aref and Hossain were ordered to remain in jail and to be brought to court again on August 10, when the indictment would be unsealed and a bail hearing would take place. The government announced that it would provide more details at that hearing, in addition to the information they had already provided, presumably to bolster their case.

Members of the Muslim community were not well informed about the grand jury proceeding. Only a dozen members of the mosque were present in court. When they came out, almost all had tears in their eyes.

That evening the government gave out yet more information, which immediately became a big news hit for the media. According to the government's sources, the U.S. military had bombed and raided a terrorist camp at Rawah in northern Iraq in June 2003, and in the litter of the burned-out and destroyed camp they found a handwritten notebook in the Kurdish language that contained Aref's name and his old 1999 address and telephone number in Albany. Military intelligence, however, presumed the notebook was written in Arabic. The government claimed that the camp was a training center for terrorists from Ansar al-Islam, a terrorist group opposed to the U.S. occupation of Iraq. "The document reveals that Aref was their commander," the government claimed.

One well-known news agency reported, "Thug's black book: U.S. troops who raided a terror training camp run by the Ansar al-Islam group in northern Iraq last summer discovered an address book among other documents. It contained personal information about Yassin Aref, one of the men arrested yesterday. His name, address, and telephone number in Albany were all in the book, according to a government official. His title is 'The Commander.'"

Most of the news reports talked a lot about Aref being referred to as "commander"—but commander of whom, or commander of what kind, was not known. The prosecutors said they were confident that when they presented this additional information during the coming bail hearing, the defendants' bail would be denied.

SPECULATIONS AND DOUBTS

The next two or three days, August 7–9, were very hectic. Some reporters seemed to be convinced that the two men really had something to do with overseas terrorist organizations. But the majority were very skeptical. Some of them suggested that if the men were really that dangerous, why did the government wait so long to move on them, with such a complicated money-laundering/sting scheme that dragged out for over a year?

Muslim leaders in the other four area mosques were not talking to the media. Muslims themselves were frightened and terrified. My house was bombarded with media telephone calls, local, national, and even some international. They wanted to hear our version and interpretation of the case. My children tried to deprive me of these telephone calls. They told me that I was not in good health, that I was too blunt, too direct, too angry with the sting, with the politicians, and with Aref and Hossain. They feared that I might make blunt, non-calculated statements that might be used against the defendants later. So Faisal and Huma responded to reporters' questions all day long. Their answers during these interviews were appropriately indirect and vague.

And my children were right: I *was* upset and angry with Aref and Hossain because of their involvement with the government's informant and his confusing loan deal, even though I thought the deal was not illegal—it was simply designed as a work of fiction to entrap them. Aref and Hossain were committed religious men and strong proponents of *Sunnah*, an Islamic term meaning actions by the Messenger of God, the Prophet Muhammad; the Prophet's teachings, including his approval or non-approval of people's practices; and by implication the teachings of other prophets, such as Abraham, Noah, Moses, Jesus, and others (may peace be upon them all). The two defendants used to advise other Muslims that they must judge every step they took in life according to *Sunnah*. So I asked myself, *did they judge themselves according to* Sunnah *when they started their friendship and dealings with a character like the FBI informant?* My blunt conclusion was: *no way*. They should have known the character of this man at the first meeting. He was not a religious person, he never came to the mosque, and he had never been known as a person of any moral values or had any standing in the Muslim community. On the contrary, he was outright dishonest, a criminal and a convict. Honest and religious Muslims should have relationships only with people of character. I still remember my first-grade teacher in Muslim school trying to implant this lesson in our minds: "If you hang around a perfume seller's shop, you will come out smelling nice. On the other hand, if you hang around a blacksmith's shop, you will come out dirty." And, "If you are drinking milk near a bar, people will judge that you were drinking alcohol. On the other hand, even if you are drinking alcohol near a milk shop, people will assume you are drinking milk." This practical wisdom and these morals are universal for Muslims in every language and in every part of the world.

I was also upset at Hossain for getting Aref involved in witnessing his loan transactions. Hossain was not living in a village in Bangladesh; he had lived in Albany long enough to know that he should have walked to the bank across the street from his house and had the loan transaction notarized by a notary public. Moreover, why did they not draw up a proper loan contract, with all terms and conditions stated, including the purpose of the loan and the repayment plan fully spelled out? Islam requires that these specifications should be dictated by the borrower of the loan, not imposed by the person who gives the loan, as it had been by the government informant.

I was less upset but still concerned about a notorious picture, shown in the media everywhere, in which Hossain was pictured looking from a distance at the informant, who was holding a missile on his shoulder. I had known Hossain very closely for about twenty years. I did not like some aspects of his personality, but I was 100% certain that he would never become involved with violence or a weapon. *So how did this picture occur, then?* I asked myself. *Is the picture fake? Was he deceived or tricked or set up in this situation? Was he blackmailed in some way?* I wasn't sure about any of this. But I was also 100% sure that no jury would ever find him innocent after seeing this picture. My children and the defendants' attorneys did not agree with me on this.

I knew that in the recent past, the FBI had succeeded in bringing convictions in several sting operations that involved weapons or missiles. They supplied a fake or disabled weapon to their informant, who carried it or pretended to sell or buy or use it. As a result, as soon as the general public heard that a weapon was involved in a sting case, they immediately jumped to the conclusion that the accused was initiating the transaction and the informant was only watching from a distance and "informing" about it. Even reporters got carried away and reported the false information cunningly planned by the FBI, rather than analyzed the facts behind the plots and the tricks involved. This was exactly the case with the missile picture: people concluded that Hossain wanted to buy the missile or was somehow involved in dealing in weapons.

THE ATTORNEYS MEET THEIR CLIENTS

The court appointed Terence Kindlon as attorney for Aref, and Kevin Luibrand, another well-known Albany attorney from the firm Tobin & Dempf, for Hossain. The two attorneys first met their clients separately at the Rensselaer County Jail for several hours. Luibrand adopted a policy of not talking to the media, or only talking to them reservedly, but Kindlon was very forthcoming and aggressive. He described his client to the media as "a deeply religious and a spiritual guy, and he has this aura

LEFT: Kevin Luibrand, Mohammed Hossain's attorney, from the law firm Tobin & Dempf, LLP (now owner of Luibrand Law Firm, PLLC).

Courtesy of Kevin Luibrand

RIGHT: Terence Kindlon, Yassin Aref's attorney, from the law firm Kindlon Shanks & Associates.

Photo from http://www.pbs.org/weta/crossroads/about/show_security_vs_liberty.html

of calm about him." He expressed skepticism about the significance of the address book found in a region where Aref had many relatives, classmates, and friends. "I want to see it and get it translated myself and see what the hell it means, and see if this group was really a terrorist group or a cultural study group," he said. "My experience with the government, when they've got all the cards and they're telling you what the cards say, is that it's a good idea not to believe them."

Kindlon also wanted to dispel any suggestion that Aref had deliberately come to Albany from overseas with a sinister plan in his mind. "This country was chosen for him, he didn't choose this country," Kindlon said. "He was sent here through a United Nation's refugee relocation program. He did not have an option to choose Albany." Kindlon added: "He told me he was so grateful to get to the U.S. He had studied religion in college, it helped him get a job as an imam in the mosque. He told me if he were under Saddam, they would just cut his head off. He knows that here he'll be treated fairly."

About the case so far, Kindlon said, "I expect the wheels of the government's case are going to come off as the national spotlight on the arrests fades. We've seen so many of these, the so-called terrorist cases, begin with a bang and end with a whimper." He also said that the government had acted questionably, and that he was going to explore the racial, religious, cultural, and political overtones in the case. "It's not exactly a secret that this case seems to be a peculiar use of the awesome power of the federal government, and a lot of people out there are thinking this may be a *misuse* of the awesome power of the federal government. I am certainly looking into using entrapment as a defense."

A National Trend of Muslim Harassment

The American-Arab Anti-Discrimination Committee (ADC) in Washington, D.C., a civil rights advocacy group, expressed similar concerns. Noting a trend of excessive scrutiny by the FBI of Muslims and Arabs, the watchdog agency proposed to monitor the Aref-Hossain case to ensure fair treatment. "We cannot rush to judgment," said Kareem W. Shora, the ADC's director. He said he was also troubled by Governor George Pataki's comment that "there are terrorists among us."

Shora said he did not expect Aref or Hossain to be classified as terrorists or enemy combatants by the Justice Department. That move, he said, would weaken the government's case, since the practice of holding "enemy combatants" without due process was under legal attack. "I believe that the Justice Department will do its best to make sure that it will be an open court, and that they are afforded the same rights as anyone charged with any federal crime," Shora said. "But we will operate as a watchdog, just to make sure due process rights are not violated."

However, I did not notice any visible role or contribution of this organization in the case later on. Perhaps it got busy with several other more pressing cases.

Many other humanitarian and civil rights organizations, as well as activists and attorneys, were puzzled by what they saw as victimization of Muslims. For example, I read in the media a statement by St. Louis attorney James Hacking, who was very familiar with these kinds of cases. He summed up the matter by accusing the FBI of conducting a "fishing trip."

CHAPTER 5

No Bail, Then Jail

BAIL HEARING

E veryone was looking toward the bail hearing on August 10 with mixed expectations. I was expecting bail to be set very high—at least a million dollars each.

On that Tuesday, as soon as I got out of my car in front of the court-house, I was shocked. It looked like a military zone. Three policemen were sitting on horseback facing the entrance door, their left hands on the reins and their right hands on their pistols. Several police cars were parked near the courthouse, and the street corners were occupied by policemen hold-ing pistols. Five cars were parked on each side of the building; security guards stood with rifles and pistols drawn. I could also see sharpshooters on rooftops, telescopic rifles in their hands. I was sure there must be many undercover officers around, particularly in the crowd of about thirty report-ers. Every parking spot was taken by media cars and satellite trucks. *Wow, I thought, what a drama, what a circus, what a show to fool everybody, what a waste of tax dollars! The feds have been secretly running after these two guys for a year, trying to entrap them without any concern about their supposed dangerousness or security risk—and today they want to tell the world that Aref and Hossain, who have been delivering pizza and driving an ambulette while minding their own business, have become such dangerous terrorists overnight that we need all this security to protect the public from them.*

After passing through the courthouse metal detector and having my ID and personal items checked, I faced five security personnel standing in line and appraising everyone who wanted to enter the courtroom. Cell phones or anything they considered suspicious had to be deposited with them. The hallway was filled with more than a dozen security guards and FBI agents. Before we could actually enter the courtroom, we faced another metal detector, another ID check, and had to sign a register with our personal information and affiliation, witnessed by the five security personnel.

I think there were six rows of benches for the audience in the courtroom. The first two were occupied by the FBI and security people, the next two by reporters, and the last two by family members of the defendants and members of the community. Additional spectators were allowed to stand against the wall. Several security guards were standing against the walls as well. I noticed a few young men and women of Southeast Asian descent; perhaps they were new FBI recruits in training. Some latecomers were denied entry due to lack of space. The prosecutors, their assistants, and the defense attorneys sat toward the front, separated from the spectators by a small wooden partition.

The defendants, in their green jail uniforms, were brought in from a side door. They seemed to be relaxed. Aref turned toward us and smiled and waved before taking his seat. Hossain did the same.

Judge Homer arrived and started the proceeding. He declared that both attorneys had been appointed by the court as public defenders; since Aref did not have enough assets, the cost of his defense would be paid by the government. Hossain's two real estate properties were registered as collateral for his defense expenses, because based on his assets he did not qualify for public funding.

"I understand that your client needs a translator," Homer said to Kindlon, who responded, "After talking to my client, I conclude that he can communicate in English adequately, therefore a translator is not necessary."

Prosecutors were asked to present their case.

Assistant U.S. Attorney David Grable, assisted by William Pericak, presented the government's case, highlighting the nineteen-count indictment filed a day earlier. Their whole strategy was to project the two defendants as predisposed to terrorism, thus ready and willing to take part in the sting scheme devised to lure them into a fictitious terrorist plot. To support their arguments, the prosecutors presented audiotapes of the defendants' discussions with the informant, Shahed Hussain, also known as Malik, as well as photos from video surveillance tapes. One such photo, a grainy black-and-white print dated November 20, 2003, depicted Hossain looking at Malik, who held a shoulder-fired missile—the same picture the media had broadcast extensively. A second photo showed Aref and Hossain at a meeting with Malik in his "office" on January 2, 2004, in which Malik was showing Hossain a supposed triggering device that was part of the missile. This device looked like a large pricing gun used by shopkeepers to put price labels on merchandise. Also shown in that picture was Aref, counting a stack of $5,000 bills and handing it to Hossain. "They essentially consummated the laundering deal," said Grable, referring to this picture.

Grable emphasized that the defendants were willing participants in the terror plot. He said that even when the government's sting grew more detailed and sinister—a plot to assassinate a Pakistani diplomat in New York City—neither man backed out.

He tried to associate Aref with a terrorist group in Iraq. As proof, he claimed that Aref's name and his original Albany address and telephone number were found in a notebook discovered in a terrorist camp in Rawah, northern Iraq that had been bombed and raided by U.S. forces in June 2003. He said Aref was referred to as "Commander."

"When questioned by the FBI agents following his arrest last Thursday about the alleged Iraqi terror connection, he had no explanation for why his name was found in this book," Grable stated. He said that Aref claimed "he's never been in the military and does not know why his name is in the book."

Grable also discussed a wire transaction in May 2000, when Aref sent $1,300 to Athens, Greece to an Iraqi man who was arrested six months later by Greek authorities for possession and production of fake identification papers, including resident permits and passports. He also alleged that Aref made $15,000 to $18,000 in wire transfers to northern Iraq.

Grable also revealed that Aref had mailed a package using a false name, and possessed a Syrian ID in his name that was valid through 2007. This ID was found in Aref's house when the FBI raided it on August 5. Grable's final accusation was that "Aref had recently applied to travel to Iraq this December."

Kindlon was asked first by the judge to respond on behalf of the defendants. Kindlon's strategy was to project his client as a nice and kind gentleman who was caught up in an entrapment scheme by the government. "He is an honest and caring man whom everyone likes," he said. He explained that Aref, being the imam of the local mosque, had an obligation to witness a loan between members of the community, just like a notary public. "Aref, who is the spiritual leader at the Masjid As-Salam mosque on Central Avenue, should be released on bond. Aref has no criminal record, owns a home, has a job, a wife and three children, and would be willing to wear an electric monitoring bracelet. He hasn't got a passport; he hasn't got bus fare to the nearest town right now. This is a good and moral man," he said. "My client's family needs him back. His people need him back."

Regarding the address book and Aref being referenced as "commander," Kindlon argued that even if Aref's name were in a notebook found in a terrorist camp, there was no evidence that he was a terrorist. Kindlon said the notebook could have been stolen, or the English translation could be flawed. He said he had not been provided a copy of the page from the notebook.

Regarding the money transfer to Greece, Kindlon explained that men had kidnapped Aref's nephew and threatened to kill him if Aref didn't pay a ransom. The federal prosecutors said they had no other information on that transfer or the men involved.

Regarding the money transfer to Iraq, Kindlon insisted that the money went to Aref's three brothers, who still lived there.

He did not address mailing the package with a false name.

Regarding the Syrian ID card, Kindlon said that Aref had been a refugee in Syria for several years, that his three children were born there, and that he had graduated from a college in Damascus.

Regarding Aref's application to travel to Iraq, he said, "The imam was merely planning to travel to see relatives."

Kindlon summed up his argument by implying that this was a case of entrapment, manipulation, and victimization. He ended by saying that the government had said that "it was not 'the case of the century.' I say it was not 'the case of the weekend.'"

Luibrand, Hossain's attorney, was more direct. He argued that the government scheme amounted to entrapment. He portrayed the two defendants as law-abiding, peaceful members of society with no criminal records. He lashed out at the government's case and characterized it as an Abscam-like sting in which agents used racial profiling to nail Muslim suspects.

"They didn't go to St. Mary's Church and they didn't go to the Jewish synagogue, they went to the Muslims," Luibrand said. "He's got a Muslim last name and that's the only reason we're here." He continued, "There are no allegations by the prosecutors of any ties between Hossain and terrorist organizations. My client could give a darn about terrorism; he could give a darn about what happens overseas." Luibrand finished by saying that the case should be dismissed and the defendants should be sent home free.

Judge Homer then called a recess, promising to be back shortly to render his judgment. The prosecutors and defense attorneys smiled at each other professionally and shook each others' hands.

Judge Homer returned after about twenty minutes. I guess his decision had already been written earlier in the day. Everybody was holding their breath.

"The evidence in this case is strong, although not overwhelming," Judge Homer began. While acknowledging that the two suspects were set up by the government, he said that an indictment outlining the FBI sting showed that the defendants took part in a scheme to help launder money in a fictitious terrorist plot: "I am, therefore, forced to view the case in a different light, and the failure of the men to walk away from the plot made them a danger to the community." Referring to the address book containing Aref's name and designation as "commander" in Arabic, he commented, "If true, that evidence carries significant weight for Mr. Aref's connection to other terrorist organizations."

Therefore, Judge Homer said, he had decided to deny bail, and he ordered Aref and Hossain to be handed over to U.S. marshals to be held until trial, which he expected to take place in six to eight months. The two were swiftly taken out of the courtroom by a side door.

We exited the court disappointed and dumbfounded, not even talking to each other. The defendants' wives and children were totally subdued. It appeared that Aref's wife, Zuhur, did not understand anything that had just taken place.

On the other hand, victory seemed to be radiating from the FBI agents' faces. They were shaking hands and congratulating each other, although without expressing any loud jubilation.

As we walked out of the courtroom, Kindlon looked at me and said, "I tried my best."

"You did," I answered him. I did not know what more to say.

FACING THE MEDIA

I walked behind Kindlon to avoid the media. As soon as he came out of the building, about two-dozen reporters rushed to surround him. At the same time, a fleet of six security cars with their sirens on was rushing the defendants to jail. Kindlon looked at the cars and, laughing bitterly, said to the reporters, "Look at this crazy stupidity. They're terrorizing the public and claiming to make the country safer."

Responding to a question, Kindlon said that in the current environment he was not surprised by the judge's decision, but he was still deeply disturbed by it. "I had the feeling that I had gone through the looking glass and fallen down the rabbit hole," he said.

"Have you been threatened by anyone, Mr. Kindlon?" another reporter asked.

"I received a threatening call as to why I'm defending a terrorist," Kindlon responded. He said he had replied to the caller, "'I am a Vietnam veteran, and I have been threatened by many ignorant people like you in the past.'" Then he assured the reporters, "Don't worry, no one can intimidate me."

Next, the reporters surrounded Faisal. They wanted to hear what he had to say on behalf of the mosque. "Obviously we are saddened and very disappointed," he said. "The case sets a dangerous precedent, whereby it is acceptable to profile the community and where just by mentioning the word 'terror' there is a presumption of guilt. The saddest thing about this case is that it will further misunderstanding about Islam. Muslims are not terrorists. They are not violent people. We are a peaceful community and have a desire to live in harmony and good understanding with everyone.

"The day of the search, the law enforcement agents entered our mosque through its back door," he continued. "We'd like to let them know that the front door is always open. I think that there's a lot that is misunderstood about Islam and about us, and we have some catching up to do."

After I got home, I saw a report on the news about a press conference that the government officials had conducted inside the courthouse after we had left. U.S. Attorney Glenn T. Suddaby, the chief prosecutor in New York's Northern District, flanked by officials from both local and federal law enforcement agencies, said that the judge's decision was a validation of the importance of the case. He said he hoped it would send a message to everybody who might be inclined to be involved in terrorism that they could never be sure the government was not watching them. "This is what law enforcement is all about and should be doing in this country," he said. Suddaby also said that the intelligence about Aref's name surfacing in a terrorist enclave in Iraq was shared with FBI agents because of changes made by the PATRIOT Act following the September 11 attacks.

A similar view was expressed by Albany FBI chief William Chase. "We're hopeful the significance of this case is really starting to come out," he said.

RENSSELAER COUNTY JAIL

Two days later, on August 12 I drove to the Rensselaer County Jail in Troy to visit Aref, who had made arrangements to see me. Apparently Hossain was not interested in meeting with anyone in the jail except for his family members and his attorney. Aref, on the other hand, was interested in seeing as many friends as possible, in addition to his family members. He was allowed only two one-hour visits per week, and had to submit his visitor's name a day or two in advance for approval. I was the first person he wanted to see.

After security checks, I was taken to a small room that was partitioned by a thick glass wall. Within minutes, a security guard brought Aref in behind the glass partition. He was fresh, energetic, and smiling. "*Assalamualaikum* (Peace be upon you)," he greeted me.

"*Wa-Alaikumassalam* (And peace be upon you too)," I replied. I tried but I could not smile.

We started talking about general topics, such as how the situation was in the jail, in the mosque, his family, my family, etc. We had been speaking in Arabic, as we used to talk most of the time in the mosque. But all of a sudden Aref became very serious, his face became somewhat red, and his smile disappeared.

"Let us talk in English," he said. "First of all, I want to apologize you. I have been at odds with you all along, having a very difficult relationship with you and opposed to you in many ways." I saw him wiping away tears. "Please forgive me. I need you in my difficult days. I know I have many friends and supporters now, but in the long run no one will be able to help me. If I thought anyone else could help me, I would not be bothering you."

Aref had been a very stubborn, opinionated, and strong-willed man, with tremendous strength and forbearance. I never imagined him crying in any circumstance. Seeing the tears in his eyes moved me greatly. It shook me inside.

I assured him that I would do whatever needed to be done. "I consider it to be my obligation and not a favor."

"Don't worry about me," he said. "I am not worried about myself. But please take care of my wife and children. They have no money and, you know, my wife is not in good health. Please take care of my children and their education."

"So long as I am around, you should not be worried," I assured him. "I will be personally responsible for taking care of them. My children are grown up now, they do not need anything from me. Allah has given me enough money, and there will be no better use of my money than spending it on your children. Plus the whole Muslim community is there."

Aref clearly relaxed. "Thank you. May Allah reward you and give you more money," he said. Then he started explaining to me that he did not do anything wrong. "Everything you hear is wrong. I was simply tricked. I did not understand many of these things."

I told him that we knew that very well. "We have no doubts whatsoever about what you are saying. We understand very well what the government wanted."

Aref is a very talkative person. When he starts talking, he forgets how to stop. He has a habit of repeating and emphasizing the same things again and again without giving the other party a chance to talk. During the rest of our time together, he kept describing how the government informant, Malik, had tricked him. "He was talking too much. I hardly paid any attention. He took me to his store full of dollar-store merchandise, showed me toothbrushes, soap, detergent, batteries. He pointed to these items and told me, 'I import these ammunitions from China and supply to local merchants and make tons of money.' Now they are telling me that he discussed missiles with me."

Aref told me that he had met Malik only a few times. Ironically, he said that Malik had talked too much about too many things. "I thought he was a confused rich businessman, a person trying to help others as a way of goodness. The guy asked my opinion about his interest in helping the people of Kashmir in India where people have been fighting for their independence for more than half a century. I told him to help the women and children, and now they are accusing me of helping terrorists in Kashmir."

Our sixty minutes together passed very quickly, as if they were only ten minutes. Then the guard appeared and ordered Aref to follow him back. Aref said "*Ma-a-assalamah*" (go with peace and safety), and returned to jail smiling at me.

CHAPTER 6

Squaring Off

NEXT STEPS

Aref and Hossain would be locked up for at least the next eight months, and possibly their incarceration would extend several more months before the trial began. The Muslim community already felt disgraced, frightened, and confused by the sting and the arrests. Many were asking, "Where we go from here?" But not many were willing to stand up and try to do something to repair the damage.

Sajid and Faisal decided to take the initiative by contacting area churches, radio and television stations, newspapers, city administrators, humanitarian groups, political and social activists, law enforcement authorities, the state legislature, and other legal entities to develop a better understanding of our religion and our community. Inviting them to the mosque or meeting with them on their home ground, and giving them some simple information and appropriate literature, was the chosen format. Faisal did most of the talking. He had at least two or three interviews every day, and also met regularly with representatives from various organizations.

Faisal asked me to participate in a meeting with several area activists. I still remember some of the discussions that took place. Once Faisal commented, "We don't want to complain about the FBI's assault on our mosque; we forgive them."

I noticed that most of the people at the gathering looked at each other with surprise. I sensed that they never expected such a passive statement.

"After what they've done to your community, how can you forgive them?" asked Joe Lombardo, a well-known area activist and a leading member of the Bethlehem Neighbors for Peace group. "How can someone forgive the FBI? They've been doing the same thing to one group after another throughout their history. Now they've found Muslims to be an easy target."

I thought it was time for me to interject. "What Faisal meant is that instead of taking a confrontational approach, we wish to adopt an approach of projecting ourselves to be exactly what we are," I explained. "Muslims are here, we are part of this society, and we are like any other regular members of it. The FBI's game plan is to make us look like bad guys and enemies of society, and we want to fight that with the help of outspoken individuals and groups such as yourselves."

THE COMMUNITY OFFERS HELP

After about two months, peace and civil liberties organizations, political forums, religious groups, and labor unions came forward to support us. They published a whole-page ad in a local newspaper, *Metroland*, on November 18 with a list of approximately seventy groups, and about the same number of individuals, expressing solidarity with our mosque and the Muslim community. The ad read: "An Open Letter to Our Friends and Neighbors: We, residents of the Capital District, are deeply troubled and concerned by patterns of profiling, stereotyping, and discrimination against our Arab and Muslim neighbors. We urge you to join us in assuring that religious freedom is protected, that cultural diversity is cherished, that political expression is encouraged, and that fear shall not divide us."

A Japanese TV group based in New York City was very interested in our Albany sting case and seemed to express solidarity with us. Their three-member crew traveled to Albany three times to explore various details of the case and to interview Faisal and other individuals from the mosque and the community. They told me that their report was being watched in Japan with great interest. "The older generation of Japanese finds something familiar in this case, and many wonder if American Muslims are going through the same cycle as the American Japanese went through during the Second World War," the producer explained.

During this time, Faisal also organized workshops, seminars, and community dinners in the mosque, to which he invited various community leaders, attorneys, professors, and civil liberties advocates to make Islam, our way of life, our difficulties, and our shortcomings known to others. At the same time we hoped that these gatherings would be beneficial to our community by helping our mosque members, many of whom were immigrants, become more aware of their rights.

I will never forget the frequent visits to our mosque by Albany City Judge Thomas Keefe, a white Catholic. After meeting with him a few times, I started to recognize him more as an intellectual and humanitarian than as a judge. He had been elected to the bench the previous year and was not up for re-election for another nine years. He mentioned this very clearly, so that no one would interpret his visits to the mosque as having any ulterior political motive.

Once he visited the mosque and, after the prayer was over, I announced his presence and invited anyone who was interested to discuss with him any aspect of the Aref-Hossain sting operation. Suddenly my wife rushed up from the back, dragging Zuhur, Aref's wife, by the hand. "Look Judge, her husband is innocent," my wife said to Keefe emotionally. "She and her children are suffering. You must release her husband. You are a city judge, and I think you can do that easily."

Judge Keefe explained to them that he shared the same sentiments and pain and wished he could do something. He had difficulty convincing my wife that the sting case was a federal court case and he had no jurisdiction over it.

On another occasion, half a dozen mosque members wanted to talk to him. We were sitting on the floor. I brought a chair for him, but he said he preferred to sit on the floor with us. During the discussion, I said to him, "I feel very guilty that we did not reach out to the general community in the past. It was our obligation to do so."

"It's a two-way street," Keefe responded. "I've lived here long enough, but never thought of reaching out to you. I feel guilty, too." His voice was choked.

I saw he was trying to hold back tears. He was able to, but I could not. My eyes flooded. But my ears began to hear an echo all around me: "Terrorists are living among us…Terrorists are living among us…" As if George Pataki were shouting at me.

Faisal decided to postpone his return to Syria for his studies and instead devote the next six months to this mission. He never admitted it directly to me, but I always suspected that he did not want to go back because he did not want to leave me alone with this mess. I think he had an inner fear that the FBI might decide to come after me at some point and try to harass me to bolster their case.

THE FBI WANTS TO INTERVIEW ME

About a week after the bail hearing, Faisal received a phone call from FBI Agent Tom Jensen, who told him, "We want to interview your father regarding the mosque's finances."

Faisal immediately called me on my cell phone. To this day I still wonder why Jensen didn't call me directly.

I called Jensen back the next day. He said that the FBI was interested in talking to me about Aref's salary and about the finances of the mosque.

"In the FBI's office?" I asked.

"Yes."

"No problem," I said. "Please give me a day or two. Let me look for an attorney who can accompany me to the interview."

"There's no need for that," Jensen said. "You can stop at any time during the interview if you feel uncomfortable."

"That's fine," I said. "But I will feel more comfortable with an attorney. Let me see if I can arrange for one."

The next afternoon I called Terence Kindlon, and after informing him about Jensen's request asked him if he would be willing to come with me to the interview. "I can't," he said. "It would be a conflict with Aref's case."

Then I called my family attorney, Paul VanRyn, a very sharp and aggressive lawyer. We had known each other very closely for almost twenty years, and he had handled more than a dozen real estate deals for me.

As soon as I told him about the FBI's request, he went ballistic. "No, Shamshad! You are not going to talk to them!" He was very emotional. "They're the nastiest people on earth. Rather than looking for real terrorists, they're running after a greedy pizzaman and wasting millions of taxpayer dollars." He commented on some details about the case; I was surprised at how well-informed he was about the whole entrapment design by the government. He mentioned two more cases where the FBI had victimized two innocent individuals and had destroyed them completely.

"But they have been very nice to me so far," I said.

"Don't be fooled," he said. "There is nothing called 'friendly talk' with the FBI around a family table. Let me call them. I'll call you back shortly."

After ten minutes, he did, and said that he had had a heated argument with them. Presumably he called Jensen, then Jensen's supervisor, and then someone else, perhaps Tim Coll. "I told them they have no business talking to my client," Paul told me. "One of them said that if they want to talk to someone, and that person doesn't want to talk to them willingly, they make an arrest and then make the person talk."

Paul said he told them, "'OK. Go ahead and arrest my client. I'll come and see what you want him to talk about. Meanwhile, you're welcome to submit your questions in writing, and we will provide the answers.'"

A few months later I happened to see Paul in his office, and he asked me, "How has the FBI been treating you?"

"Since you shouted at them, they have left me alone," I said.

He smiled. "They should be out looking for real terrorists somewhere."

I was sure Jensen would call me again. I was dead right. He called me again, but it was a year later.

THE FBI REACHES OUT TO THE MUSLIM COMMUNITY

Shortly after this incident, Tariq Niazi, president of the Islamic Center of the Capital District, a suburban area mosque run mostly by professionals, contacted me. The ICCD was the first mosque opened in the Capital District, and I had been a very active member until 2000, when the Masjid As-Salam opened. Niazi informed me that at the request of the FBI, he had arranged a meeting with them at the ICCD: "They want to reach out to the Muslim community, and they want representatives of all area mosques to be present in this meeting. Everyone is coming, and you should come too, with some Albany mosque members."

On the day of the meeting, about twenty people were at the table. Masjid As-Salam was represented by Sajid, Faisal, and myself. No one else was willing to attend.

The FBI was represented by William Chase, head of the Albany Division; Special Agent Darren Semprebon; and another special agent whose name I do not recall, even though I still remember his face. Everyone from the mosques reassured them that Muslims were law-abiding citizens who practiced their religion peacefully and who had no interest in violence or any illegal acts.

Semprebon did most of the talking for the FBI. Again and again he wanted to justify why the FBI kicked and smashed so many doors at Masjid As-Salam during their raid on the night of August 5: "It was simply to protect my people," he claimed. The other agent emphasized the difficult position and task of the FBI. "If another event like 9/11 takes place in this country, we as the FBI will not be able to survive," he said. "Therefore we aren't willing to take any chances, and we have to move in every direction."

Chase suggested that the arrest of Aref and Hossain was by no means a profiled targeting—rather it was part of an ongoing investigation.

Sajid and Faisal mostly talked about the life hereafter, when the "judge of all the judges will reward us or punish us according to our deeds here." Needless to say, the FBI was hardly interested in the hereafter or any religious preaching.

I remember finishing up the meeting by saying, "I simply dare to mention to you three very intelligent men of a national intelligence agency that your present indictment is not simply an indictment of two individuals from our community. Rather it is an indictment of the whole Muslim community."

I found Chase intelligent and impressive. Sensing an opportunity, I called him over to a corner and told him that his agents had wanted to interview me, but that I had wished to avoid it. "I had a heart attack two years ago, and my health is somewhat fragile—"

"Really!" He was clearly surprised. "They told me that you are very cooperative. Don't worry. If need be, I'll interview you myself." He put his hand on my shoulder, and I felt as though a weight had dropped from my mind. I thanked him. I thought that if he asked to talk to me in the future, I would do it even without the presence of an attorney.

"Why do you think the FBI called that meeting with us?" I asked Faisal the next day at the breakfast table.

"Come on, Daddy! You're always skeptical of them," he responded.

Later in the day, after returning from the mosque, I met Faisal on our porch. I was smiling broadly. "What's up?" he asked.

"I found the answer to the question I asked you earlier," I said. I handed him a copy of a news story that was headlined, "NO MORE 'COMMANDER'—Wrong Translation."

COMMANDER NO MORE

The notebook with Aref's name and first Albany address and phone number that was found in a military raid on June 11, 2003 in Rawah,

Iraq, about 200 miles north of Baghdad, was classified as "pocket litter," a term used by the military for objects recovered from the bodies of those killed. The notebook was brought to the U.S. in November 2003 and sent to the FBI for translation. This process was credited to the inter-agency coordination that the Bush Administration had been promoting between different intelligence agencies.

The "pocket litter" was written in Kurdish, but the FBI, thinking that it was Arabic, sent it to an FBI Arabic translating unit. Both languages are written from right to left and follow similar, but not the same, scripts. Some words are common between the two languages, but they are two distinct languages, as close perhaps as English and German are. The FBI's Arabic translator, however, had translated the key word *kak*—one of the most common words in Kurdish, meaning "brother," an honorific term of respect—as "commander."

Many FBI translators are paid quite well, something like 30¢ a word. So they don't mind translating "tea" as "cup," or "bathtub" as "sink." I have talked to several senior physics professors who described the CIA's translation of some important scientific papers by Soviet scientists during the Cold War era in the same way. It is ironic that one important method by which the U.S. military and intelligence agencies get their information about foreign terrorists is through such translations.

In the Muslim communities of the world, there exists a well-known example of an Arabic translation flop. Nawa is a village in Syria. A very famous Islamic scholar and author born in that village many centuries ago used the village name as his last name, and thus he is known as Imam Nawawi. This practice of being named after one's birthplace has been common throughout Islamic history, including the present time. Nawawi wrote a widely read book that includes forty statements from the Prophet, and people normally refer to this world-famous book as *40 of Nawawi*. *Nawa* in Arabic means "pit" or "nut," like the seed of a peach or a similar fruit. The same term is also used for the nucleus of an atom. Thus many Arabic translators for Western intelligence agencies commonly translate *40 of Nawawi* as "40 nuclear bombs." Translations of intercepts of dis-cussions among Muslims about this book have caused security alerts in several countries on several occasions. Muslims often joke that "if a book can become a nuclear bomb in the sight of the government, why wonder if an innocent Muslim becomes a terrorist?"

In Aref's case, the translator had translated *Kak* Aref—which means "Brother" Aref or "Mister" Aref—as "Commander" Aref. I think either the translator was too dumb or too smart: too dumb because he could not distinguish Kurdish from Arabic, or too smart because he thought the agency would value his mistranslation more than the true translation. How should we categorize the intelligence of the people who were handling the notebook? I will leave it up to the reader to judge. But they judged immediately that the man who came to Albany in 1999 was a "commander" of terrorists in northern Iraq.

I have read many versions of the reports about this raid on the Rawah camp. The U.S. military claims that it was an Ansar al-Islam terrorist training camp; according to Lieutenant General David McKiernan, the bombing killed eighty people, leaving only two survivors. However, some reports say that it was not a terrorist training camp but rather a camp comprised of Saddam loyalists and Baathists trying to evade U.S. forces. Other reports suggest that it was a refugee camp, and that one night they were celebrating someone's wedding by lighting fireworks, which attracted the attention of the U.S. Air Force. Remember our military's rule of engagement in Iraq: "Anything that seems like an enemy action, shoot first and ask questions later." Still other reports say that the camp served as a stopover or resting place for locals and refugees going between Syria and Jordan. Rawah is in a totally Sunni area, and its residents are mostly pro-American. I have also read that after the bombing, survivors were massacred; one tribal chief told an Islam Online News correspondent that the bodies of twelve young men were found tied together with a rope, and all of them had been shot in the head at close range.

Ansar al-Islam did not even exist in 1999 when Aref left Syria for the U.S.; it was founded toward the end of 2001. But Aref's Albany address and telephone number found in the pocket litter were three years old. The same pocket litter had the addresses and telephone numbers of many other individuals around the world. The FBI, and to some extent the media, presented this "evidence" as if it had been Aref's own diary that was found in the camp. Consequently, the defense had a hard time arguing that Aref had nothing to do with this pocket litter and that he was unconnected to the presence in it of his name and address, along with so many others'.

THE PROSECUTION'S CASE IS SHAKEN

The translation mistake seemed to call into question the very basis for the sting. The search warrants, affidavits, indictments, and bail denial were all based on the assumption that the defendants had ties with foreign terrorists, so the mistranslation seemed to raise questions about whether the government overstated these allegations. Thus the case against Aref and Hossain did not seem as strong as once it looked.

On August 17, U.S. Attorney Glenn Suddaby issued a document admitting that the translation "commander" in the document was wrong, and that it should have been "brother." He informed Judge Homer about this error in a letter. But he claimed that the error would not affect the case against Aref. "The proof of what they are charged with is not concerned with whether his name was in the book, which it was," Suddaby told the media. When reporters pushed him hard to describe how such a mistake could happen, he replied, "Apparently the military translator said it means one thing. The FBI felt it means something else. Regardless of what the translation is, it does not change a thing."

The defense attorneys saw it very differently. "What is troubling about this is that when they [the prosecutors] were in court, they were talking about a document they had never seen, and the information they gave turned out to be wrong. And that's very disturbing," said Kindlon. "This has become the pattern of the authorities, encouraged by the present administration, to leap to conclusions with booms, and then fizzle down when the facts emerge."

Luibrand lashed out at the government, declaring that the mistake had undermined the entire case. "They targeted these Albany residents by their own words because they had a notebook obtained from Iraq that had Aref's name and the phrase 'commander,'" Luibrand said. "That notebook has been in the government's possession for fourteen months, and now they report to us they were mistaken and the word is not 'commander.' In affidavits used to obtain search warrants, the FBI cited the notebook, along with evidence that Hossain might have connections to a political extremist group in Pakistan. This whole investigation, the whole targeting of Aref and Hossain, was seemingly prompted by this document, and it was wrong from the very beginning." He demanded a copy of the "pocket litter," along with any intelligence about the camp at Rawah.

This cartoon by John deRosier appeared
in the Albany *Times Union* in 2004.

Courtesy of John deRosier

Both attorneys suggested that their clients should be released on bail now that the government's case was significantly weakened because of this mistake. Judge Homer directed the government to provide the page to Aref's attorney by the end of the same day.

HERE COMES UNCLE SAM

But just when it seemed that the defense had wrapped the prosecutors in their own net and the "commander" mistranslation would blow the case apart, a huge surprise arrived from Washington, D.C. On the same day that Suddaby admitted the error, Uncle Sam invoked the Classified Information Procedures Act (CIPA) to block any further disclosure of information the defense was after. In a twelve-page motion, the Justice Department declared it would block the information the government did not want to provide: "The United States believes that disclosure of this material would raise issues of national security that the court should address before any of this material is provided to the defense."

When I heard this, I started shaking, and I almost fainted. I knew that with this declaration, the fate of the two defendants was sealed. *This is a tool with which a fair trial for a Muslim will always be denied,* I thought. *How can a trial be called fair if a defendant, or even a defendant's attorney, cannot challenge the evidence of the accusation against him? Is this happening in broad daylight in America, an icon of justice and fairness to all?* For me, America has always been a model democracy, a champion of freedom and justice, where everyone is entitled to due process and a fair trial. I had heard about the 1980 CIPA provision in the past. Despite fierce opposition by defense attorneys, this law had been invoked in a smattering of cases involving suspected terrorists, spies, or military personnel charged with crimes. But hearing about it, and seeing it in action, were two different things.

I wrote a letter to President Clinton during his first term when some debates were going on about CIPA, the only letter I ever wrote to a president of the United States on this subject. I said that this provision was a disgrace to the justice of America.

For me personally, the government's CIPA claim was very hard to take due to my religious viewpoint. According to Islam, every child born is innocent and free of sin. It is his actions that make him guilty or a sinner.

Similarly, a person is innocent of an accusation until proven otherwise. The burden of proof is on the accuser. Proper evidence must be brought forward rightfully by the accuser. "Secret" or "classified" evidence that the accused cannot challenge violates his God-given right.

The defense attorneys were shocked, too. "They made this big show of terrorism charges based on provocative, damaging information that is shown to be false, and now they want to shut everything down to make us helpless," Kindlon commented. "How can we respond? What have we got to defend with?"

One mosque member commented philosophically, "The days are of two kinds—one for you, and the other, upon you. Today is for them, and today is upon us. They can do anything they wish."

The newspapers and other media were also disappointed and upset. Rex Smith, editor of the biggest newspaper in the area, the Albany *Times Union*, wrote: "The Constitution clearly gives citizens the right to know what is going on in American courtrooms. Sometimes it falls to the press to undertake the job of making sure the government honors that right. We'll do that in this case."

I felt that after invoking CIPA, the prosecution was laughing at the defense. But Judge Homer was not laughing.

A SECOND BAIL HEARING

Evidently Judge Homer was not happy with the FBI's misinformation regarding the "commander" document. He thought they had misled him. He indicated to defense attorneys that they should request another bail hearing. The attorneys filed for a second bail hearing immediately; it was scheduled for August 24.

On that day, the whole scene of the previous bail hearing was repeated everywhere—inside the courthouse as well as outside. Perhaps security was even tighter than the previous time. The prosecutors seemed to be more prepared; they brought more ammunition to the courtroom to fight the case, including real ammunition: a SAM missile packed in a casket-like box. The courtroom was completely overrun with reporters, mosque members, and the defendants' wives and children.

The lead prosecutor, David Grable, was once again assisted by Assistant U.S. Attorney Greg West and, this time, FBI Special Agent Tim Coll.

Next to them was the box with the SAM, presumably to be displayed during the proceeding. Judge Homer presided again. The prosecutors repeated the same arguments they had presented during the first bail hearing, adding some minor details here and there. They also accused Aref of making fourteen calls between October 1999 and October 2001 to the office of the Islamic Movement of Kurdistan (IMK) in Damascus, Syria, and they accused Hossain of making eight overseas calls during approximately the same period of time, implying that the defendants had foreign terrorist connections. "This makes them dangerous to the community and a flight risk. Therefore they should not be allowed bail."

Kindlon presented his defense the same way he did the first time, countering each accusation point by point. "If making telephone calls to a foreign country is a crime, then I should be punished first. I call my two children who are overseas now very often. Why is the government not showing us the contents of these calls?" he argued. "Aref was an employee in the IMK office in Damascus, and after coming to Albany he kept in touch with his colleagues there, and sometimes he called to say hello to them. If Americans don't make telephone calls overseas, how will the telephone companies pay their expenses? My client's connection with foreign terrorists is just a fiction in the agents' minds."

Then Kindlon pointed to the casket-like box and emotionally and aggressively accused the prosecutors of "bringing that thing here to exploit the paranoia and fear of the people and create a stunt. My client is a deeply religious and peaceful man. He should be released to his family and to his community." Then he told the court, "They should go and look for real terrorists. There are plenty of them, I suppose." He folded his file. Then very quickly, looking at the bench, he said, "Sorry, judge, I got carried away."

The prosecutors didn't mention or display the SAM. Did Kindlon's blunt remark stop them from doing so? We will never know. But they did show the SAM later, on a bigger occasion—the first day of the trial.

Luibrand also argued very forcefully in favor of granting bail to Hossain. Holding up a page of the supposed overseas telephone numbers dialed by Hossain, and while looking at the prosecutors, he said, "They say these are the overseas calls my client made. None of these numbers are more than four or five digits long. These are numbers Hossain's children punched in while playing with the telephone at home." Luibrand continued, "They have so far turned over sixteen hours of surveillance tapes and two-inch-thick transcripts, with more to come, that show that Hossain was misled and induced by the informant. In these recordings, my client insists that he's a good citizen of this country, that this is not the time for violent jihad, that we need to follow the path of God peacefully. This is a fictional case. Let it be a fiction, and let the case be dismissed."

In his decision, Judge Homer said that the whole case was based on a sting operation and that the government's mistakes had weakened the evidence. "After one year's undercover operation and surveillance, the government and the FBI have come up with no real evidence that the men are connected with terrorist groups," the judge said. "There are some serious questions about the facts. Recent developments convince me that the men are not as dangerous to the community as previously thought. Therefore, they will be released on bond while awaiting trial."

The defendants and their attorneys seemed relieved. I heard "*Alhamdulillah* (Thanks be to God)" coming simultaneously out of the mouths of several members of the Muslim community.

The terms of bail were set at $250,000 worth of real estate properties for each defendant; four individuals with good standing in the community, and having reasonable earnings, as guarantors for each man; house arrest until trial with electronic monitoring devices; telephones to be monitored; travel not allowed beyond the boundaries of Albany County; and the defendants restricted to home during night hours.

I was happy that no cash was involved. Arranging $500,000 in cash would have been a gigantic task.

The defense attorneys praised the judge and called his decision courageous. The prosecutors did not entertain the media that day.

All of us were happy. I felt very much relieved. But deep down inside me was a concern: would the FBI let it go the way it was going, or take it as a challenge and try to hit back at us later with a bigger punch? The next hearing in the case was scheduled for September 15, when the court would decide how much of the classified material the government would have to share with the defense attorneys.

ARRANGING BAIL

That night I went to see Hossain's wife, Fatima, to talk about some technicalities of the bail. As soon as she saw me, she started to cry.

"Everyone is scared, no one wants to associate with me, no one wants to talk to me, no one returns my phone calls," she said, wiping her tears. "What will happen to me and my children, to my husband? How can I arrange his bail? People in the mosque might bail out the imam, but who will help my husband?"

I consoled her. "Their cases are being tried together, therefore everything will be worked out together. Don't worry, I will work it out, insha-Allah (God willing). Everything will be fine. When they are out, they will handle everything themselves." Her children were looking at me as if I were an angel of mercy.

After the night prayer, I explained the bail requirements to the attendees in the mosque, about twenty of them. I said that offering their own properties and themselves as guarantors for bail purposes had no danger of any loss. Both the defendants also had properties, family, and children, but they had no travel documents and they were to be monitored by electronic devices, so they could go nowhere. "We must feel obligated to help them out," I said.

Four individuals volunteered immediately to offer themselves as guarantors. The remaining guarantors and properties, and the other details, were worked out the next day.

I had instructed everyone involved to gather in the mosque with their identification cards, pay stubs, income tax returns, or property deeds one hour before the scheduled court appearance. We planned to proceed together to court. But as the scheduled time approached, we did not have everyone or every document. Luibrand had been calling me every few minutes, telling me that Judge Homer was getting nervous and wasn't sure if people would show up. So we rushed to court without having the full number of people or documents. I left a few people in the mosque to drive any latecomer to court the moment he arrived.

Luibrand hurried toward me in the hallway. "Thank God you guys showed up," he said. "The judge is really getting upset. I had almost lost hope."

"Me too," I said. "I was considering the option of postponing it until tomorrow. Our people are not very punctual. But let us proceed." We rushed toward the courtroom.

Upon my suggestion, Kindlon informed Judge Homer that some people were still on their way, but since the proceeding would take some time, he should begin. The judge agreed, and one by one he began to interview the seven people who had come: two engineers, a salesperson, a therapist, two businessmen, and a store worker. He checked their documents, including the deeds of their real estate properties, and explained to them that in case of default by the defendants they would lose their security. Everyone assured the judge that they understood his explanation and accepted the risk involved. Each document was checked by an FBI representative as well, and after some brief questions all were approved.

Fortunately, these individuals were not too scared of the FBI to risk their money and property to obtain Aref and Hossain's release. But later on, some mosque members were upset when they heard that two of these individuals were harassed by the FBI, perhaps because they had stepped forward to help fellow Muslims in trouble. I heard from mosque members that the offices and businesses of these two individuals were searched, and permits, licenses, and all business-related papers were investigated. They were questioned in a harassing manner, as if they had committed a crime. One of them felt so harassed and hurt that he decided to leave the country.

Judge Homer ordered the release of the defendants from jail. We were told that the pre-release formalities would take about two hours. So we decided to go back to the mosque, do the afternoon prayer, and arrange some transportation for the defendants' wives and children to the jail and back to their homes. One member of the mosque offered a limousine ride. He collected the families and drove us all to the jail.

As soon as I got out of the limousine, I saw a crowd in front of the jail. The defendants were already outside, holding plastic bags in their hands containing their personal belongings. They were surrounded by more than two-dozen media reporters and about the same number of people from the Muslim community. The two men were beaming with joy and happiness in being able to breathe the air of freedom after twenty days of imprisonment. Hossain in particular was talking to the crowd very excitedly: "I am a peaceful man. I am a true American. I love this country. Even after going through this, I am not angry with anyone, I have even more respect for the United States of America."

While all this was going on, my cell phone rang. It was Luibrand. "Please ask Hossain not to talk to the media," he told me. Presumably he was watching everything live on TV. But it was too late; Hossain had already finished talking. It was Faisal's turn, and he talked to the media on behalf of the mosque and the Muslim community.

We took the men and their families home. I thought that at least the first phase of torment of the families and of the Muslim community was over, and that my obligation and responsibility were over. The rest of the defense could now be handled by the defendants and their attorneys.

After bail was granted, public skepticism about the case grew, and people began to question whether the intention of the government was nothing more than racial and religious profiling. Fred LeBrun, a veteran columnist at the Albany *Times Union*, asked in his column,

> Why did they come just as the government was being challenged about questionable "terrorist alerts"? Was it a case of the government preferring to see what it expected or wanted to see? Why did evidence in the case, which the government initially shared with apparent plea- sure, suddenly become a matter of national security that needed to be protected when the shaky nature of it became apparent?
>
> There are fundamental questions, such as, what should we demand of our government in times of fear? When government panders to the lowest forms of fear—racism and fear of those deemed "other"— what must we do? Demand justice. Call on elected officials to stop fear-mongering. Those outside the Muslim community must reject comments by politicians, neighbors and their own friends and family who rail against all Muslims (or immigrants or people of Middle Eastern descent) upon hearing about unproven accusations against a few—or any time. Demand justice. With justice will come what we all desire—peace.

This cartoon by John deRosier appeared in the
Albany *Times Union* in 2004.

Courtesy of John deRosier

CHAPTER 7

The Sting

WHAT IS A STING OPERATION?

In a sting operation, a situation is created in which it appears that a real crime is taking place, although in fact the "crime" is just a fiction being acted out by the law enforcement authorities according to a plan to see if someone will join in the illegal act. For example, a person may pose as a drug dealer to catch drug users who may try to buy from him. Or a person may pose as a drug user to catch a drug dealer willing to make a sale to him. Or a woman may pose as a prostitute to catch men who are willing to solicit her for sex. These operations (termed "stings" because the unwitting target is surprised and hurt in many ways, as though he has been stung by an insect) are commonly and frequently employed by law enforcement agencies.

However, if you are not a drug user and have no interest in buying drugs from someone posing as a dealer, but the dealer pressures you or somehow induces you to buy the drug, then it is entrapment. Sometimes authorities employ coercive methods to get targets to become involved in illegal activities, but this is improper, and courts usually dismiss criminal charges based on such coercive tactics.

Consider a situation in which someone develops a friendship with you, and at some point confesses to you that sometimes he sells drugs to make money. One day he invites you to go for lunch. You are driving him in your car, and he asks you to stop at an ATM so that he can withdraw some cash. While he is at the ATM, the police bust you and recover drugs in your friend's backpack that he had left in your car. You are charged with promoting drug trafficking because your "friend" turns out to be an FBI operative. This is an example of a setup.

Now consider a case in which two of your friends explain to you that one of them needs to repair his car, and is borrowing $200 from the other who has some extra cash to lend. They want you to witness the loan so that there will be no confusion or dispute about the repayment. Later, however, you are charged with money laundering, because part of the $200 was earned by illegal means, or the borrower intended to use the money for illegal purposes. This situation might sound unfair or bizarre to you, but not to the FBI. For them, this kind of setup is a sophisticated scheme to frame a person whom they could never otherwise grab because he would never otherwise commit a crime. Albany's sting operation to frame Yassin Aref and Mohammed Hossain was of this kind.

The person employed in these schemes to help the government frame the unsuspecting target is called "the undercover," or "the informant," or "the confidential informant," or "the cooperating witness." But in fact, all of these terms are misnomers with regard to the Albany sting operation. These terms are applicable to an individual who infiltrates criminal enterprises and gathers information about the crime or the criminals, and who then reports back to the law enforcement authorities. But an individual who pretends to commit a crime in order to be watched by others present on the scene, or an individual who pretends to have committed a crime and describes it to others who unwittingly participate in it by listening to his claim, should be called something else—perhaps a "provocateur," or a "fraud," or a similar term.

The sting operation to catch Aref and Hossain was similar to the latter situation, and the informant was simply an operative, a "fraud" or an *agent provocateur*, as one journalist called him. The "fraud" informant employed by the FBI in the Albany sting was Shahed Hussain (not to be confused with, and no relation to, defendant Mohammed Hossain). In legal papers, he is commonly referred as Malik.

The sting began with Malik befriending Hossain and taking him into confidence. Then Malik showed Hossain a shoulder-fired SAM missile and told him that he (Malik) was involved in a lucrative secret weapons business by importing SAMs from China and supplying them to some terrorists in New York City. Malik invited Hossain to join him in this weapons business, but Hossain flatly refused, telling Malik that he was not interested because the business was illegal. Then Malik offered Hossain a desperately needed cash loan of $50,000 with strangely attractive terms.

Hossain was asked to return the loan in installments by means of checks—
so it could be interpreted later, in a tricky way, that the whole loan deal
was an illegal money-laundering scheme. Aref, as an imam and an honest
intermediary, witnessed the loan arrangement as part of his religious duty
and as per Muslim custom. After many manipulations and distortions, the
FBI declared that Aref was an accomplice in the illegal money-laundering
deal between Malik and Hossain.

The whole sting operation progressed slowly and took a year to
materialize (to get a full picture of its evolution and progression, see Appendices A and B, Sting Tapes 2003 and 2004). A lot of gossip, loose talk,
and irrelevant discussions between the three were taken out of context,
mistranslated, misinterpreted, and distorted to support the contention of
illegality of the loan deal.

THE GOVERNMENT'S SO-CALLED CONFIDENTIAL INFORMANT

According to a rumor in the Pakistani community of Albany, Malik
had fled Pakistan after allegedly getting involved in a murder-related
crime. He managed to land in the U.S. in the mid-Eighties as a young man
of about twenty-eight. Luibrand asked the FBI to give him information
about Malik's criminal past in Pakistan, but the FBI refused to respond.

Malik succeeded in acquiring a retail business and a gas station in
Albany. He also worked as a translator in the Department of Motor Vehicles for immigrants taking driving tests. During his employment there, he
developed a scam of selling illegal driver's licenses to immigrants for prices
ranging up to $1,000. After successfully selling approximately ninety illegal licenses, he was finally caught and arrested on January 23, 2002 and
subsequently convicted. He faced up to fifteen years in prison, $250,000
in fines, and deportation to Pakistan, according to some reports.

Being a Pakistani, a Muslim, a master criminal, and very cunning, deceptive, and talkative, he seemed to be of great interest to the FBI. They
were looking for someone like him to entrap or set up some Muslims
from the Albany mosque. In Malik, they found the ideal candidate. They
offered to set him free and give him both U.S. citizenship and cash if he
would help them. "The FBI was too generous. This characterless slime
would have done that gladly for free," said a Pakistani who knew him

well. One area storekeeper to whom Malik used to supply candy and chips told me that he stopped buying from him because Malik used to cheat by not delivering the full amount or count, and by mixing some expired items into the supplies.

On October 15, 2003, Malik's house in Latham, a village near Albany, burned down. Some speculate that he burned it down to collect from the insurance company, although local authorities think it was an accident. The insurance company refused to pay on technical grounds. According to a rumor, the FBI called the insurance company on Malik's behalf. You can do the rest of the math!

After the Albany sting case broke, the FBI took Malik under their protection, hid him in secret locations, and kept his identity secret. They prevented the Albany *Times Union*, which had information about him, from publishing anything about him. I heard about two FBI agents who questioned a merchant next to the mosque and accused him of threatening harm to their informant, Malik. They told him that he was their guy and they were protecting his back. Some Pakistanis also speculate that the FBI paid Malik a lot of cash and bought some businesses for him, although in court they admitted paying him only $32,000.

In a well-known sting operation in Lodi, California, the FBI admitted paying their single informant $250,000 over a sixteen-month period.

This is the background of the government's entrapper: ready to trick some Muslims from the mosque and put them into the FBI's net. In time, Malik was trained, coached, and sent on his mission.

WAS I THE FIRST TO BE TARGETED?

I knew nothing about Malik, nor had I ever heard of him, seen him, or met him. He was not an attendee at the mosque. When and where he first started his mission, I have no idea. Was I the first target? I can't be sure. But perhaps I was.

One afternoon in September 2002, my home telephone rang. On the other end of the line was a person who said he was Shahed Hussain. He told me he was calling at the suggestion of Imam Yassin Aref to look into the possibility of providing shelter in the mosque for a battered Pakistani woman with two small children who had been kicked out by her husband and had no place to go.

I sensed immediately that something was not right. I had heard about this situation because my daughters had been contacted a few days earlier to provide some help to the woman and her children. The story was real, but Shahed's request was extremely odd: first, a Muslim woman without her husband seeking shelter in a mosque is unthinkable culturally as well as religiously. Second, an unrelated man, Shahed, was trying to take up her problem. Normally women handle this kind of problem and men stay at a distance. Third, how could Imam Aref suggest such a solution? Could this be the same imam who did not like women coming to the mosque even for prayers after sunset? Fourth, Imam Aref and everyone else knew that we did not have a facility for a woman with children to stay in the mosque.

In a domestic situation like this, people normally approach others within the same ethnic group and make some sort of accommodation within a closer circle, or suggest the woman go to a recognized women's shelter. So I was puzzled and curious to know who this Shahed was and what he intended. My first thought was that he was most likely an ignorant, characterless young man who had been having an illicit relationship with the woman.

"Are you related to this woman?" I asked.

"No," he replied.

"Then why are you trying to help her, rather than some Pakistani women helping her?" I asked.

"Nobody wants to help her," he said. "I have heard a lot of praise about you. I thought you would be able to help."

"Have we met each other? Would you recognize me?"

"No."

"Do you come to masjid?"

"Yes, every Friday."

"Do you remember the person who makes announcements after the prayer?" I asked.

He hesitated, and after a long silence said, "No."

"That's me," I said. "Do you recognize me now?"

Again, after a long silence and hesitation, he said, "No."

By this time I had become absolutely sure that Shahed was a liar. Perhaps he never came for Friday prayers.

"What is your background?" I asked directly.

"I am a businessman," he said very confidently. "I have gas stations and do a lot of community service in the Muslim community."

That was it for me. He was supposedly a person in this area who was doing a lot of community service, and I did not know him? How come? I knew every community servant in the area thoroughly. All my life I had been meeting community servants, and I knew their style of talking and their approaches to other community leaders. He was definitely an odd case. I became anxious to meet this fraud.

"Look," I said. "There is no place in the masjid for this woman. Try with some Pakistani families. Meanwhile, if you need any help from the mosque, talk to Yassin. Can we meet sometime?"

He agreed readily and happily to meet me the next day at 4 p.m.

Normally I meet people in the mosque, but being sure that he was a total fraud, I did not want to see him in the mosque. I asked him to meet me next door to the mosque, in the Sabah food store. I frequently used one of the tables in the store to carry out personal business or transactions. Muslims are not supposed to use the mosque premises for buying or selling or conducting personal business. It is regarded as a place to do business only with the Almighty.

Shahed did not show up the next day. Thus I never met him or found out who he was, and I never heard of him again until the next March.

After the sting case broke, it was easy for me to figure out that perhaps FBI Special Agent Tim Coll had been trying to entrap me through Malik. Presumably the FBI had put my home telephone under surveillance, and through it knew the story of the battered woman from my daughters' conversations. Coll might have thought that since the story was genuine, I might not question anything and would simply drop into his net. Until now, I have not figured out the scheme through which he was attempting to entrap me. However, I have good and valid reasons to suspect that the FBI tried to entrap me through others as well.

In March 2003, Aref drove me, along with some other members of the mosque, to a house in Latham to offer condolences to the family of an elderly regular of the mosque who had passed away suddenly. This is a common tradition among Muslims. We visit the family of the deceased, offer condolences and some words of advice to the family members, and pray for the departed soul. Once we got there, we were introduced to— Shahed Hussain. He talked to me unusually politely and humbly, so much so that I realized there was something wrong with him. But at the time, I had no clue that his fraud would help the FBI bring disaster to us and disgrace to the whole Muslim community.

It appeared that Shahed Hussain and Aref did not know each other, nor did any other member of the mosque who came with us that day. Hussain came out to the car in the snowy weather to say goodbye to me.

"Why did you not come to the Sabah food store a few months ago when we were supposed to meet?" I asked.

"I forgot," he replied politely. I immediately became very suspicious of him all over again.

I saw him only once more, a few months later when he walked into the mosque presumably to attend a meeting with some members of the Jamaat Tabligh who were conducting a weekly meeting there. Jamaat Tabligh (Group for Propagation) is a very powerful movement that originated in India in the early Thirties. Its members are extremely devoted and observant Muslims whose mission is to emulate the first generation of Muslims in all aspects, including dress and physical appearance. Malik simply did not fit with the group. I remember greeting him in the mosque while looking at him with a questionable expression. He answered the greeting, but avoided direct eye contact with me. I became suspicious but just brushed aside my thoughts, thinking that he might have come to see one of the members for some personal reason. I wish I could have become suspicious enough to inquire about him further.

MALIK'S FIRST SUCCESS

It is very difficult to determine how many people from the mosque or the Muslim community Malik tried to entrap, or in how many ways. I have received many reports in which he tried to make some illegal dealings of one sort or another, though he did not make much progress beyond initial contacts. But it seems that he had his first breakthrough in July 2003, when he dropped by Hossain's Little Italy pizzeria and introduced himself as an area businessman. He found Hossain very receptive.

We know from trial testimony that Malik was coached and instructed by the FBI, and after being fitted with a body tape recorder he was sent to Hossain on July 28 to start his game. Malik presented himself as a very rich businessman, an importer of Chinese goods and a wholesale distributor of grocery merchandise in the area, with an enormous amount of money and several cars, including a Mercedes and BMWs. He told Hossain he was so rich that people called him Malik (meaning "king") rather than his real name of Shahed Hussain. He expressed interest in buying some businesses in the area. He also indicated some interest in buying Hossain's pizzeria. Hossain was desperately trying to sell his pizzeria because the business was not doing well. Hossain told Malik that he had already been offered $50,000 for it, which he would not consider. However, he was willing to sell it to Malik for $75,000.

Malik also pretended to be very generous and helpful to others. He told Hossain that he was a community servant and was interested in helping the members of his community by giving loans left and right. After talking about many things, Hossain expressed a desire to secure a loan from Malik for an amount up to $5,000.

Requesting a loan from a person with financial resources is a very common practice among third world Muslims. Throughout their history, they have had no practice in borrowing money from banks or other financial institutions. Rather, they seek loans from their relatives, friends, and acquaintances, and rich people feel a social and religious obligation to help others by extending loans, all interest-free, since taking or giving interest on loans is forbidden in Islam.

On August 7, Malik offered Hossain an opportunity to fraudulently arrange, through the Department of Motor Vehicles, an identification card for Hossain's developmentally disabled brother, who did not know English, by arranging for the brother to take a fake test. Malik boasted of having arranged hundreds of licenses for immigrants, normally at a charge of $500 apiece. This time, Malik explained that he simply wanted to do a favor for Hossain and help him. Hossain agreed, obtained the ID, and paid Malik $75 for his services. (See Appendix A, Sting Tapes 2003, August 7.)

According to the FBI's plan, Malik was supposed to develop a friendship with Hossain in the coming weeks and then, depending upon its progress, move to the actual plan that perhaps was not exactly defined at that stage. The FBI had marked three weak points in Hossain, and their plan depended on the exploitation of these three weaknesses: that Hossain was financially greedy, that he had a streak of religious zeal, and that he was prone to rambling in disjointed conversations that jumped from one subject to another.

To achieve Hossain's trust and confidence, Malik brought expensive toys, including a toy helicopter, for all of Hossain's five children. This was a ploy to convince Hossain that Malik was a sincere and caring friend. At one point, Hossain told me that all along he had some skepticism about Malik's sincerity and generosity, but that on the day that Malik brought the toys for his children his wall of skepticism came crashing down.

Malik also told Hossain that he didn't trust anyone in Albany except him. He said he trusted him fully and was very interested in their friendship because he wanted to learn Islam from him. I think this gesture by Malik psychologically flattered Hossain by conferring on him a degree of recognition of his religious scholarship. Hossain's joy had no limits at this flattery. In this way, the FBI exploited the religious zeal they perceived in Hossain.

In the subsequent weeks and months, Malik met Hossain on more than fifty occasions and secretly recorded their conversations—over fifty hours on audio tapes, mostly in broken Urdu with occasional lapses into English. Malik secretly secured some surveillance videotapes as well. Mostly they talked, chatted, and gossiped from topic to topic, covering Southeast Asian politics, Middle Eastern conflicts, business, religion, jihad, violence, terrorism, etc. Malik posed as a radical Muslim interested in violent jihad, while Hossain tried to talk about peaceful jihad, implying a rightful struggle through religion and peaceful efforts.

During these discussions, Malik usually talked too fast and about too many things, mixing one topic with another in such a way that a listener would not be able to sort out the relevant parts of the discussion from the irrelevant ones. He hardly ever answered a question in a straight way. His answers were twisted or mixed with irrelevant things. As soon as he realized that Aref's or Hossain's statements were not favorable to the FBI's plans, he would cut them off and not give them a chance to say anything more on the subject. Pretending to be an extremist, he would frequently inject into their discussions questions or statements out of nowhere to emotionally incite Aref or Hossain to make statements more to the FBI's liking. Hossain was also very talkative and injected many irrelevant topics into the conversations, and sometimes became hyperexcited during the discussions.

Before every meeting, Malik went to the FBI building, where Special Agent Tim Coll attached a recording device to Malik's body. In the absence of Coll, Special Agent Christopher Bean performed the same task. The recording device remained on while Malik drove looking for the target, or answered or made telephone calls, or discussed personal or business topics. Sometimes Coll would monitor the conversations from his car parked in a nearby location.

After the meeting, Malik would return to the FBI building or to another designated place, where the device was removed. Sometimes Malik met Coll or another agent near a Home Depot store two miles away from the mosque, or at the OTB (Off-Track Betting) building on Central Avenue, only a mile away from the mosque. Sometimes prior to a meeting or after it, Coll called Malik to check on where he was. On one tape I heard the FBI receptionist ask Malik not to go any further into the building, and she called Tim Coll to come and attend to him. On occasion, Malik was simply watched from a distance by an agent in his car.

After every meeting, Coll and Malik would exchange notes. Before the next meeting was to take place, Coll would coach and instruct Malik about how to induce the target to say certain things that might prove valuable in court during a trial, and valuable as well for media propaganda against Muslims.

At one point I was interested in listening to all of the tapes—over fifty hours of recordings—but after listening to only one tape I became so frustrated that I gave up the idea and did not listen to any more until two years later. I eventually did listen to all of them, some of them several times, before writing these pages. Malik mostly asked questions about violence and jihad, and Hossain did most of the talking and explaining, like a teacher talking to a student. Hossain spoke in broken Urdu with incomplete sentences, and like Malik often jumped from one topic to the other without logical links. Sometimes it became difficult to figure out what he wanted to say. Many of the recordings were done in Hossain's pizzeria where customers were also talking; sometimes a TV was on too. This made the conversations difficult to follow on occasion.

See Appendix A and B, Sting Tapes 2003 and 2004, for dated transcriptions of many of the tapes.

CHAPTER 8

The Legal Battle Begins

THE CLASSIFIED INFORMATION PROCEDURES ACT (CIPA)

On August 17, 2004, when the government had invoked the Classified Information Procedures Act (CIPA) to block the disclosure of information sought by the defense, attention was centered at the time on the "pocket litter" that described Aref as "commander." But we also suspected that the FBI might have some secret surveillance recordings of Aref's telephone conversations overseas, because this was alluded to during the bail hearings.

During a court proceeding on September 15 that was presided over by Senior U.S. District Judge Thomas J. McAvoy, who was assigned the case for the trial, Assistant U.S. Attorney Gregg N. Sofer, a member of the Justice Department's Counterterrorism Section, informed the court that the federal authorities needed at least two months to analyze volumes of classified material before they would know what type of information they had and where it came from. McAvoy agreed, but told prosecutors to conduct their review of the documents swiftly because the lives of two men were at stake and they had a right to a speedy trial. The prosecutors responded that they might need more than the sixty days allotted by him to analyze intelligence documents, but McAvoy hinted that he might schedule the case for trial in three months, saying that the defendants had lives to live and should not exist under this cloud for too long.

We in the Muslim community concluded from this that the FBI had no substantive proof of terrorism, and therefore the government wanted to hide behind the classified evidence so they would not have to show how weak their case was. In other words, we felt the government was saying, "The intelligence community knows things that you don't know, but those things are all secret and classified, so we cannot tell them to you." The Muslim community knew that one such piece of classified evidence was nothing more than the same "commander" page of the notebook already known to everyone, and discredited.

But prosecutors brought two officials from the Justice Department's Security and Emergency Planning Office into court to convince McAvoy to establish security procedures for the case. We came to know that the government planned to construct a special cell inside the courthouse building itself, where the classified materials would be placed under guard around the clock and to which only the defense attorneys and court personnel with security clearances would have access. Presumably this was standard procedure in cases involving classified evidence. Of course, the defense attorneys had to first go through a lengthy process of getting security clearances before they could have access to this cell. Moreover, they would not be allowed to take notes on what they saw, could not make copies of any documents, and would be prohibited from disclosing the information. A federal security officer would be present in the room at all times, even when the attorneys were having discussions with their clients. What this meant was that none of these documents or their contents would ever be made public unless they were brought forward by the government during the trial.

We considered all these procedures nothing but a drama, and we were almost certain that no documents would ever be made public, because either they did not exist, were fraudulent, or were of no probative value. Of course, one obvious reason for all this was to withhold the "commander" page of the notebook from the public and press, since everyone was more than curious to see it (a small part of it, translated into English, was released in March 2006).

While talking to a reporter about this special cell and the security procedures around it, Kindlon jokingly said that it was like the movie *Men in Black*, and that maybe the government would use a device to erase his memory. McAvoy did not like Kindlon's comment. He became angry and essentially imposed an unofficial gag order on the attorneys after that point.

Luibrand, Hossain's attorney, tried to argue that the indictments brought against the defendants were just money-laundering charges. The government had had all these months to use its intelligence capabilities, he said, but had come up with nothing, so "why make a fuss now?"

On September 19, in its commentary about the government's delay tactics in the case, the Albany *Times Union* wrote, "With that in mind, we repeat this most basic tenet of the American legal system: Justice delayed is justice denied."

On October 22, Kindlon and Luibrand both filed motions to reject the government's request to keep portions of the evidence secret. They said it was premature for the government to ask for special protection of classified materials, because prosecutors had been unable or unwilling to tell the judge if such classified material even existed. In turn, the prosecutors argued that they had to restrict the flow of information for national security reasons, and to support their claim they informed the judge that such measures had been taken by courts in the past, citing some prosecutions of real terrorism cases.

We were optimistic that the court would see the fundamental difference between an actual terror-related case and a bogus, fictional, tricky, and deceptive money-laundering scheme.

A few days later, the prosecutors filed a motion in support of their argument to keep the classified evidence secret. They did not mention the classified evidence itself, but offered to show it to the judge so that he could decide if and to what extent restrictions should be applied to its disclosure.

Two weeks later the prosecutors met privately with McAvoy and showed him a document that they said was a matter of national security and should be kept sealed. On November 11, McAvoy ruled that the classified information in the case would be sealed and not made public— and the prosecution scored its greatest victory. With this document, we thought, the mind of the judge had been poisoned. The ruling not only sealed the documents; it sealed the fate of the defendants.

On January 14, 2005, Assistant U.S. Attorney David Grable submitted a request to McAvoy to extend the trial date for another eight months. He wanted more time to sift through volumes of documents before getting ready for the trial. He submitted a four-page document that was classified as "secret." The defense attorneys were not allowed to see it because its disclosure could "cause serious damage to the national security of the United States." The judge reviewed the document in chambers and granted a three-month extension. He said that an eight-month period was too long and that the court wanted to move the case along as fast as humanly possible.

A version of this document was so heavily redacted before being made public that no one could figure out anything about it.

But our skepticism remained. We felt that besides the "commander" page, the FBI had nothing against Aref and was struggling to come up with something else, and that was the reason the government kept delaying the trial.

An Angry, Desperate, and Busy FBI

Sometime toward the end of spring 2005, Special Agent Jensen called me again. He invited me to come to the FBI office to pick up an envelope containing some foreign coins that the FBI had found in the mosque during the raid on August 5, 2004. I was a little surprised because there had been no mention of these in the inventory of the items the FBI had taken from the mosque. Jensen also said, "We might also have a little discussion about the mosque's finances and Aref's salary."

"Shouldn't the coins be sent to the attorney's office?" I asked.

"No," replied Jensen. "We have to give them to you. They are of no value to us. Their total worth is only 68 cents."

Then why were they so anxious to return 68 cents' worth of coins to me? They had never returned anything else taken from the mosque. I was unable to make any sense out of it. If they intended to prove that our mosque received foreign donations, they would bring the coins to court as evidence; why give them back to me?

"Please send them by mail," I suggested.

"No, we want to hand them over to you," Jensen said.

"Okay, I will make arrangements to pick them up," I said.

"Was it your attorney who called us last time?" he asked, referring to Paul VanRyn, who had called the FBI about a year ago when they wanted to interview me.

"Yes. He has been handling my real estate deals for a number of years. Did you check with Mr. Chase [the bureau chief] about having an interview with me?"

"No, why?"

"Well, the last time I met with him, I requested that he spare me from any interviews because of my health," I said. "I had a heart attack not too long ago, and he told me that if and when an interview would be necessary, he would interview me himself. Please check with him."

"Oh, okay, I didn't know you had a heart attack," Jensen said.

I never heard from him again after that.

In the morning during summer vacations, normally I sit on a recliner on my porch, which is about twelve steps higher than road level, with a mug of tea and read the newspaper. One day I was reading the paper when I saw a car stop in front of the house. Two men got out and very briskly climbed to the top of the stairs. It was Special Agent Tim Coll with another young FBI agent.

"Here he is," said Coll, approaching me. We shook hands and he handed me a book-size brown envelope and a typed sheet of paper. He was very casually dressed in a T-shirt and pants. He looked carefully at the dirty wooden railing of the porch and sat down on it, primly keeping his feet on the floor.

"I want you to sign the receipt for this envelope. It just says that the envelope contains some foreign coins," he said.

I signed the receipt.

"We want to talk to you about the finances of the mosque," Coll said. "I hope you'll be willing to talk."

I was quite at ease and composed. I wasn't sure if it was a threat; I didn't take it as such.

"Have you checked with Mr. Chase?" I asked.

"Yes," Coll said. "I talked to him about it this morning."

"I want to cooperate and I will see how best to handle it," I said to him.

Coll then asked me to talk to the U.S. Attorney, Glenn Suddaby. I asked him if he had Suddaby's card or phone number. He did not. He took a piece of paper from the other agent, jotted on it "Glenn Suddaby," and gave it to me. Then we shook hands again, and he and the other agent left the porch and drove away quickly.

Faisal and I talked about it. We could not figure out anything about the return of the envelope except that it was perhaps an easy excuse to contact me in person. Faisal was of the opinion that I should talk to Suddaby. I debated within myself and could not reach any decision about contacting him, so I did not. I am still not sure whether I should have. I told

Kindlon about the envelope with the foreign coins. He too was puzzled, but could not make anything out of it.

My speculation was that the prosecutors were looking for some evidence by which to bring additional charges against Aref regarding his salary payments. Perhaps they hoped he had understated his salary amount to them during one of his interviews, or under-reported his earnings to the IRS or the Department of Social Services, from which he had received some benefits as a refugee. This might have been a possible indication that they did not have anything solid against Aref with respect to terrorism, so they wanted to bring any other kind of charge against him. This has been a common pattern in many cases around the country—for example, in the case of Dr. Rafil Dhafir in Syracuse, which began with claims that it was one of the biggest terrorism-related cases in the country and ended up with only medical billing fraud charges.

We heard rumors that at least a dozen FBI agents were busy working on the case locally, as well as overseas in Syria, Palestine, Jordan, and Iraq—all looking for something solid to bring against Aref. Later we heard from some reliable civil right activists that the FBI had hinted to them about the importance of the case, that it was being regularly mentioned in very high-level briefings, including perhaps to the president and the vice-president. I was shocked when I heard that, and found it very difficult to believe.

Supposedly the FBI suspected Aref of several terrorism-related possibilities and was desperate to find something credible against him to present in court. But they were unable to discover anything real. A member of the mosque reported to me that he had gone to the FBI office for some other business and happened to see Coll, who told him to "tell Aref that he should not think he will go free." According to Coll, Aref was involved in radical things in the name of religion.

I think the case was a very big challenge to the FBI. If they failed to obtain a conviction, it would be a great embarrassment for them. They were already embarrassed about the "commander" flop. Moreover, they were angry with Aref for some reason and seemed determined to punish him. They apparently felt secure enough with their classified material, but they were looking for anything else that could help the case.

Ali Yaghi called me one day from Jordan and told me that FBI agents had offered him a large sum of money and U.S. citizenship if he would come back and give testimony against Aref—to the effect that some terrorists had traveled to Albany and had stayed with Aref while they were here. In his usual style, Yaghi told me that he had replied with a big "f-word" to the agents. I did not pay much attention to Yaghi's statement, thinking it might be a distortion or an exaggeration or some sort of trick by the agents. A few weeks later, however, Aref told me in the mosque that he had heard from his friends overseas that the agents really had made such an offer to Yaghi, as well as similar offers to some individuals in Syria if they would be willing to testify against him.

One day Aref told me that two FBI cars followed him all the time. He said that in the beginning he only suspected that he was being followed, and he tried to verify it by stopping or making turns abruptly while driving. Indeed they were following him. Whenever he was home or in the mosque, the agents would remain in their cars, parked at far corners from his house or the mosque. But whenever he went to the park with his children, the same two agents would follow him on bicycles (they carried the bicycles in their cars). Strangely enough, they would quit in the evening and leave him alone at night. Once I gave Aref a ride to Schenectady to attend a funeral. From the time we started out from the mosque, and then all the way back from the funeral, he kept telling me about two cars that were following us. Twice I stopped rather abruptly and noticed that the cars turned into side streets and parked at a distance, then began to follow us again as we proceeded.

Once a *Times Union* reporter called the mosque to find out whether there was anything special happening with Aref's family that day. He had heard on his scanner that a helicopter was following Aref's jeep, which his wife was driving while taking her children to a diner. Aref was not in the car. Exploring the information further, we came to know that Aref and his family were under aerial and satellite surveillance as well.

Meanwhile, the prosecution managed to get another three-month extension. On August 5, 2005, the government filed a forty-page, heavily redacted motion that outlined the details of the sting operation, indicating that it suspected Aref of having terrorist connections overseas and that the sting operation had targeted him, though it had begun first with Hossain because it was difficult to entrap Aref directly. According to Agent Tim Coll, the initial intent was to engage Aref in conversations to find out whether he had any terrorist connections. The motion requested that the court limit the amount of information the government would have to disclose about its investigation and intelligence-gathering techniques.

On August 9, at the end of a court conference, McAvoy announced that he expected the trial to begin early in 2006. He gave the government until October 11 to submit any remaining material. The government was still loathe to specify what evidence it would use, and the prosecutors were still talking about the volumes of material they were looking at to present as secret evidence. They also demanded that the court should prohibit Aref from using entrapment as a defense because he had been brought into the case by Hossain to witness his transactions, and not by Malik. We learned that if a defendant were entrapped in a scheme by someone other than the government's informant, then the entrapment defense was not available to him.

McAvoy scheduled the next court date for October 11. He also instructed defense attorneys not to discuss the case.

We were very frustrated with these constant postponements. I was skeptical that the trial would really start at the beginning of 2006, more than a year and a half after the defendants' arrest; I thought it would most likely drag on even further. I remembered very clearly when McAvoy initially gave the government sixty days to prepare the case for trial, and had said, "They have lives to live and the right to a speedy trial." He had hinted at that time that he would schedule the trial within ninety days. But he seemed to have become a different judge.

A few weeks later, when we invited Kindlon to the mosque for a dinner, I asked him about the "cell" in the courthouse. "It's all trash," he answered angrily. "Nothing is there." When I asked him about his security background check, he answered, "It wasn't worth it. They ripped me and everyone in my office off. They checked all my papers, including all my tax returns, and turned the office upside down, but despite giving us security clearances they showed me nothing of their documents." He was very upset and disappointed. Both defense attorneys were military veterans and eventually were given security clearances, but they got little else.

WHY WAS AREF TARGETED?

Apparently the FBI could not find an easy target among the Masjid As-Salam's members, including myself, to make a case, so they decided to focus on Aref. He matched the FBI's profile of a target of interest in several ways. He was an immigrant from Iraq, he had lived in Syria, and he spoke Arabic. He was a stubborn, practicing, and committed Muslim who was usually present in the mosque interacting with other Muslims. He had a thick long beard, wore Arabic dress and cap, and looked like a "typical" terrorist. He was an imam and leader of an inner-city mosque, which had as worshippers a number of apparently "anti-government" ex-convicts who hung around with him most of the time. His public teachings, speeches, and sermons were more often than not critical of some policies of U.S., European, and Middle Eastern governments. His voice was loud, and in his speeches he often spoke very emotionally. His language was tough, full of rhetoric, and his English was less than perfect, which made his words sound rougher than they actually were. While discussing the affairs of the Middle East, it seemed as though he knew every leader and every group personally and that he had been physically present whenever a major political or religious decision was made. In a nutshell, there was much on the surface to draw the FBI's attention to Aref in the post-9/11 atmosphere. Their instincts must have caused them to assume he was anti-American and possessed an abundance of knowledge about matters overseas. Thus targeting him was natural and imperative, according to the FBI's textbook, since that was the trend throughout the country at the time.

During the FBI's investigation of Ali Yaghi, they found that Aref's past had included political activity in northern Iraq as well as in Damascus. Aref was apparently in contact with many groups and their leaders, including some important power players and political figures. The alleged "pocket litter" notebook found at Rawah on June 11, 2003, in which he was mentioned as "commander" (actually "brother"), along with some important suspicious names like Dr. Rafil Dhafir of Syracuse and Mullah Krekar of Norway, must have added fuel to the fire. Aref had worked in the office of the Islamic Movement of Kurdistan (IMK), a nationalist organization fighting for the independence of Kurdistan from Saddam's Iraq, one of whose leaders had been Krekar. At the end of 2001, about two years after Aref stopped working for the IMK and two years after Aref had come to the U.S., Krekar founded Ansar al-Islam, which was designated a terrorist organization by the U.S. in 2003. Perhaps this last factor truly made Aref a high-level target in their estimation. The ultimate aim of U.S. intelligence agencies is to reach the leadership of al-Qaeda; linking Aref to the IMK, to Krekar, to al-Qaeda, and thus to Osama bin Laden seemed to be a pretty good hypothesis.

I believe the FBI started digging deep around each and every suspicious thing about Aref. They dug harder and harder and deeper and deeper, but the suspicious things never turned into positive leads. Either those "leads" proved to be negative, or they remained mere suspicions, or both. Clearly the FBI was disappointed with each empty investigation, but after going so far they did not want to give up and walk away from him. Perhaps they wanted to take revenge on him for their failed digging. We are of the opinion that if they had found anything substantive or definitive against Aref, they would have taken him directly to Guantanamo.

MULLAH KREKAR

ullah Krekar, a Sunni Kurd whose real name is Najmuddin Faraj Ahmad, was born in Kurdistan in 1956. He moved to Norway in 1991 and has been living there ever since as a refugee, playing a long-distance role in the Kurdish struggle for independence. Prior to 2001, he traveled back and forth between Kurdistan and Norway via Syria, and had been one of the leaders of the IMK. Until 2001, neither he nor the IMK were considered to be involved in terrorism. But toward the end of 2001, Krekar formed an armed group, Ansar al-Islam, which was later alleged to be involved in attacks on U.S. forces in Iraq. Mullah Krekar claimed that such attacks were not done with his knowledge or under his leadership.

Krekar was arrested in the Netherlands in September 2002 and held in prison for a few months. He was interviewed by FBI agents there, but no request was made for his extradition to the U.S. In January 2003 he was deported to Norway, and in February 2003 the U.S. State Department designated Ansar al-Islam a "foreign terrorist organization" (FTO). Krekar has since been regarded by U.S. intelligence agencies as a high-value terrorist and an al-Qaeda and Osama bin Laden sympathizer.

According to Krekar, he and his group were targeted by the U.S. because he refused to support the Iraqi occupation by Coalition forces. He also claimed that a drug-smuggling charge filed against him by the Jordanian government was manufactured under U.S. pressure.

According to some reports, at one time the CIA planned to kidnap Krekar and bring him to Guantanamo. Their attempt was foiled by the Norwegian authorities, who became aware of the plan and were not willing to approve it. The CIA's plan was similar to a previous one in which two agents, Cynthia Dame Logan and Gregory Asherleighs, succeeded in kidnapping an Egyptian suspect, Osama Mustafa Nasr, off the streets of Milan, Italy.

However, the Norwegian government was not happy with Krekar's presence in the country. His refugee status was cancelled in February 2003 and he was ordered deported to Iraq. But the government did not force the deportation because it was believed that Krekar would be tortured or executed by the Iraqi authorities. Norwegian laws forbid a foreigner to be deported if he faces a risk of torture or execution. I have heard that many Muslims in Norway are not happy with Mullah Krekar, either. They feel he has been a source of embarrassment for them.

On March 21, 2003, Krekar was arrested by Norwegian authorities and charged with aiding and financing overseas terrorists, although the charges were later dropped for lack of evidence. Apparently Norwegian courts do not entertain secret evidence!

AREF'S OLD SPEECHES AND DIARY ARE TRANSLATED

We heard that after more than a year, the FBI had finally been able to translate Aref's personal journal that he had kept while in Syria. The FBI also translated some of his speeches delivered in Kurdistan in 1994, when he was traveling back and forth from college in Syria. The journal and tapes of his speeches, all of which were in Kurdish, were confiscated from his house during his arrest on August 4, 2004.

In the journal, Aref mentioned meeting two strangers who showed up at his house in Damascus. According to Muslim custom, he invited them to come in and eat with him. It is not uncommon in third world countries that unknown individuals knock at a person's door without any appointment or expectation, and as a courtesy the owner invites them in. The FBI knows better than anyone else that whenever they knock at a Muslim's door, more often than not they are invited inside and offered at least a cup of tea with cookies.

According to Aref, at the dinner table the young men chatted about some radical things like carrying jihad to the West, particularly the U.S. and Israel. There was no mention of these two individuals in Aref's journal either before or after that one meeting, but the FBI concluded that since the two individuals were at Aref's dinner table and sounded like terrorists, Aref must be connected to them and must have terrorist contacts. According to his journal, in 1999 Aref also met Mullah Krekar, then a leader of the IMK. Aref was an employee in the Damascus office of the IMK at that time, and he met Krekar along with the rest of the IMK staff when Krekar visited Syria from Norway for one month during the summer. The FBI must have concluded that Aref was a terrorist because he was associated with Mullah Krekar, who two years later founded Ansar al-Islam, and that Aref must have been a member of the IMK because he worked in its office and knew important people in the organization. The FBI probably had suspicions that the IMK might have connections with terrorist organizations, although it was never declared a terrorist organization by the U.S. Aref insisted that he was never a member of the IMK and that he did not know Krekar personally.

In many places in his journal, Aref wrote that "we went there" or "we met that person," always in connection with his job as a driver for the IMK. I tend to think that this was his style of writing about events, and I think he actually meant "*they* went there" or "*they* met that person," meaning the IMK officials whom he drove to appointments. Aref was simply a driver or chauffeur, and part of his job was to transport important people or leaders to various places and meetings. One should note that all of this took place in a third world situation, in which leaders conduct their meetings at dinner and everyone participates, including the driver. It is not a Western-style meeting in which there is a written agenda, minutes are taken, and the meeting starts and finishes at a specific time in a specific place. And when people travel together in the Middle East, it is considered very impolite to leave the driver on his own while the important people see to their own welfare independently. But because of Aref's style of writing in his journal, the FBI must have concluded that Aref was equivalent to those important leaders with whom he was traveling. The FBI also argued that Aref had mentioned in his journal about meeting with Hamas representatives, and according to them Hamas had strict security precautions that did not allow anyone into a meeting unless he was approved. I would think that would be true in Palestine, but security was probably not as strictly followed in Damascus in 1999 in the situations Aref described.

According to the FBI's interpretation, Aref invited Mullah Krekar and his group to his house for dinner. This information bothered the FBI a lot. They must have concluded from this invitation that Aref had a personal relationship with Krekar. But this is not necessarily true in Middle Eastern culture. Low-level employees very often invite visiting high-level leaders or important people and their groups for a feast in their houses, even if they have no personal relationship with them. It is something Westerners find hard to comprehend. Moreover, according to Aref, he invited a number of people to his house and was not able to recall whether Mullah Krekar was among them or not. It is very common that a member of a mosque invites some new faces in the mosque to have lunch or dinner with him and chat. Aref used to do that on a regular basis in the Albany mosque. He would take them home to eat with him and his family, or bring them food from his house—even people who came to the mosque for the first time.

In his speeches, delivered in 1994, Aref discouraged his fellow Kurdish citizens from emigrating to the West lest they lose their culture, traditions, and religion due to interaction with the heavily corrupt political and social environment of the West—both government and society. But from the text of his speeches, the FBI concluded that Aref was a radical interested in waging war against the West, and they prepared excerpts from Aref's journal and speeches to present as non-classified evidence against Aref in court. They did not appear to notice that they were going to put on trial in a U.S. court someone's opinions and viewpoints expressed years ago in a foreign land.

Aref was aware of the FBI's witch hunt against him. At the same time, he was very frustrated with his defense. He told me that Kindlon was doing nothing, and that Kindlon had not gone through any of the fifty hours of sting tapes that the FBI had provided him, nor had he gone through any other material. Aref was expecting Kindlon to listen to all the tapes, or to go through the FBI transcripts and then discuss various things with him to really understand what was said and how the discussions had developed over time.

I had no experience with trials, and Kindlon had no business discussing the case with me in any detail, but occasionally I used to call him for a few minutes to assess how the case was developing. I used to console Aref by saying that attorneys do not prepare the case until close to the trial date. But Aref was not satisfied, nor did he know what to do.

When I heard that the FBI had sent the translations of Aref's journal and speeches to Kindlon and had hinted at the possibility of bringing additional charges against Aref based on this translated material, I became alarmed. Common sense told me that they must be more prepared now with these new documents than previously. I had heard of several sting operations in the country that in the beginning seemed to be big terrorism cases, but had ended up with plea bargains to minor charges. Based on this analysis, I advised Aref one day to unilaterally offer to leave the U.S. and be deported to Syria or Iraq. I told him, "Even if you win at trial, the FBI will never let you live freely in this country." Aref agreed and planned to discuss this with Kindlon the next day—but after discussion with him and others, Aref changed his mind. I have no idea whether or not the FBI would have accepted his offer to leave the country; some attorneys told me later it was highly unlikely that the government would have gone for it.

A few days later Aref told me that Malik had sent word to him that he had misled and tricked him and Hossain in the sting plot under the impression that they would receive a prison sentence of a few months to a year, and that after that everything would be fine. Based on this, Aref and Hossain thought perhaps that was what the FBI intended, and Malik had gotten this information from the feds. But I didn't buy it. "The FBI uses criminal informants as tools and does not make them partners to share plans and policies," I told them. I am not sure if they understood me.

CHAPTER 9

Blows for the Defense

SUPERSEDING INDICTMENT

oward the middle of September 2005, it became obvious that the prosecutors were planning to add some new charges against Aref in a superseding indictment. If so, his bail conditions might change or be revoked. We were very concerned, but felt totally helpless. On September 29, a grand jury charged the defendants with eight new counts related to providing material support to the terrorist group Jaish-e-Mohammad (JEM) and money laundering in the sting. JEM was a group in Kashmir that was fighting for Kashmir's independence from India, the group that Malik said he was supposedly helping.

"One reason they did that was that the new charges carried a presumption of pre-trial detention, whereas the old charges were under a section that did not have that presumption," Kathy Manley, the assisting attorney in Kindlon's office, explained to me. "The fact that none of the earlier charges carried a presumption of pre-trial detention had some bearing on the defendants' earlier release on bail, even though the main reason was the flop of the mistranslation of 'commander,'" she added. Kindlon had pointed this out to the court during the first detention hearing.

On top of that, Aref was charged with three extra counts related to his alleged contacts with terrorists and terrorist organizations overseas: lying to the FBI about his association with Mullah Krekar, and lying on his refugee and immigration applications about his association with and membership in the IMK. During his interrogation by the FBI on the night of his arrest, Aref had told them that Mullah Krekar was a famous man and that he did not know him personally. The FBI claimed that since Aref met Krekar with a group of IMK staff on a few occasions, this meant that he did indeed know the man "personally."

Aref's application for UN refugee status in 1999 in Syria was marked "none" in answer to a question that asked the applicant to list the political organizations with which he had been associated. Apparently someone had filled in that form for Aref, because he did not know any English at the time. On February 13, 2002, "none" was marked again when he applied to change his immigration status from a refugee to a permanent resident; the question asked the applicant to list all the organizations he had belonged to after his sixteenth birthday. Once again, someone in the Albany office of the U.S. Committee for Refugees and Immigrants had filled in the form for Aref, without the help of a translator. Because of communication problems with immigrants who speak little English, it is common for applicants to enter "none." In fact, most applicants do this to simplify the application process, even if they speak some English.

The prosecutors filed a forty-eight-page memorandum detailing the background of the new charges and urged the court to revoke the defendants' bail and to send them both back to prison pending trial. In the memorandum, the prosecutors included the translation of seventeen pages of Aref's diary, the translation of one of his poems written in 1999 in which he discussed revolutionary ideas and jihad, and a printout of the telephone numbers of his overseas calls. In this way, they bolstered their claim that Aref was a danger to the community due to his radical ideas and contact with overseas terrorists. They also claimed that Aref had ties with Dr. Rafil Dhafir, a Syracuse oncologist and ethnic Iraqi who had been arrested for violating the Embargo Act against Iraq when he sent, via his own charity, medical supplies and food to Iraq to help alleviate the suffering caused by the U.S. embargo of the 1990s. During a search of Dhafir's office about two years earlier, the FBI had supposedly discovered in a trash bin a fax sent from Iraq by an Islamic center seeking financial assistance from Dhafir's charity. In the fax, the organization had mentioned Aref, the imam of the mosque in Albany, as a "representative" of their center.

The FBI alleged that Dhafir posed a national security threat through his connections to terrorist organizations overseas, although he was never charged with any terrorism-related crimes. He had transferred money to Iraqi charities to help children there, but for some reason the authorities were interested in punishing him, and so they did: Dhafir received a twenty-two-year prison sentence, and is serving his time at the federal prison in Terre Haute, Indiana in its Communication Management

Unit—one of the most restrictive units, especially designed for Muslim "terrorists"—even though Dhafir was convicted of embargo violations and medical billing fraud and not of any terrorism-related charges. But according to the FBI, Aref had associations with Dhafir, who allegedly had associations with unknown terrorists in Iraq— and they used this logic to conclude that Aref must be treated as a terrorist because of his alleged association with someone who was alleged to be associated with an alleged unknown terrorist group overseas. No one should underestimate the power and the imagination of the FBI!

Meanwhile, Aref was totally exhausted by the pressure surrounding the case—the surveillance, the possibility of additional charges and bail revocation. On the night of September 29, 2005, after the night prayer at the mosque, he briefly addressed the attendees. He recited from the Qur'an, Verse 177 of Chapter 2 ("The Cow"): "—and the righteous are those who are firm and patient in pain and suffering and adversity and throughout all periods of panic; such are the ones who are truthful and who are God-fearing." After explaining these virtuous characteristics of a compassionate Muslim, he said, "As you all know, tomorrow is the court date. I may not come back from there. Please don't worry about me, just pray for me and for my family, and please take care of my children."

AREF'S BAIL IS REVOKED

The packed court session on September 30 was an exact repeat of the first and second bail proceedings. The original judge, Homer, was on the bench. The charges brought by the prosecution were more or less the same, even though the number of counts had increased. The only difference was that the prosecution claimed to have more evidence this time, from the translations of Aref's journal and his speeches, and they had very artfully assembled—from "facts" selected here and there—a fictional picture of suspicious activities in Aref's life.

As an example, Aref had written in his journal from time to time about "America's plan," referring to the Iraq Liberation Act passed by the U.S. Congress in 1998, a plan by the U.S. to topple Saddam Hussein with Kurdish help. But this phrase was mistranslated by the FBI as the "Plan in America," and was then misinterpreted as a scheme that involved Aref entering the U.S. to do harm through terrorist activities. The government tried to present Aref as if every movement in his life had had something to do with terrorism, and therefore he was a danger to the community and must be put away from human and societal contact. Someone who did not know about the mistranslations, the misrepresented facts, the false connections, and the illogical conclusions would have agreed with the FBI's version. It was a masterful piece of fiction. I was of the opinion that the government had already convinced the judge through its memoranda to imprison Aref, and that the court proceeding was simply a formality.

Kindlon's job was to present the opposite view. As he had done previously, he argued very forcefully, item by item. His arguments were factual and convincing. Essentially he wanted to convince the judge that the whole assertion of the government's allegations was an artfully woven fiction. According to Kindlon, Aref lived a regular life in a third world country in the circumstances of the time and place. His alleged interactions with various individuals were also regular, and either related to his employment or were commensurate with the norms of the society. As a refugee himself, helping hundreds of other refugees flee from Saddam's Iraq required Aref in his daily routine to meet and interact with a variety of people. As a bright college student, he recorded in his journal all these events, meetings, and news items. His journal, Kindlon said, was not a blueprint of terrorism plots or a guide to terrorist activities; such routine, normal contacts and interactions gave no basis to claim terrorism: "Therefore I request you to leave my client free on bond the way he has been for the last thirteen months. He has demonstrated that he is a law-abiding member of society and will remain so pending trial." Kindlon also said it would be too burdensome to prepare a defense if Aref was imprisoned.

We were very satisfied with his arguments, but it remained to be seen if the judge was convinced. Luibrand's job was much easier that day. He only said that the prosecutors did not show any foreign terrorist contacts of his client, and that his overall status remained the same. Therefore, there was no point in altering Hossain's bail conditions. Both the prosecution and the judge appeared agreeable to Luibrand's request.

After about a twenty-minute recess, Homer came back to the bench to render his decision. He said, "There is no evidence Hossain has any connection to terrorism other than his alleged participation in the FBI sting." But Homer characterized Aref's journal entries, taped speeches, and alleged contacts with top terrorist figures in Syria and Iraq as troubling. "The new evidence, in my judgment, is significant," he said. "This makes Aref a danger to the community."

He ordered Aref's bail revoked and that he be handed over to U.S. marshals, who were waiting with handcuffs. Aref was promptly taken away, but he turned toward us in the back of the room and smiled. We could not smile back. Many eyes became tearful.

The defense attorneys could not make any statements outside the courthouse because they had been instructed not to discuss the case. Of course, the prosecutors were much elevated due to their victory. They did not make any outrageous statements, except that Suddaby was reported to have said that with the new charges, Aref faced up to 470 years in prison and $7.2 million in fines if convicted, and Hossain up to 450 years in prison and $6.7 million in fines. Under the original charges, the men faced from seventeen-and-a-half to twenty-two years in prison. One very angry member of the mosque commented, "If both these fines are collected, it will probably cover only part of the cost the government has already spent so far trying to convict the two men."

In addition, the prosecutors had been very smart to tell McAvoy, the trial judge, that all the classified materials they were submitting involved national security and therefore must be sealed after he had viewed them. McAvoy readily consented to do this. The defense attorneys were at a loss as to how to rebut these secret documents, but on October 14 they requested that the court give them access to the documents. Nothing came out of this, and to this day the defense has never had access to any of the secret material.

HOSSAIN TRIES FOR A SEPARATE TRIAL

Hossain and his attorney did not want to share anything with anybody, including me, about the case. However, in the middle of November 2005, Hossain told me that his attorney was trying to separate his case from Aref's. He did not give any reason for this. I suspected immediately that it was a prelude to a plea deal on his part. In many joint cases, prosecutors let one person plead guilty for a reduced charge and use that person to help prosecute the other. It was not a big surprise, particularly when the government had by then clearly stated that Aref was their ultimate target. I confided my concerns to Aref, who said, "No, he is a good brother. He will not do that." Ultimately I did not pay much attention to this attempt, because after talking to other attorneys I found out that such a request was unlikely to be granted. Also, the government would resist it lest they had to deal with a twofold case. Kindlon told me he did not care, because it would make no difference to his defense.

Kathy Manley, the assisting attorney, told me that I was very much wrong on this. She said that the request for separate trials was a standard motion that both defendants filed. It was done because all the alleged terrorist connections were against Aref, not Hossain, and this motion would simply prevent prejudicial evidence about one being used against the other. In case of a plea deal, there was no need to sever the case.

On December 9, in a sixty-four-page motion, Luibrand requested that the court separate Hossain's case from Aref's, essentially arguing that because of Aref's alleged contacts with overseas terrorists, it would be very difficult for this information not to prejudice the jury against Hossain also, who, Luibrand said, had nothing to do with such things. Hossain's charges concerned money laundering, and since he had been misled, induced, and coerced to take part in a very sophisticated scheme devised by the FBI, he was entrapped. Based on the clear entrapment that had occurred, Luibrand said, he was requesting that the court dismiss Hossain's charges.

The government had to respond to this brief by December 23, giving Luibrand until December 29 to reply. McAvoy said he would announce his decision during a court session on January 9, 2006.

NSA WIRETAP

On December 28, the *New York Times* reported in a front-page article that the National Security Agency had tapped into some of the country's main telephone arteries to conduct broader data-mining operations in the search for terrorists. The article pointed out the illegality of the NSA's practice of wiretapping many defendants in high-profile terrorism-related cases without a warrant, and that many defense attorneys in such cases were planning to file briefs to their respective courts to force the prosecution to reveal whether they had used illegal wiretapping of their clients without court approval. Many in the legal community wondered why the president had bypassed the FISA court that had been granting warrants in terrorism and espionage cases since 1978. They challenged President Bush's authority to have secretly ordered the NSA on October 30, 2001 to wiretap suspected individuals without court approval. The White House and the Justice Department, on the other hand, insisted that the president did have such authority, and that such an order did not violate the Constitution or American civil liberties.

Kindlon and Luibrand immediately wrote letters to the U.S. Attorney requesting disclosure of any warrantless wiretapping or eavesdropping. After receiving no response, they filed omnibus court motions comprising eight requests, including one to determine whether their clients had been subjected to any illegal wiretapping. They hoped that the bogus sting operation would lose ground if it were proven that the defendants' telephones or e-mails had been tapped without a warrant. We were all sure that Aref, his residence, and the mosque had been subjected to surveillance long before the sting operation began, but the question was whether the prosecutors would acknowledge this. The defense attorneys did their job knowing all too well that the chances of learning the truth were zero, because so far they had not been allowed to see even a single piece of sealed evidence.

On January 9, 2006, McAvoy denied each motion, request, and everything the defense attorneys had requested, including information about the illegal wiretapping. "The judge denied everything from the beginning to the middle to the end," commented Kindlon. He said he felt like a spectator guessing about the drama being played out on the other side of a closed curtain. And—after seventeen months, after so many anticipated dates for the trial had come and gone—a trial date was still not in sight. "My client is miserable. He is locked down twenty-three hours a day," Kindlon said. "He is at the end of his rope."

We all were totally frustrated. The situation of the defendants' families and children was indescribable. I was losing confidence in McAvoy as a neutral arbitrator with every passing court date. Members of the mosque were forced to look at him like a top FBI agent in another kind of robe.

On January 17, 2006 the *New York Times* published another article about the NSA that quoted law enforcement and terrorism officials as saying that the NSA eavesdropping program "might have helped uncover people having ties with Al-Qaeda in Albany... ." The article featured as its lead illustration a color photograph of Aref in chains.

On January 20, 2006, Kindlon filed a seventeen-page motion to dismiss the case against Aref, based only on the NSA's illegality in gathering information about Aref before initiation of the sting operation.

YET ANOTHER BAIL HEARING

Immediately after his bail had been revoked on September 30, 2005, Aref had started complaining more and more about Kindlon. His main complaint was that Kindlon had hardly any time for him. The accusation was genuine. In the last four months or so, Kindlon had seen Aref briefly only a few times; he would promise to see him in the next few days, and then skip several weeks. At one point Aref even refused to see him. I called Kindlon several times to try to understand the situation, but Kindlon did not have any genuine excuse to offer me. At the time, he was very busy preparing for the trial of Christopher Porco, a high-profile murder case, and he had many other cases to take care of as well, as did most successful lawyers. But I was extremely concerned about Aref's dissatisfaction with Kindlon. I sensed that Aref was being advised by some inmates inside the prison, and I suspected that he might fire Kindlon, or perhaps decide to act as his own attorney.

Despite my strong advice to be patient and wait a little more, on January 16, 2006 Aref wrote directly to McAvoy from his jail cell and requested that the judge grant him bail. He said that whatever had been presented by the prosecutors during the last bail hearing was not true. Moreover, he wrote, "I have four children, including a three-week-old baby, and they all are suffering, my wife is not well, and I am the only one with a job. I believe I have a right to a bail hearing." McAvoy forwarded Aref's application to Kindlon, stating that he did not intend to act on his application and that any future request must come to him through Kindlon.

My thinking was that the court had gone back and forth on Aref's bail three times already, and unless there was any compelling change in the situation it would be very difficult for the judge to rescind his last decision. However, a new bail hearing was granted for February 10.

That day was simply a repeat of the earlier detention hearings under Judge Homer, and he presided once again. As usual, Kindlon argued strongly that the whole case was an artful fabrication by the government and that his client was only a victim of that fabrication. He had nothing to do with terrorism. He also emphasized that the decision on the illegal NSA wiretap would take some time, and if there were an appeal of that decision, the future trial might drag on much further. In response, William Pericak, the prosecutor, suggested that the NSA matter was scheduled to be discussed in court on March 13 and he did not expect the trial to be postponed too much longer. He also said that the suffering of Aref and his wife and children should not be given any consideration because that was part of the judicial process. Judge Homer, as well as the prosecutors, suggested that a waiting period before trial of about two years was not uncommon in Albany County, and that Aref had been in prison for only the last five months. Referring to Kindlon's arguments item by item, Homer commented, "Even though each incident may have an innocent explanation, collectively put together they give the impression that Aref once had ties with people involved with terrorism." He denied bail. Aref lifted his handcuffed hands and gestured toward us before he was taken out.

Outside the court, Kindlon said that he was very disappointed with Homer's decision. One reporter asked if he thought his phones were being tapped. "Anyone's phones may be tapped," Kindlon lashed out. "The Bush Administration is acting lawlessly and they don't give damn about the Constitution."

Despite this defeat in court, we were satisfied with Kindlon's arguments and presentation. But Aref was furious. He thought Kindlon had failed him and had not argued the way Aref wanted him to. He was so angry that he told me over the phone that he did not want Kindlon to represent him anymore. "Perhaps he is representing them," he said. About three weeks later, Aref wrote a long letter to McAvoy requesting that he remove Kindlon as his defense attorney and appoint someone else instead. He complained that Kindlon had hardly any time for him, never kept his promises to meet him, did not present his defense the way he wanted it presented, and gave him wrong and misleading information. McAvoy refused to accept Aref's request and sent the letter to Kindlon, asking him to resolve the problem with his client.

I knew very well that there was a big communication gap between Aref and Kindlon. Aref had no legal background, and Kindlon did not have much sense of Aref's behavioral background. Aref needed someone to sit down and listen to him hour after hour and plan arguments for the defense the way he wanted. But Kindlon was not meant for that.

Things might have fallen apart tragically if, by mere luck, another attorney had not appeared on the scene. Steve Downs, who had recently retired as head counsel for the State Commission on Judicial Conduct, volunteered to become part of the defense team and accepted the responsibility to interact with Aref in jail. As soon as Kindlon told me about it, I was hugely relieved. I invited Downs to come to the mosque after the Friday prayer to talk to the gathering about the progress of the case. He did so willingly. His presentation touched everyone. The mosque members liked him right away. He was an activist, had been a Peace Corps volunteer in India, and had a charming personality. I bonded with him immediately, and I adopted him as caretaker of the mosque and its members in legal matters. We started calling him "one of us."

Aref liked him very much as well, and Downs had plenty of time and patience for Aref. Downs sat with Aref in jail day after day for months and sorted out the many distortions that the government had fabricated about his past to associate him with terrorism.

THE NEW YORK CIVIL LIBERTIES UNION

Before the last court hearing on February 10, I was told that the NYCLU would organize a demonstration and press conference in front of the courthouse in support of the defense and against the government's position on the illegal NSA wiretapping, but on that day I did not see anyone from the group there. Instead, on February 17 we heard that the NYCLU was going to file motions on behalf of the defendants in relation to the wiretapping.

Meanwhile, the prosecutors obtained another extension until March 16 to submit more documents under seal. McAvoy scheduled a pretrial conference on March 24 in Binghamton, where he also held court. It was a two-hour drive from Albany. But on March 10, McAvoy issued a classified ruling denying Kindlon's motion filed in January that specifically sought information on the NSA warrantless wiretapping. McAvoy did something else too on that day: he sealed his own ruling immediately, only a few minutes after he received a sealed motion filed by the Justice Department. The defense team, as well as the whole legal community, was stunned. It was particularly difficult for me to take. I was very angry. I thought to myself, *are we living in a third world country, or in the former*

Soviet Union? How could the FBI and the prosecutors sit down privately, in confidence with the judge, and say to him and show him whatever they wanted, and the defendants and the defense attorneys would never know about the contents? How could this ever be called due process?

LEFT: Kathy Manley, Aref's assisting/appeal attorney, from the law firm Kindlon Shanks & Associates.

Photo from http://www.kindlon.com/attorneys.htm

RIGHT: Steve Downs, Aref's volunteer attorney.

Photo by Katherine Hughes

CHAPTER 10

Classified

SOME CLASSIFIED MATERIAL IS RELEASED

On March 16, 2006, McAvoy ordered the Justice Department to turn over some classified material to the defense. This decision was made in response to the numerous defense requests and was the result of more than twenty private meetings between the judge and federal prosecutors, during which they had haggled about what classified information the government was required to disclose to the defense. But the ruling was not clear as to what documents the government was supposed to reveal and what it could withhold.

The prosecutors ultimately sent ten documents to the defense attorneys on March 21. A day later, I found two of the documents in the mosque mailbox with a note attached to them: "This is the [obscenity] FBI's secret evidence now made public." I guessed they had been put in the mailbox for me by a mosque member, who might have obtained them through a media reporter, one of the defendants or their attorneys, or from the Internet. But I wondered, *why the dirty language?* When I looked at the documents, I understood.

The two documents were the criminal histories of Ali Yaghi and John Earl Johnson. Their criminal reports had already been well publicized in local newspapers, and I did not find anything in them that could have been labeled "secret" or "classified." I had also heard that it was routine for the government to release the criminal history reports of people it intended to call as witnesses at trial. I verified that the prosecutors were intending to use the two men as witnesses, although I remembered that Yaghi had told me that the FBI had offered him a lot of money and U.S. citizenship to testify against Aref, but that he said he "gave them a big

'F.'" (The prosecutors did not ultimately call either man during the trial; perhaps something went wrong and they changed their minds.)

I called Kindlon and asked him about the much-discussed released documents. "All nonsense and all useless," he said. "Everything was known already."

I have earlier discussed Ali Yaghi and his arrest, imprisonment, and deportation to Jordan. John Earl Johnson, an African American born in 1979, was also a member of the Albany mosque. He was known by the name Yaya or Yahya in our community. He lived in a building next door to the mosque. According to some newspaper reports, Johnson was convicted in 1996 for a residential burglary in Chicago and was sentenced to seven years in state prison, where he converted to Islam. After his release, he spent some time overseas in Pakistan, Afghanistan, and Syria. In 2000 he was arrested in Afghanistan for carrying computer disks that contained information about chemicals and explosives. He then spent some time in Damascus going to school to learn Arabic with other foreign students from Western countries. After his return to the U.S. he settled in Albany, where it appears he was under surveillance by the FBI either as an individual or as a profiled member of the mosque. He was arrested by Albany police in December 2001 for carrying a rifle as he exited his apartment. It was a weak case and languished in court.

A year later, on December 27, 2002, the FBI noticed him putting two rifles into the trunk of his car, which was parked behind his apartment near the back door of the mosque. He was followed and arrested on a highway outside of Albany. From the trunk of his car, two rifles and four 3.5-inch computer diskettes were confiscated. According to Johnson, the two rifles had been legally purchased by his wife; he had the receipts in his wallet. He had downloaded the information on the computer disks from the Internet, he said, because he had been interested in researching the history of explosive chemicals. The FBI claimed that the disks contained information about chemicals, explosives, and bomb-making devices, and that he had been arrested in Afghanistan for having similar computer disks in his possession. In July 2003, Johnson pleaded guilty to the FBI's charges and was sentenced to forty-six months in jail. After serving his term, he returned to Albany and became a regular and peaceful member of the mosque community.

I did not know much about Johnson except that he used to regularly attend prayers in the mosque. One day, a few months prior to his arrest, he saw me in front of the mosque and said, "Oh, I missed you before the prayer. I intended to ask your permission to raise some money in the mosque during the prayer." He explained to me that a friend of his who was visiting Pakistan had sent him an e-mail requesting some money to buy a return ticket to the U.S.

I told him, "What has the mosque got to do with him? He is your friend, and he has sent an e-mail to you, so you should help him or not help him. It is your personal business. Nobody else knows who he is. Why would somebody else bother helping him?"

He did not like my response. Very soon the exchange became heated. I recall telling him that unless someone had a return ticket, he should not be visiting overseas in the first place. But Johnson said, "People go overseas because there is no freedom to practice Islam in this country."

Normally I avoid getting engaged in this kind of argument, but this time I took the opposite position. "Tell me a single Islamic thing you cannot practice in this country," I said.

He was silent for awhile and then said, "You cannot marry four wives in this country."

I had heard that kind of argument before. "When you are able to take care of even one wife nicely," I said, "we will discuss this topic further. I will wait until then." That was the end of my argument with him.

After seeing Johnson's criminal report in the form of the prosecutors' "declassified" document, I momentarily wondered if the FBI had been trying to use him to raise a few dollars in the mosque to be sent overseas, in order to later accuse the mosque of financially supporting foreign terrorists. But I had no corroboration for this idea, and I am inclined to think that was not the case.

Yaghi's criminal report contained his personal data, documentation of his conviction for illegal possession of a loaded gun, and his release certificate from prison. It also had some additional information/instructions for law enforcement:

** DO NOT ALERT THIS INDIVIDUAL TO THIS NOTICE. **

THE PERSON QUERIED THROUGH THIS SEARCH MAY BE AN INDIVIDUAL IDENTIFIED BY INTELLIGENCE INFORMATION

AS HAVING POSSIBLE TIES WITH TERRORISM. CONTACT
THE TERRORIST SCREENING CENTER AT (866) 872-9001 FOR
ADDITIONAL IDENTIFYING INFORMATION AVAILABLE TO
ASSIST YOU IN MAKING THIS DETERMINATION.

DO NOT ARREST THIS INDIVIDUAL UNLESS THERE IS EV-
IDENCE OF A VIOLATION OF FEDERAL, STATE OR LOCAL
STATUTES. CONDUCT A LOGICAL INVESTIGATION USING
TECHNIQUES AUTHORIZED IN YOUR JURISDICTION
AND ASK PROBING QUESTIONS TO DETERMINE IF THIS
INDIVIDUAL IS IDENTICAL TO THE PERSON OF LAW EN-
FORCEMENT INTEREST.

WARNING—APPROACH WITH CAUTION.

IF YOU ARE A BORDER PATROL OFFICER, IMMEDIATELY
CALL THE NTC.

***DO NOT ADVISE THIS INDIVIDUAL THAT HE IS ON A
TERRORIST WATCH LIST. ***

MKE/TERRORIST ORGANIZATION MEMBER — CAUTION

THE "COMMANDER" PAGE IS RELEASED

Besides the criminal reports of Johnson and Yaghi, the prosecutors
also released translations of five entries from the black-and-white
"pocket litter" notebook found in the U.S. military raid at Rawah on June
11, 2003. The original entries were handwritten in Kurdish, and were
translated as follows:

(1) Yassin Aref
8 Leonard Place
Albany
NY 222   Important
USA
0015184279892
Brother [Commander] Yassin America—New York

Note that the zip code is incomplete (and that instead of starting correctly as 122, it starts as 222), and that Aref's first address in 1999, which he moved from six months later, was more than three and a half years old. Did the FBI really think that terrorists were so stupid as to carry a three-and-a-half-year-old address of their "commander," where he no longer lived? Of course, the original mistranslation of "Brother"—in Kurdish, the word was written as *Kak*, an honorific term of respect like "Mister" or "Sir"—was "Commander," and it was this mistranslation that had created all the controversy. When this "secret" document was finally released, no one found any interest in it because it was so meaningless. Now I really understood the meaning of "making a mountain out of a molehill."

> (2) Norway—Teacher Krekar—home 004722572688
> Mosque 004722207247

These are Mullah Krekar's contact numbers in Norway.

> (3) The movement's office/Damascus 2760482

> (4) Syria Office—Ha' 2760482

[Ha' are the first two letters of *Hatif*, which means "telephone"]

> Office fax 5112347

These are contact numbers for the office of the Islamic Movement of Kurdistan (IMK) in Damascus, Syria.

> 5) Dr. Rafael Abu-Ahmad 0013156373495

This is the nickname of Dr. Rafil Dhafir of Syracuse, who was arrested and prosecuted later.

The prosecutors also provided a document with the following entries:

> (a) Yassin Aref, 8 Leonard Place, Albany, NY 222, USA 0015184279892
> Obtained in March 2003, in a military raid in Mosul on a suspected safe house.

> (b) Yasin 0015184279892
> Obtained in March 2003, in a military raid at Khurmal, a suspected Ansar al-Islam facility near the village of Sargat.

They also provided a page that was about 60% redacted and appeared as follows:

> (c) XXXXXXXXXXXXXXXXXXXXXXXXXXXXX

An Individual, who is in a position to testify, provided the following information:

Individual stated that during October 2001, the individual was approached by XXXXXXXXXXXXXXXXXXXXXXXXXXXXXXXXX XXXXXXXXXXXXXXXXXXXXXXXXXXXXXXXXXXXXXXXXXXX XXXXXXXXXXXXXXXXXXXXXXXXXXXXXXXXXXXXXXXXX

XXXXXXXXXXXXXXXXX told the Individual that USAMA BIN LADEN had requested the following information, to include flight training schools, access to airports in XXXXXXXXXXXXXX and XXXXXXXXXXXXXXXX

also asked the Individual how close the Individual could get to an XXXXXXXXXXX aircraft, XXXXX XXXXXXXXXXXXXXXXXXXXXXXXX   XXXXXXXXXXX XXXXXXXXXXXXXXXXXXXXXXXXXXXXXXXXXXXXXXXXX XXXXXXXXXXXXXXXXXXXXXXXXX

XXXXXXXXXXXXXXXXXXXXX further told the Individual that when the Individual obtained this information he could get in contact with the "brothers" through the following Syrian fax numbers: 963-112760482 and 963-115112347 in Damascus, Syria.

XXXXXXXXXXXXXXXXXXXXXXXXXXXXXXXXXXXXXXXXXX XXXXXXXXXXXXXXXXXXXXXXXXXXXXXXXXXXXXXXXXXX XXXXXXXXXXXXXXXXXXXXXXXXXXXXXXXXXXXXXXXXXX XXXXXXXXXXXXXXXXXXXXXXXXXXXXXXXXXXXXXXXXXX XXXXXXXXXXXXXXXXXXXXXXXXXXXXXXXXXXXXXXXXXX XXXXXXXXXXXXXXXXXXXXXXXXXXXXXXXXXXXXXXXXXX XXXXXXXXXXXXXXXXXXXXXXXXX

XXXXXXXXXXXXXXXXXXXXXXXXXXXXXXXXXXXXXXXXXX XXXXXXXXXXXXXXXXXXXXXXXXXXXXXXXXXXXXXXXXXX XXXXXXX.

The telephone and fax numbers are the numbers of the IMK office in Damascus, Syria, where Aref worked for about ten months in 1999 before being sent to Albany by the UN refugee organization. The FBI claimed that after coming to Albany, Aref called the IMK number fourteen times. Aref admitted making these calls to say hello to his colleagues and friends there.

The FBI refused to reveal the nature of the calls or state whether they had transcripts of them. We believed that these calls were monitored under the NSA's illegal wiretapping program. Kathy Manley, Kindlon's assisting attorney, explained to me that as a result of a case called Brady, the prosecution has to provide evidence favorable to the defense. Kindlon had made a Brady motion to obtain the contents of those calls to counter the government's implications that the calls were sinister, but the motion was denied in the judge's classified order. The prosecution never said that they did not have the contents of the calls, or that the information was not favorable to the defense—they just claimed it all was classified. This was completely in violation of due process and the Sixth Amendment.

AN APPEAL TO THE SECOND CIRCUIT

On March 24, Kindlon and Luibrand requested that the U.S. Second Circuit Court of Appeals in Manhattan review Judge McAvoy's denial of their January 20, 2006 motion to determine whether their clients had been subjected to warrantless wiretapping. Kindlon explained to me, "This legal move, known as a writ of mandamus, which challenges the decision-making of a lower court judge presiding over a case that hasn't reached trial, is used rarely. Our aim is to force the federal government to disclose whether it used warrantless wiretaps to spy on the defendants before they were targeted in the FBI sting. If that was the case, the indictment will no longer be valid."

The writ attacked McAvoy for holding numerous private meetings with government prosecutors, for limiting the release of classified information to the defense team, and for issuing rulings that were immediately sealed, thus depriving the defense of an opportunity to participate. By doing this, the court had deprived the defendants of due process, the right to counsel, and the right to confront the evidence against them. Kindlon wasn't sure about the outcome of the appeal, however, because even though it was a relatively new issue and it was being raised before trial rather than after conviction, it was the first appeal on the topic.

We were all anxious to see the reaction of the Second Circuit, but Aref was not happy with this writ. "This wiretapping is irrelevant to me," he told me. "I did not say whatever they say I said. I did not do whatever they say I did. I am not whatever they say I was. I want to be defended based on the truth and the truth only."

"The defense here is all legal matters, all technicalities," I tried to explain to him. "If it is proven that evidence was obtained illegally, the whole case will collapse. We must not neglect to pursue this aspect."

Three days later, the New York Civil Liberties Union asked the same Second Circuit court for the same relief: to unseal the ruling McAvoy had made regarding the government's warrantless wiretapping program against Aref. The NYCLU argued in its brief that the First Amendment required McAvoy's ruling in the case to be made public. "Courts do not have the authority to issue entire opinions in secret," the NYCLU said. The brief stated that it was unprecedented that a judge would seal a ruling without explaining why.

The NYCLU noted that the judge had rejected the defendants' suppression motion on March 10 less than two hours after the government had submitted a secret court document opposing it. In its writ, the NYCLU asked the appeals court for something very reasonable: "To order the judge to release his opinion publicly, with redactions only to the extent necessary to protect classified information."

"We do not have secret courts in this country," said Chris Dunn, the NYCLU's associate legal director. "It's not a surprise that the government wants this to be secret, but it's extraordinary for a court to go along."

While all these efforts were going on, in our case as well as in several other cases around the country, the White House and other government agencies were busy trying to defend Bush's warrantless wiretapping program. An example of this is the statement given by Louis J. Freeh, the former director of the FBI, when he came to Albany on March 31 to receive an award from a local bar association. He said, "I believe President Bush has the Constitutional authority to spy on Americans if they are suspected of being linked to terrorism. However, it should be left to the courts to decide whether the National Security Agency went too far in a controversial eavesdropping program."

THE TRIAL DATE IS FINALLY SET

We had become used to one trial date after another being scheduled but no actual progress being made toward the trial. April 14, 2006 was one such court day in which we expected nothing new, but we were surprised to hear from prosecutor William Pericak that the prosecution was ready to take the case to trial and was looking forward to presenting its evidence. McAvoy announced the trial would begin on September 6, 2006. This was still five and a half months away, but we felt confident of it.

McAvoy did not say anything regarding a request that Kindlon had submitted to him earlier, asking the government to turn over any tape recordings of calls that Aref had made to the IMK office number. This request challenged the redacted sheet released by the prosecutors on March 16 in response to McAvoy's order of March 10, 2006. This redacted page (detailed earlier) implied that Aref aided terrorists when he called the Syrian IMK number fourteen times between 1999 and 2001. Kindlon had reiterated that those calls—which the government claimed connected Aref to a terrorist organization, Ansar al-Islam—were actually personal in nature and did not in any way connect him to any alleged terrorist activity. Kindlon hoped that the release of the recordings of these calls would remove any suspicion that his client had any links with terrorists.

On May 23, a three-judge panel of the Second Circuit Court of Appeals refused to rule on the request by the New York Civil Liberties Union to require McAvoy to make public his secret court ruling regarding the government's wiretapping program. The panel expressed doubt that the NYCLU had standing to challenge McAvoy's ruling. In essence, the NYCLU was advised that it had to start the challenge in McAvoy's court to begin with before it tried to bring an appeal. To us it sounded like Catch-22 or going in circles. What did "to begin with" mean? Hadn't McAvoy originally refused to comply with the defense's request to release his rulings? One of the panel judges, Chief Judge Dennis Jacobs, did express that it was "fairly unusual" for a judge to file an opinion under seal.

Meanwhile, in spite of everyone's suggestion to the contrary, Aref had been insisting since his last bail hearing failed that he wanted to file a request for yet another hearing. I tried very hard to convince him that unless a drastic change in the situation occurred, the judge would not rescind his last decision. But Aref insisted. "We have nothing to lose," he said. "Let us give it a try."

On June 6, Kindlon filed a forty-three-page memorandum outlining the government's misrepresentation of facts concerning Aref's past and the twists and manipulations of the translation of his journal. Steve

Downs and Kathy Manley had spent long hours putting these facts to-gether to help Kindlon prepare his memorandum, and before that Downs had spent many hours with Aref sorting out the facts. Downs's aim was to prepare a document that would reflect the truth rather than the gov-ernment's lies, and with his help every falsehood and mischaracterization artfully presented by the government was exposed. The government had avoided presenting certain portions of Aref's journal that reflected his opposition to terrorism and leaders who supported violence. Contrary to the government's assertion that he was anti-American, the document noted that Aref supported the U.S. alliance to depose Saddam Hussein ("America's plan," the Iraq Liberation Act of 1998). The government had painted a very sinister picture by translating "America's plan" from the journal as "Plan in America," to imply that Aref had entered America to carry out a terror scheme. In reality, the diary clearly referred to "Amer-ica's plan" to topple Saddam Hussein through an alliance of Kurds and Iraqis. The government simply twisted the translation, the diary, and the truth at will. Similarly, a letter with Aref's name on it, clearly from Islamic Cintral in Irbil, a Kurdish nationalist organization, was claimed by the government to have come from the IMK—an entirely different organiza-tion. Finally, the document also reflected that not only did Aref not have any alliance with Mullah Krekar, he was opposed to Krekar taking over the IMK's leadership.

Kindlon explained that the government's lie that Aref was a member or representative of IMK was very crucial, because it formed the whole basis through which the government tried to connect Aref to Mullah Krekar and to other suspected individuals and organizations. In fact, it was the existence of those charges that allowed the prosecutors to bring in much of the journal material as evidence relating to those charges. This was one of the main reasons they brought the superseding indict-ment, and then it became very difficult for the defense to challenge the introduction of the journal as evidence.

On June 7, McAvoy issued a pretrial order directing the prosecutors to disclose their expert witnesses, including translators. Pursuant to this order, on June 12 the prosecutors released three more entries from the black-and-white "pocket litter" notebook found at Rawah in June 2003. The address and telephone numbers indicate that these three individuals of Middle Eastern origin lived in the New York City/Long Island area:

1. Musad Yasin   Musaab As-Samarrai
   97E Mineala Lane, Valley Stream, NY 11580, USA   Very Important
   Tel 516-561-6210, E-mail FUTUREL@IDT.NET

2. Dr. Walid Al-Samaraii, America, 516-593-7476

3. Mus'ab Saeed   00/1516-561-6210

I had no idea who these individuals were, and I did not try to investigate them due to security reasons—mine as well as theirs. I simply guessed that they were active Muslims/leaders/imams in their localities. In the beginning, when the mistranslation of "commander/brother" was a flop, there was a rumor that the "pocket litter" notebook contained the names, addresses, and telephone numbers of 100 Muslim leaders around the world, presumably collected by some Kurdish individual or organization to seek financial, religious, or political help for their cause.

On the other front, on June 23 a three-judge panel of the Second Circuit Court of Appeals in Manhattan made its decision on the appeal filed by Kindlon to force the government to say whether any of the evidence against Aref had been gathered with the assistance of the warrantless electronic surveillance program. The panel denied the appeal based on procedural grounds. In a brief opinion, the panel said it did not have jurisdiction to grant what Kindlon requested. They dismissed other aspects of Kindlon's petition as well, for technical reasons.

On July 13, Judge Homer once again rejected Aref's request for bail pending trial. Even though Kindlon's forty-three-page memorandum filed on June 6 had exposed many false and illogical claims in the government's position, the prosecutors emphasized that it essentially changed nothing. Homer was inclined to agree with them. He stated, "On September 30, 2005, the court had assumed Aref to pose a flight risk and a danger to the community, and he was ordered detained. The evidence presented now does not persuade the court to reconsider that."

At this stage, it seemed that everything was over and the defense had no more cards left to play. We simply had to wait for the trial to begin.

CHAPTER 11

Waiting

PREPARING FOR TRIAL

B y the middle of August 2006, we were awaiting jury selection and the beginning of the trial. Kindlon and his assistant, Kent Sprotbery, would defend Aref, and Luibrand would defend Hossain. Assistant U.S. Attorneys William Pericak and Elizabeth Coombe, assisted by FBI Special Agent Tim Coll, would prosecute the case. The FBI's and the prosecutors' prestige was on the line. They had admitted that their real target was Aref, and it appeared that they wanted to punish him by bringing a successful conviction against him. Hossain seemed to be a secondary concern for them.

We in the Muslim community believed they had no concrete evidence whatsoever against Aref—nothing—but we also knew very well that they were desperate to get a conviction and would do anything to achieve that goal. So we were not expecting a fair and honest presentation from the prosecutors in court. In our judgment, they had already brought McAvoy to their side by privately sharing with him their thoughts and so many secret documents. They had translated Aref's old speeches and journal in a way that slanted the meaning from innocent to sinister. They had piled up plenty of video and audio surveillance tapes with suggestive images and phrases. They had spent a good amount of the FBI's manpower and resources over a two-year period to pick out specific portions of these materials to use in court. We knew they would present lies, distortions, twists, and fabrications. They would present surveillance gossip and discussions between Malik and the defendants out of context, and make responses to Malik's provocative questions appear to be the original thoughts of the defendants. They had practiced and rehearsed their presentation under the guidance of FBI psychologists to ensure that the jury believed the defendants were dangerous terrorists just looking for an opportunity to strike. If the jury believed this, then a conviction based on money-laundering charges would be the natural outcome, even if there were no evidence to support the charges. We were aware that their awesome power and their presentation techniques would put the defense at a substantial disadvantage. But we did not know what to do.

The FBI had already given incentives to tempt Ali Yaghi to testify in court that some terrorists had traveled to Albany and had stayed in Aref's house as his guest. They were prepared to use John Johnson to testify about some incident or conversation or circumstance concerning Aref, but we did not know how they wanted to use him; perhaps it would be a conversation in the mosque taken out of context, or perhaps it would be Aref's past in Damascus, where Johnson had lived for some time. They pressured Kassim Shaar, a friend of Aref's, to say he would testify that Aref and Malik discussed in his presence shooting down the Pakistani ambassador's plane in New York City, and told him that if he did not testify they would charge him for being an accomplice in the phony plot. They forced Abul Kashem, owner of the diner next door to Hossain's pizzeria, to say he would testify against Hossain by threatening to charge him with buying a fraudulent driver's license for his daughter from Malik. They wanted him to say that he had heard Hossain praising Osama bin Laden at one point. If such testimony were given, we believed that it would be false, or at least grossly out of context. We learned that they tried similar tactics with several other members of the Muslim community to get them to testify against the defendants.

One day Hossain told me that the FBI had approached his ex-wife, Rosemary, to testify against him and had threatened her, if she did not, to charge her with marrying Hossain only to help him get a green card. She was an American white woman, several years older than Hossain, who had converted to Islam. She had married and divorced a few times prior to marrying Hossain, and she had adult children from a previous marriage. She divorced Hossain in 1992 after only a few years of marriage, and they had no children together.

I knew Rosemary, her previous husband, and their two children, a boy and a girl, very well. On August 12, I read the following in the Albany *Times Union*: "The ex-wife of a city pizza owner charged in an FBI counterterrorism sting is ready to testify next month that he once told her he hates Jews, according to court papers filed by federal prosecutors. The woman, who split from Mohammed Mosharref Hossain in 1992, also claims he married her to obtain a green card and then divorced her once he was naturalized, documents said."

Hossain told me later that perhaps she was referring to him as a Jew-hater because of seeing his anger at a television news report that they had watched together sometime in the mid-Eighties. The report was about Israeli soldiers who had killed several Palestinian women and children. "For the FBI these days, anyone who expresses sympathy for Palestinians' suffering is an anti-Semite Hamas terrorist," said an angry mosque member. "Besides, the guy [Hossain] is charged with money laundering, not for being an anti-Semite."

Around the same time, Hossain also told me that Rosemary's daughter worked for the FBI. In fact, I had seen her a few times in and around the federal court. One local TV channel aired an interview with her, face blurred, in which she accused Hossain of being an abusive stepfather. She said Hossain did not let her and her brother celebrate Christmas when they were living with her mother, who at the time was married to Hossain. I was surprised by this accusation, because she was supposedly a Muslim girl who had a Pakistani Muslim father and a Muslim mother. I used to see Rosemary and her daughter frequently at the Islamic Center of the Capital District.

On August 22, the prosecutors requested of the court that FBI language specialists (Urdu, Kurdish, Arabic, and Bengali) should be allowed to hide their identities by using pseudonyms and physical disguises when they testified during the trial. To us, this appeared to be a move to intimidate the jury into believing that the defendants were so dangerous that even the translators' lives were not safe, while at the same time putting the defense in the disadvantaged position of cross-examining disguised individuals. Professor Stephen Gottlieb of Albany Law School, whom we had invited to the mosque a few times, was surprised. "I have never heard of something like this before," he told me. "This is expected in a mobster's trial, where real dangers do exist." But here it was just a bogus sting case, where it was obvious even to the government that the defendants had no connection to any real terrorists.

The prosecutors also told the court that they wanted Rohan Gunaratna, a Sri Lankan who belonged to a research group in Singapore, to testify in the case as an expert. Gunaratna, a Hindu anti-Muslim TV pundit, was well known to be more than willing, for a fee, to go anywhere in the world to testify in favor of his sponsors. Many Muslims fear pundits like him more than they fear the FBI. A Malaysian student told me, after having read some of Gunaratna's statements, that "his kind are so brilliant, and such experts on terrorism, that after putting a bunch of hair on a piece of furniture they can prove that the piece of furniture is nothing but a terrorist with a beard." Gunaratna's mere presence in the court was supposed to prove to the jury that the defendants were such high-value terrorists that he was willing to travel all the way from Singapore to Albany to testify against them.

After making some more inquiries, I concluded that there were a number of people like Gunaratna who were making a fortune from the sponsorship of the FBI by testifying in one court proceeding after another. The credentials and authority of such experts on terrorism rank from 95% to 100%—they understand 95% of what the FBI wants from them when they receive the first call, and they deliver 100% of what the FBI wants from them in court. Their rewards are very understandable: after paying for the best possible transportation, hotel, and food, the FBI offers them a modest honorarium starting at a minimum of $5,000 for a few minutes' testimony. "Shame on U.S. university professors and researchers who kill themselves day and night discovering facts. They should resign, surrender their Ph.D.s, and go testify for the FBI!" a member of the mosque lashed out.

In essence, the FBI expected Gunaratna to pick out a few words and phrases from the surveillance discussion tapes and, pointing to the defendants, claim through his authoritative expertise that such statements were found 99% of the time among al-Qaeda terrorists and global jihadists: "Therefore I certify that the two individuals in front of me in this court are really dangerous terrorists."

The FBI also wanted to bring in a high-level weapons expert from the military to describe to the jury just how real and dangerous the missile was that the FBI's informant, Malik, had in his possession. Since Hossain saw such a dangerous weapon once on Malik's shoulder, therefore Hossain must be a very dangerous terrorist. To this end, they submitted the name of Rodney Ratledge, Chief of the Division of Short-Range Surface-to-Air Missile Systems at the Alabama Defense Intelligence Agency, Missile and Space Intelligence Center, at Red Stone Arsenal in Huntsville, Alabama. His task was to tell the jury that the SAM in question was the same kind of missile being used by overseas terrorists as a weapon of mass destruction. His expertise would suggest to the jury that through his association with this weapon, Hossain must be like one of those terrorists.

I had no clue about the defense's preparation for the trial. Sometimes I thought the defense attorneys had no independent preparations, that their plan was only to counter the arguments presented by the prosecutors in court. I thought Kindlon was confident that the government would not be able to prove Aref guilty of anything. Luibrand planned to use the entrapment defense, and so perhaps he did not need much preparation for that.

THE FBI'S INTERROGATION OF AREF

ⓦe were also sure that the FBI would present some details from their interrogation of Aref on the night of his arrest to discredit him or implicate him in terror-related activities. The interrogation was not recorded, and thus no transcript had been made of what was actually asked or said, so the FBI was relatively free to make up claims as to what Aref may have said. The FBI described Aref's interrogation as follows:

> Date of transcription 08/05/2004
>
> YASSIN MUHIDDIN AREF, born July 1, 1970, social security account number XXX-XX-XXXX [omission mine], who resides at 44 West Street, Albany, New York, was interviewed at the Federal Bureau of Investigation (FBI), Albany, New York, subsequent to his arrest. The following individuals were present at various times during the interview:
>
> Special Agents ZACHARY DELECKI, TIMOTHY COLL, LAURA YOUNGBLOOD, JAMES P. BEANE, and JONATHAN L. RUDD, and two FBI linguists. After being advised of the identities of the interviewing agents, AREF was advised of his rights in English and, thereafter, waived his rights by signing an Advice of Rights form. A second Advice of Rights form (identical to the first form) was provided to an FBI linguist who explained the form to AREF in the Sorani dialect of Kurdish. AREF stated that he understood and had no problem speaking with the interviewing agents. AREF then signed the second form and provided the following information:
>
> AREF is the imam at the Albany Mosque. AREF has known MALIK for 5 to 6 months but does not know his real name. AREF has known

MOHAMMED HOSSAIN for approximately five years. AREF admitted witnessing a loan, as imam of the mosque, between MALIK and HOSSAIN for $45,000.00 to $50,000.00. AREF acted as an intermediary for the transaction, counted the money and signed receipts for the loan payments. The agreement was for HOSSAIN to repay MALIK two thousand dollars a month, which AREF would witness. The money for the loan did not come from the sale of a missile or ammunition. AREF stated that he did not understand the English term missile and the FBI linguist explained that term to him in Sorani. AREF did not know the term "chaudry." Additionally, AREF never heard of and did not know about an organization named Jaish-e-Mohammad, or JEM. AREF believed MALIK to be a wholesaler but did not know anything about MALIK's business and was just a witness to the loan. AREF never saw a trigger mechanism for a missile. After being shown a picture of the trigger mechanism, AREF stated that he had never seen it before.

AREF believed MALIK was a wholesaler and the cash came from his wholesale business.

AREF never served in the military and does not know why anyone would refer to him as "commander." AREF left Iraq in 1995 and has never returned to Iraq. AREF was a student in Iraq and had no affiliation with any political party or terrorist group. When asked if he knew of any terrorist organizations in Iraq, AREF stated that he had heard of a group called Ansar Al-Islam. AREF has no information about terrorists and stated that if he did, it would be his duty to stop them.

AREF has two older brothers in Iraq who are members of the Patriotic Union of Kurdistan (PUK)—MOSIN MUHIDDIN AREF (phonetic) and IBRAHIM MUHIDDIN AREF (phonetic). AREF also has a cousin, MAROF (phonetic), who has a Ph.D. in International Law and works for the PUK. MAROF is currently in Chicago visiting from Iraq. AREF never worked for the PUK. AREF does not know any Kurds in the Albany area. AREF knew that DR. DHAFIR was arrested in Syracuse, New York. However, AREF does not know DHAFIR and, other than one time DHAFIR visited the mosque a couple of years ago, AREF has never been in contact with DHAFIR, telephonic or otherwise.

AREF had limited contact with the Kurdistan Islamic Center in Syria, which he referred to as the Islamic Movement in Kurdistan (IMK). AREF is from the BARZANJI tribe and at one time, many years ago, may have participated in a rally sponsored by the IMK, but he is not part of the organization.

AREF left Iraq in 1995 and went to Syria where he worked as a gardener in Damascus. During AREF's last five months in Syria, he worked in the office of a man named MUSHID MUSTAFA AB-DULLA (phonetic). ABDULLA was a member of the IMK. Although AREF was not a member of the group, because he worked for AB-DULLA, some people might have thought he was an IMK member. AREF did cleaning in ABDULLA's office and other odd jobs for AB-DULLA, including transporting people from the airport and handling documents. AREF believes that ABDULLA has since left Syria and is now in England. AREF was shown a copy of a fax, in Arabic, that was recovered in the search of DHAFIR's place and asked why a letter was sent from the Islamic Center to DHAFIR vouching for AREF. AREF stated that he thinks he remembers seeing the letter in Syria and that they send letters of recommendation for people all the time.

Ansar Al-Islam (AI) was not in existence when AREF was in Iraq and he learned about the organization from the news in the United States. He also heard about ZARQAWI in the news but has no affiliation with AI or ZARQAWI. There are lots of groups in Iraq and things have changed over time. AREF may have known people in the past who are now members of AI but he cannot be sure. AREF knows the founder of AI to be MULLAH KREKAR. AREF knows of KREKAR because he is a famous person; however, he does not know KREKAR personally.

AREF's wife has a cousin who lives in Seattle. AREF's wife and daughter are planning to visit them in Seattle on August 17, 2004. AREF went to Ohio last year to visit a friend named EDRISS (phonetic). AREF also went to Florida to visit HASSIN KARIM (phonetic), who was his high school English teacher for three years.

Since coming to the United States, AREF has only sent a limited amount of money to Iraq—about $600 to $700. He has also sent money on two occasions to help a nephew, ABDULRAHMAN AB-DULLA GUL (phonetic), in Greece a few years ago. The total amount sent to his nephew was about $1,500. His nephew now lives in England and has dropped the "GUL" from the end of his name. The last time AREF sent any money to Iraq was two to three years ago.

AREF has never heard of anyone named LALO GORAN and he has never used that name himself. AREF knows someone he met in Syria, who now lives in Atlanta, with the last name of GORAN.

Little Italy, Mohammed Hossain's pizzeria,
continues to be run by his wife and family.

Photo by Jeanne Finley

CHAPTER 12

The Trial Begins

Because Sprotbery had to have an emergency appendectomy, the trial was postponed by one week and jury selection started on September 12, 2006. Out of more than a hundred individuals who had responded to a very detailed questionnaire sent by McAvoy, sixty-five prospective jurors were called to court. McAvoy interviewed them on a variety of topics. Pericak and Coombe asked them questions before approving them. Sprotbery and Luibrand tried to eliminate individuals who had racial or religious prejudices. They asked the prospective jurors if they would be able to consider the defendants as people like Smith and McDonald from their home towns, or would consider them Aref and Hossain, immigrants born in Iraq and Bangladesh. There were some who openly admitted considering the defendants terrorists, and who regarded the prosecutors as being good guys, and they were not chosen. Finally six men and six women, and one substitute, were chosen and sworn in.

I had to struggle to understand how this jury could be considered capable of reaching a fair decision. None of the jurors had anything remotely in common with the defendants and Malik—religion, race, language, culture, upbringing, style of talking, views. Only a person of the defendants' background could really understand what was meant when they said something or acted in a particular fashion. A mere transcript of a translation would not necessarily tell the true story.

I talked about this language problem with the mosque members, often giving them an example of a transcript of a translation that read: "John left Jack, saying, 'Okay, I will remember that, and take care of you soon.'" The prosecutors, I said, might claim that John became angry with Jack and threatened him harm, while the defense might claim that John wanted to help his friend Jack and promised to do his best to help him soon. In reality, this was not a joking matter; several times in court the jury was presented with transcripts containing contradictory interpretations.

THE PROSECUTION'S CASE

*T*he trial began on September 13, 2006. The intense security inside and outside the court was a repeat of the past. Pericak laid out the basis of his case by telling the jury that a sting operation had been conducted, in which a government informant had provided the opportunity for a crime and the defendants had participated of their own choice. Luibrand, on the other hand, informed the jury that the man whom the government called an "informant" was nothing but a convict and a con man who misled his FBI handlers and tricked the defendants into an elaborate scheme of "loaning" money to a fellow Muslim, which would later be defined as "money laundering."

As expected, the first day's testimony started with a big and spectacular stunt. Rodney Ratledge of the Alabama Defense Intelligence Agency displayed the SAM missile, putting it on his shoulder and explaining to the jury about its power and ability to shoot down airplanes. With this display, the prosecutors clearly wanted to implant a seed in the jurors' minds that the defendants had been running around with missiles like that all their lives. The defense referred to this weapon as a "barrel": "That's exactly what it was. You could have not fired it, you could have not caused any damage to anything with it; it was simply an empty barrel of a particular shape," was the description of the weapon by the defense.

On the following day, September 14, there was testimony by an Iraqi Kurdish refugee, Mohammad Aziz, who lived in Nashville, Tennessee. Several of his family members and thousands of Kurds had died when Saddam's troops had dropped mustard gas on the Kurdish population near the Iranian border in 1988. Aziz survived the gas attack but had a damaged lung and had to carry an oxygen tank by his side to breathe.

I was confused as to why the government wanted his testimony. He was extremely happy to see Aref in court, and praised him for his relentless service to Kurdish refugees in Syria through the IMK's office in Damascus, where Aref had been employed with Aziz's nephew. According to Aziz, the IMK's three-man office was basically a refugee help center. Aziz, while staying in Damascus during 1998–1999, used to go to the IMK office frequently to read newspapers and meet newly arriving refugees to get fresh news about the situation in his native land. Perhaps the prosecutors wanted to mislead the jury through Aziz's testimony into believing that Aref was a member of the IMK and not only a simple employee. But to my recollection, neither the prosecutors nor the defense asked Aziz if he had any knowledge of Aref's membership in the IMK. My take on this absence of questioning was that the prosecutors did not want to take the chance of hearing directly from Aziz that Aref was not a member of the IMK. On the other hand, since Aref was not a member of the IMK, and the prosecutors would never be able to prove that, why would they bother to ask Aziz about Aref's membership in the IMK?

However, there was another reason offered, from the defense. Aziz did not know English, and testified in Kurdish. But the FBI translator was very manipulative and began mistranslating the prosecutor's questions and Aziz's answers. Of course, no one in court had any inkling of this because no one else spoke Kurdish—except Aref, who became so disturbed and agitated that Kindlon had to ask McAvoy for a conference to raise the issue about the false translations. Kindlon proposed bringing a tape recorder into court to record everything Aziz said in Kurdish, so it could be translated later by an independent translator and compared with the FBI translation. A recorder was not introduced, but suddenly the translations improved and the government may have decided not to put mistranslated words into the witness' mouth.

On September 15, the jury listened to hours of surveillance tapes recorded during the sting. Transcripts were displayed via a large projector facing the jurors. One segment of a transcript included a discussion between Aref and Malik that had taken place on January 14, 2004 (see Appendix B, Sting Tapes 2004), in which Malik sought Aref's opinion about whether he should help Jaish-e-Mohammed (JEM) in Kashmir. Aref told him that he did not know enough about that group to give an opinion, and gave Malik a rule of thumb to make a decision: "I say if you believe they are doing right and working for Allah and you help them for Allah, go ahead. But of course, you should to be careful and...you should to know they [government] looking for any person they have any kind of link with that group. And if they find any link between you and that group, you should to know, you are going to be in the trouble."

This was a prevalent feeling among Muslims at that time, that law enforcement authorities in the U.S. penalized Muslims mercilessly based on mere suspicions. Therefore a word of caution to a prospective donor to a Muslim organization was expected from an imam, even though the organization may have been working for Allah's cause.

The next witness was Kassim Shaar, who was from northern Iraq and was a family friend of Aref's. He was the first person whom Aref met at the Albany airport when he landed in the U.S. The church that was helping Aref and his family settle in Albany had sought Shaar as a translator. He was present at Aref's house on February 12, 2004, when Malik made a payment of $10,000 to Hossain (see Appendix B, Sting Tapes 2004). He testified that Malik, whom he had never met, arrived with Hossain at Aref's house and the three men exchanged money and papers. "Out of the blue," Shaar said, "Malik blurted out that Aref or Hossain should not go to New York City next week because 'there was an attack coming to New York City, a missile attack coming there.'" Shaar testified that he could not connect that statement to anything that was occurring at the time. Aref told him that Malik was talking crazy, it was a sort of joke. But Aref was surprised with that irrelevant statement himself, and asked if Malik had any design to record such a statement in the presence of others for some sinister purpose. Malik lifted his shirt to show that he did not have any recording device on his body. Aref apparently was convinced that it was all a nonsensical joke.

"You thought he was joking, didn't you?" asked Kindlon.

"Right," Shaar replied.

According to Malik, his body recorder had fallen off in his car, so their discussion inside Aref's house was not recorded. However, the FBI claimed that Malik's transmitter was still on his body and that Special Agent Tim Coll listened to their discussion from a car parked outside of Aref's house.

On September 18, Coll took the stand and spent almost seven hours testifying. He seemed to be enjoying it. He gave his background as an FBI agent, and then talked about how he had envisioned the sting operation and how he had executed it to its conclusion over more than a year. He explained how he coached Malik before sending him to his targets, how he debriefed Malik after the meetings were over, how he installed the surveillance equipment, and how he monitored and listened to their conversations from a nearby parked van disguised as a cable repair vehicle. Whenever he said anything from the witness stand, he made sure to look at the jurors and make pleasant facial gestures to impress them.

The following day I missed the trial because I had two classes to teach.

But I was told in the evening by two mosque members who had been at-tending the trial every day from start to finish that it had been a really hard day for Coll in court. "So hard that he forgot to look at the jurors," they told me. "During his cross-examination, Sprotbery made him almost cry." I am sure they exaggerated. But the next morning I read in the *Times Union* that "Special Agent Timothy Coll became agitated at points during his testimony, characterizing questions as 'not fair' and defending the FBI's tactics of using an informant with a long history of criminal conduct."

Jurors were shown the surveillance video clip of January 2, 2004 on the projector screen, with a transcript of the conversation printed below. On the tape, while Aref counted the money, Malik pulled out a trigger device that looked like a mechanism for putting price labels on cans in supermarkets and showed it to Hossain by moving it toward him. Pros-ecutors told the jury that Aref saw the trigger mechanism and knew what it was, while the defense insisted that he was busy counting the money and never looked at it.

The public spectator section of the courtroom consisted of six rows. Each row could accommodate about twelve people. Normally during the trial, the court was overfilled; at times, people were refused entry into the building due to lack of space. The first two rows were usual-ly occupied by FBI agents and media people, who were recognizable by their styles. The last two rows were occupied by people from the mosque, and one could recognize them easily as well. The occupants of the middle two rows, however, were somewhat of a mystery to me. Some of them were well dressed and looked like attorneys or professionals, others looked very scholarly and paid a lot of attention to the proceed-ings, while others were casually dressed. It appeared that many of them knew each other. I kept guessing and speculating about their identity.

One day during a recess. I made a point of listening to their discus-sions to try and figure out who they were. Four of them were engaged in a conversation. I sat down on the bench behind them, fixing my eyes on my newspaper and my ears on their words. They expressed their total skepticism about the case. One man said that this case was typical of hun-dreds of others. "After 9/11, several thousand Muslims were arrested, but not a single real terrorist was ever found. Many accused of terrorism were finally tried for immigration violations or other minor charges. Many of them were deported or released for time served." It seemed the other three were in total agreement with him. He showed them a photocopy of an Associated Press report that said that in the last six months, Justice Department attorneys had declined to prosecute more than nine out of every ten terrorism cases sent to them by the FBI, Immigration and Customs Enforcement, and other federal agencies.

I was shaken emotionally after hearing this comment. But still I was not sure who they were. I decided to ask. I moved to their bench and told them that I had overheard part of their discussion and wondered who they were. They told me that there were about two dozen of them, and that they had been attending court every day to understand the case firsthand. "We are either independent individuals or we belong to some peace or justice or human rights group," one man said.

That same afternoon at the end of the session, a tall, well-dressed man came to me and said, "I was always skeptical of the case, but after hearing three days of testimony I am totally disgusted at the behavior of our government." He gave me some money. He did not want to take a receipt for it, and he did not want to tell me who he was. "Please help Aref's children with this on my behalf," he said, and walked away. I could not hold back my tears.

On September 17, Fred LeBrun wrote in his column in the *Times Union*:

> Frankly, it's difficult to get past the poisoned fruit of the poisoned tree metaphor lawyers like to toss about the original sting operation. It stinks. All the charges and supposed "crimes" stem from that very shaky government set-up that to this day remains a murky, inclusive mess. When the fast-talking informant produced a supposed surface-to-air missile at a private meeting, Hossain had to be told what it was. According to the government's own videotape at the trial, all the inflammatory terrorist rhetoric came from the informant, not from Hossain. If anything, Hossain looks like a guy humoring someone he believed to be a wealthy businessman who was going to make him a desperately needed loan.
>
> By Islamic custom and law, Hossain needed a witness to the financial transaction. He called his imam, Yassin M. Aref, to be the witness, and that eventually led to charges against Aref. Even though Aref was never present when the supposed missile was around, we're now told Aref was really the fellow the feds were trying to nab in the first place,

apparently on the basis of foreign intelligence. Intelligence that in recent years has also inspired little confidence, or less.

So now we're up to our earlobes in the government's interpreting what all this means through a host of difficult-to-understand witnesses, conflicting translations, contradictory statements, and confusing video footage. And a constant parading of the bogus surface-to-air missile for the jury to contemplate.

Straight up, if the defendants were not a couple of swarthy Middle Easterners who fit the profile, this case would be a laugher. But to the contrary, for reasons that have little to do with Aref and Hossain, I fear what can happen here is no laughing matter at all. Justice is on trial.

I openly wonder if they can even get a fair trial.

THE INFORMANT AND AREF'S SPEECHES AND JOURNAL

September 18th's proceeding basically dealt with the accuracy of the translations, with contradictions and discrepancies in the transcripts and the tape recordings, and with what Malik reported to Coll after the conclusion of his meetings with the targets. The defense pointed out that Malik was not only deceitful to the defendants but to the FBI as well. Sprotbery and Luibrand selected several instances in the FBI surveillance recordings and accused the prosecution of distorting and twisting the facts. The prosecutors in turn accused them of picking only selective pieces and using them out of context.

The testimony of September 19 was marked by Malik's presence on the witness stand. Since the arrest of the defendants on August 5, 2004, he had been in hiding. Dressed in a business suit, he was escorted into court by several FBI agents. The defendants showed hardly any emotion in his presence. They must have felt very sheepish; this was the cunning con man who had outsmarted them and tricked them into the FBI's trap.

On the witness stand, Malik talked too fast and too much, just as he did during the sting. Several times during his five-hour-long testimony he engaged in arguments with the defense attorneys, and several times the judge intervened, reminding him to only answer the question and not to argue. Sometimes, to avoid straight answers to the defense's questions, he gave irrelevant answers. Once the judge scolded him for this and instructed him, "Think about a question and then answer it."

When the defense pressed him hard to accept that he was a convicted criminal, he said that he had not committed any crime prior to the crime for which the FBI had caught him. When asked why, during discussions about his business, he had told the defendants that he was not breaking any laws, he said he meant Islamic laws, not American laws. When asked if, after the meetings with the defendants, he had told Coll things that the defendants had never said, he replied that he used to tell Coll what the defendants meant, not what they said. Toward the end of his testimony, he gave the same answer to every question: "I said or did whatever Agent Coll instructed me to say or do. Please ask him about it." After his testimony was finished, Malik was taken out of court, escorted by about a half-dozen FBI agents.

On September 20, an FBI translator presented a translation of two tape-recorded speeches that Aref had delivered in a town hall in his hometown in Kurdistan in 1994. The tapes of these speeches had been seized from Aref's home during the FBI raid on August 5, 2004. A transcript was also made available to the jury.

In 1994, Aref was a twenty-four-year-old college student in Syria, and he was visiting at home when some town authorities asked him to deliver those speeches to discourage Kurdish youths from abandoning Kurdistan and migrating to Western countries. In the speeches, Aref did just that: he warned young people not to lose their religion, culture, or identity by settling in Western countries, and he described to them the difficulties and realities of immigrants in those countries. Thus the speeches contained much negative rhetoric about Western culture. Aref called Western ethics "rotten" and Western politicians "immoral." He asked young people to resist the temptation of immigration, to remain steadfast, to stay in their homeland and serve their people. He also advised them to stay away from violence: "Allah the Great does not allow Muslims to oppress people—to shed other people's blood."

However, the prosecutors clearly wanted to convince the jurors that Aref had been carrying radical Islamic views from the very beginning, even when he was a young college student. Some of us were lost by this: were a college student's personal beliefs and opinions from twelve years earlier on trial, or was a man on trial for witnessing a loan involving money laundering?

Several FBI agents and police investigators also took the witness stand that day, testifying about various documents and other materials taken from the defendants' houses or Hossain's car during the raid on August 5, 2004.

On September 21, prosecutors devoted the whole day to presenting material against Aref alone. With the help of a projector, they presented visual translations of selected portions of Aref's journal. A Kurdish translator was on hand to explain any linguistic queries about the material. Aref had mentioned a few things in his journal, written while he was working for the IMK in Syria, that were of interest to the FBI, including meeting Mullah Krekar and some individuals whom the FBI suspected of being terrorists. By showing certain excerpts from the journal, they intended to convince the jury that Aref was a member of the IMK and had contacts with terrorists for a purpose.

Kindlon's argument was the same as he had presented earlier during the bail hearings: Aref was an IMK employee who had met Mullah Krekar and others casually in connection with his employment. FBI agent Zachary Delecki testified that when Aref was arrested and questioned at the FBI building on August 5, 2004, he told them he was not a member of the IMK and did not know Mullah Krekar personally, but did know that he was a famous man and the founder of Ansar al-Islam. The government charged that both of these statements were false.

The prosecutors also projected on the screen a letter issued by Islamic Cintral of Kurdistan in Irbil with Aref's name on it, and tried to confuse the jurors into believing that the letter was issued by the Islamic Movement in Kurdistan. They also showed jurors an IMK pamphlet and two photographs of Aref with IMK leaders, as well as a business card belonging to a representative of the IMK that the FBI had discovered during the search of Aref's house, which they said proved his membership in the IMK. One writer-activist sitting next to me laughed and said, "What kind of proof of membership is this?"

I said, "In my pocket I have a letter sent to me by the FBI. I have FBI pamphlets, I have the cards of several FBI agents, I have had my picture taken with them, I have shaken hands with them, I have eaten with them, I have participated in discussions with them, and I have taken part in their presentations. Am I a member of the FBI?"

Sensing the FBI's effort to connect Aref to the IMK, and thus to Krekar and Ansar al-Islam, Kindlon had once commented, "Connecting Aref to Ansar al-Islam would be analogous to saying that someone who was friends with Timothy McVeigh when he was a member of the United States Armed Forces is somehow connected to terrorism, because Mr. McVeigh later carried out the attacks in Oklahoma City."

The government also charged that Aref had lied on his immigration application. When he filled in a four-page application for permanent residency in February 2002, he had marked "no" in answer to a question that asked if he had been a member of any political organization since his sixteen birthday. Aref's English was very poor at that time, and the form had been filled in at the U.S. Committee for Refugees and Immigrants (USCRI) center in the Capital Region by its then-director, Helene Smith. Smith died in 2003, and the center that functioned like an immigrant support organization had become defunct. Thuy Nguyen, a woman who had worked at the center as a translator at the time, was brought by the prosecutors to testify. Her testimony confirmed that the form was actually filled in by Smith, but that Smith was very careful to make sure the applicants understood every item in the application before they signed. The problem was that neither Smith nor Aref spoke the other's language.

THE GOVERNMENT'S EXPERT WITNESS

There was no testimony scheduled for the next two working days in court because the FBI was busy looking for a terrorism expert as a replacement for Gunaratna, who supposedly had expressed his inability to attend the trial. Two days later we learned that someone named Evan Kohlmann had been invited by the prosecution to take the place of Gunaratna. I wondered why they wanted the testimony of a terrorism expert anyway: this was a money-laundering sting operation, not an actual case where an act of terrorism had been carried out. But after discussing the matter with the attorneys, I concluded that the prosecutors wanted to frighten the jury so that they would not even think of letting the defendants walk the streets again.

The prosecutor's plan was to use Kohlmann's testimony to link Aref to people and organizations overseas known to be involved with terrorism. Even though Hossain was not accused of any links to terrorism, they wanted Kohlmann to link him up, too. During one of his discussions with Malik, Hossain had mentioned that he was a member of the Jamaat-e-Islami (JEI) of Bangladesh. The prosecutors wanted Kohlmann to tell the jury that this was an organization involved in terrorism.

I made some inquiries and discovered that Kohlmann was a twenty-seven-year-old recent law school graduate and a self-proclaimed "international terror expert" who lived in a Manhattan basement apartment that was referred to as his "office." "Actually," a retired attorney told me "his office travels with him, or he travels with his office, because it consists of a cell phone and a laptop." This retired attorney, whom I had known for a number of years and who knew every detail of the case and Kohlmann's background, told me, "This kid knows nothing except for what he learned by Googling the Internet. He's memorized the names of about a dozen suspected terrorists and organizations and recites them in the courtroom like a parrot, and links all of them to each other and ultimately all of them to al-Qaeda terrorists. But his real expertise is his ability to somehow tie defendants to such individuals and create a fearful sensation in the jurors' hearts. The FBI loves that." The attorney continued: "I've followed his testimony in four different cases and it's the same, irrespective of the case. He's become the FBI's darling, and they're grooming him to use in many more terror trials."

Thinking that this attorney might be exaggerating, I made further inquiries. I found descriptions of Kohlmann's supposed expertise on the Internet, one of which read: "Is Kohlmann any more an expert than a blogger? If the judge cares about being fair, he'll knock him out because he doesn't know anything. He reads the Internet...repackages it and claims he's an expert." This was posted by Marvin Miller, a Virginia attorney who cross-examined Kohlmann while defending a man on terrorism charges. Miller continued: "He gives an argument to scare the jury about terror and fear. He has no master's degree, no Ph.D., he cannot speak, read or write Arabic, Kurdish or Urdu. It sounds like he's managed to bootstrap his way up from college kid/law student to international expert-witness-scourge in a few easy bounces, with the first couple of bounces taking place in, not surprisingly, the Fourth Circuit. It sounds like this young man is an 'expert' not because of any actual qualifications, but because of his well-developed ability to tell the government what it wants to hear. All smoke and one mirror. Is terrorism expertise going to be the next form of junk science?"

I called the retired attorney for advice. "My God," I said, "it is frightening. What should we do?" He replied, "Don't try to block his testimony or stop his fast tongue in court. McAvoy will never agree to that. Take advantage of Kohlmann's ignorance. He's so ignorant that he doesn't know if Bangladesh is a city or a country. If you asked him to locate Bangladesh on the world map, most likely he'd put his finger on Brazil. According to him, there's not a single Islamic organization in the world that doesn't have ties to al-Qaeda. He might tell the court that the IMK was established by Osama bin Laden's brother-in-law, and that it's a secret bank that funnels money to al-Qaeda. Ask your attorneys to exploit his ignorance in front of the jury before the FBI is able to coach him to tear the defendants apart." He also told me that our defense had made a serious mistake in not inviting an expert to nullify Kohlmann's dangerous misinformation.

The defense had tried to find some honest, knowledgeable experts to testify about the IMK and related matters, but they could not get hold of any. There were experts who had knowledge of Islam and its practices, but after some debate the defense decided not to bring in any of them.

During his deposition by Sprotbery in the presence of prosecutors Pericak and Coombe, Kohlmann revealed that he had originally been met in person by both Pericak and Gregg Sofer, an assistant U.S. Attorney, sometime in early summer in Washington, D.C., and that they had talked to him about the possibility of testifying in the Albany sting case. He was later contacted on the evening of Thursday, September 21 while he was in a taxi in New York City. He came to Albany the next day by train and met Coll, Pericak, and Coombe, who briefed him and showed him translations of Aref's diary and his two speeches, some video clips of the surveillance tapes, and Gunaratna's expert report. (Although Gunaratna did not testify, he submitted a report, which had been sealed by McAvoy weeks earlier.) With lightning speed, Kohlmann submitted his "expert report" on the IMK, Mullah Krekar, Ansar al-Islam, and Jamaat-e-Islami (JEI) of Bangladesh the next day, Saturday.

Kohlmann's information on the first three had been downloaded from a single article in a single magazine. His information on JEI had been downloaded from the website Jamaat.org of Jamaat-e-Islami of Pakistan, because he could not find any source for information on JEI of Bangladesh. He justified this by saying that since both of these countries had been one country some thirty-five years ago, similarly named organizations in the two countries must be the same. When I heard this logic from the FBI's expert witness, I almost fainted. I have known this organization, and its very different roles in the three countries of the Indian subcontinent, reasonably well.

I think Luibrand was on the same frequency as the retired attorney who knew a lot about Kohlmann. After Sprotbery was finished questioning Kohlmann, Luibrand deposed Kohlmann regarding JEI of Bangladesh, with which Hossain was accused of having ties. Here is how Luibrand questioned Kohlmann with respect to the latter's knowledge of JEI:

> Q: Have you written any papers on the topic of JEI Bangladesh?
> A: No.
>
> Q: Have you ever interviewed any members of JEI Bangladesh?
> A: No.
>
> Q: And have you ever been interviewed on MSNBC or NBC News on the topic of JEI Bangladesh? [On his resumé, Kohlmann claimed to have consulted for these news media.]
> A: No.
>
> Q: How many political parties are there in Bangladesh?
> A: Off the top of my head, I really couldn't tell you.
>
> Q: Who is the current prime minister of Bangladesh?
> A: I don't know.
>
> Q: Who was the prime minister in 2003?
> A: Don't know.
>
> Q: Who was the leader of JEI in 2003?
> A: In Bangladesh?
>
> Q: In Bangladesh.
> A: I am sorry, I don't know.
>
> Q: Did JEI Bangladesh have a platform for its political party in 2003?
> A: When you say platform, a written platform?

Q: Yes.
A: I don't have a copy if they did.

Q: Have you ever seen it?
A: No.

Q: Have you ever been to Bangladesh?
A: No.

Q: Do you know what role, if any, JEI Bangladesh has in the current Bangladeshi government?
A: I believe that they're a minority party involved in Parliament. I know they're active politically, in terms of acquiring more seats, but I couldn't tell you more than that.

Q: What role, if any, does JEI Bangladesh have in the current executive branch for the Bangladesh government?
A: It's, I believe again, a minority involved in Parliament, but I don't know about that, the executive powers.

Q: Does JEI have any role in the actual running of the Bangladeshi government?
A: Well, informally. But, formally, again, I don't know.

Q: Are there any elected JEI Bangladesh officials in the Bangladeshi government?
A: I don't know.

Q: Can you name any of the major political parties in Bangladesh from the year 2000 to the year 2004?
A: Other than Jamaat-e-Islami?

Q: Yes.
A: That's—I'm not familiar off the top of my head.

Q: Have you ever heard of an organization known as the Bangladesh National Party?
A: Vaguely.

Q: Do you know what it is?
A: I'm assuming it's a political party, but, again—the name vaguely sounds familiar, but…

Q: Do you know what, if anything, it stands for politically within Bangladesh?
A: Sorry, can't tell ya.

Q: You can't tell me because you don't know?
A: I don't know off the top of my head.

Following this deposition testimony, which confirmed that Kohlmann was not an expert on the topic of JEI, Luibrand filed a motion to preclude his testimony on JEI on the grounds that Kohlmann was unqualified as an expert against Hossain. But his motion was rejected. Kindlon made fun of the "kid" but did not make any motion to prevent him from testifying, so Kohlmann was allowed to testify on the morning of September 27, two days after his deposition. At that time—given overnight coaching by the FBI and time for considerable Internet surfing—his knowledge of Bangladesh and its Jamaat-e-Islami was at its peak, and it must have impressed the jury.

Luibrand repeated some of the questions he had asked during the deposition—and now Kohlmann had answers. In my judgment, the most absurd answer he gave was that "the JEI was formed in Pakistan in 1941 as a political party with paramilitary elements in it."

Pakistan did not exist until August 14, 1947. JEI was founded in 1941 in British-ruled India as a religious organization with some elements of political thought, including the concept of a modern democracy based on Islamic principles. As I myself knew well, India was not a Muslim country, and its Muslim population was a minority. JEI leaders were accused of being too liberal by the conservative Muslim population, and some even accused its founder, Maulana Maudoodi, of being an American agent. His mission was to propagate changes in the society through education. JEI never had any ties, even remotely, with violence.

However, when Luibrand pushed Kohlmann hard to expand on the paramilitary element of JEI Bangladesh, he cited criticism by Amnesty International of the human rights violations of the Bangladesh government, in which JEI Bangladesh was a minor coalition partner. This "expert" had no clue that the same organization had criticized the U.S. administration for more severe human rights violations.

I used to laugh at the court proceedings of many third world countries, but after seeing the role in this court of Kohlmann and his testimony—not anymore!

Kohlmann also described Mullah Krekar and his relationship with the IMK and Ansar al-Islam in exactly the same way the information had been floating on the Internet for the last few years—except he said that several other organizations and their leaders were linked with each other and thus with the IMK and Ansar. He claimed that they were all enemies of the U.S., even those that had been fighting against Saddam with America's blessing and those that were not designated as terrorist organizations by the U.S.

When Sprotbery tried to ridicule his "expert" qualifications, McAvoy jumped in and said that the jurors would have to assess Kohlmann's qualifications for themselves before they accepted or rejected his testimony.

I cannot resist mentioning that in 2005, while waiting for a flight in India, I met the leader of an extremist Hindu faction at the Varanasi airport. He was very upset with Christians because missionaries had converted two Hindus from his village to Christianity. There had been some attacks and assaults on churches, nuns, and other missionaries for similar reasons. This faction was extremely hostile to both Christians and Muslims in India. Arguing with me, he said, "Christianity is an evil and militant religion. Its main leader named Pope maintains an office in Rome, Italy and appoints homosexuals as leaders of various churches who sexually assault young boys. Its paramilitary wing is engaged in bombing buildings and women's clinics in the U.S.A." He was carrying documents that listed the names of the people killed in the 1995 Oklahoma City bombing, and lists of many churches and priests accused of sexual misconduct. He was enthusiastically showing newspaper clippings to his disciples and anyone else sitting around. "These are the people who colonized the poor countries of the world and converted them to Christianity by force!" he claimed.

I wanted to talk to him about Mother Teresa and charitable works by Christian charities, but he was not willing to listen. How nonsensical and far from reality does his description sound to a sincere Christian? Well, that's how it sounds to us Muslims most of the time when radio talk-show hosts or TV pundits or "experts" characterize Islam and Muslims!

With the expert testimony of Evan Kohlmann, the prosecutors wrapped up their case. Then it was the defense's turn.

CHAPTER 13

In Defense

AREF TESTIFIES IN HIS OWN DEFENSE

The defense immediately moved that the charges should be dismissed, citing insufficient evidence. Pericak countered by saying that it was up to the jury to sort out the evidence. McAvoy did not rule on the motion.

After an hour's lunch break, Kindlon put Aref on the witness stand as the first defense witness. Not many were expecting this move. We were happy, because we thought he would be the best person to speak for himself. Aref wanted it that way too, and everyone was curious to hear from him firsthand.

Kindlon's questioning of Aref was designed to let the jury know about his background, from childhood in Kurdistan to being a refugee in Syria and then to his life in Albany. Aref spoke straightforwardly, and it seemed to us that the jurors believed in his integrity and found him to be a different person than the prosecutors had depicted. Aref claimed that he had never promoted violence in his life. His struggle, he said, had been to oppose the tyrannical regime of Saddam Hussein and the genocide on Aref's people, the Kurds, and the words *jihad* or *mujahideen* found in his journal should be interpreted in that context, not in the context of violence against America or against the "unbelievers." He expressed his sadness at the FBI's misinterpretations and mistranslations.

Aref spent about four hours on the witness stand that day, and continued his testimony the next morning, September 28. He told the court that after his arrest on August 5, 2004, he was taken to the FBI building, chained to a chair with hands and feet tied, and interrogated until morning by five FBI agents and two translators. He was roughed up, shouted at, and frequently threatened during the interrogation. He was told he would never see his children again. Once, he said, Agent Coll had rushed toward him with a closed fist and threatened to punch him in the face.

Kindlon asked him to clarify the record in his diary about two youths, one Libyan and one Palestinian, who were at his house and talked about carrying violence to America and Israel. He said he simply recorded whatever they discussed. He did not share their views and he never had any contact with them before or after that day. Regarding a notation in his journal about the death of Abu Sayyaf in the Philippines, who belonged to a U.S.-designated terrorist group, Aref said he had never heard of that person or group before, but recorded it since it was sad news in certain Muslim circles in the Philippines, where Sayyaf had been regarded as a champion in fighting for peoples' rights.

Kindlon also went over portions of the diary in which Aref mentioned that while in Syria, he supported "America's plan" to remove Saddam Hussein from power in Iraq. His diary also mentioned that he was very hopeful and optimistic about moving to America as a United Nations refugee, while at the same time he was critical of American culture and its corruption, such as the scandal over the illicit relationship of then-President Bill Clinton with Monica Lewinsky. On occasion, the jurors enjoyed listening to Aref and smiled at some of his statements.

At one point, Aref mentioned in his diary that he refused to become a member of the IMK when they wanted to force him to accept membership and become their representative in the U.S. after his immigration. As a religious person, Aref did not want to confine his ideology by accepting membership in a particular group such as the IMK. "If you want to preach, if you want to advise—you should be an independent person," Aref said. "I see Islam as bigger than any group's policies."

He spent the whole day on the witness stand.

Friday, September 29 was the day for cross-examination by the prosecutors. Pericak asked Aref why he did not call the FBI when, on February 12, 2004, he heard Malik in his house talk about a missile attack in New York City. Aref responded that he never believed Malik's abrupt statement, and that he was a hundred percent sure that whatever Malik was saying was not true. "We was talking, my guest was there and all of sudden, without warning, he says don't go to New York City next week," Aref told the jury. "I said why? He said next week will be attack day. I kicked him out of my house, and he said he was joking."

Because of his poor command of English at that time, there was a lot of discussion as to whether Aref ever understood the words "missile" or "ammunition" during his discussions with Malik, particularly with regard to the way Malik mispronounced these words. Regarding the money-laundering allegations, Aref claimed he had no sense of any illegal activity. He thought it was a simple loan transaction between two community members. Aref pointed out that at one point during his conversation with Malik, he had said, "I think Hossain is borrowing more money than he needs. I am concerned about his ability to pay back."

It was somewhat strange that Kindlon did not present any corroborating witnesses or any other evidence to support Aref's innocence. Instead, he totally depended upon directly countering the evidence presented by the prosecutors. In his opinion, they had proven nothing against Aref, and the jury would have to find some proof beyond reasonable doubt to convict him. There was some difficulty in finding character witnesses for Aref, too. There was debate as to whether I should be called as a character witness, but for some reason Kindlon decided against it. And mosque members were so scared that they were not willing to come forward. So I talked to them and requested that they help Aref by offering themselves as character witnesses. At first, about ten members volunteered, but when Steve Downs, the volunteer attorney for the defense team, contacted them to prepare them for the task, one by one almost all decided to drop out and not face possible targeting by the FBI for being witnesses against the government. I would have liked to see subpoenas for several members for whom Aref, over the years, had arranged or witnessed loans. As is common among Muslims from third world countries, many members were involved in taking or giving personal or business loans among themselves, and several used Aref as an intermediary or witness. In my judgment, it would have helped the jury to understand that Aref's involvement in the Malik-Hossain loan deal was not based on any sinister idea, but was rather the routine duty of an imam, similar to a notary public's function.

HOSSAIN'S ENTRAPMENT DEFENSE

Since Luibrand's defense was based on entrapment, most likely he did not find a pressing need for character witnesses. But the same difficulties would have existed in finding them for Hossain as well.

Monday, October 2 was the last day of arguments. Luibrand displayed on the screen translations of segments of conversation in Urdu between Hossain and Malik. These translations had been done by a professional translator, who was present in court. A female FBI translator was scheduled to testify. But the professional translator's version gave a very different picture of the conversation than what the FBI's female translator presented.

This Urdu translator, who by her features appeared to be a Pakistani, looked extremely funny in her headscarf. It appeared that she had tucked a white piece of cloth torn from a bed sheet over her head, without attention to shape or style. I immediately realized that she did not know how to wear a headscarf, and had perhaps never used one before. *What's the purpose of this scarf?* I could not help but ask myself.

I got the answer as soon as she took the witness stand for Luibrand's cross-examination: the FBI wanted to display this woman as a religious Muslim. They projected an Urdu word, *madrasa*, on the screen and asked her to translate it. "It means a 'radical propaganda center,'" she pronounced, as if she had already practiced a few times. I became furious at this, and felt like pulling off my shoes and throwing them in her face. Luibrand then showed her a translation of the same word, by two different translators, as a "religious school" and a "children's school." Both are exactly what it means, but she kept on saying it meant a "radical propaganda center," and Luibrand knew very well why she had been instructed to do that. Hossain had mentioned to Malik in one of their conversations that Hossain was sending donations to a *madrasa* in his hometown in Bangladesh. The FBI wanted to convince the jury that Hossain was sending his money to a "radical propaganda center"—which, they implied, was nothing but a terrorist center!

A mosque member told me that he had seen the woman earlier without a headscarf. Kathy Manley told me that her headscarf might have been her "disguise"— remember that the court allowed translators to use false names and wear glasses or similar things to obscure their identities.

Even though I found the FBI's whole case, with only some exceptions, full of distortions and manipulations, I had become very upset on only two other occasions. Once, on a loan transaction receipt, Hossain had noted, in very poor handwriting, "$2000 for Shahed." The context of the monthly amount of repayment of the loan to Shahed (Malik)

Hussein was obvious. But Pericak kept insisting that it read "$2000 for Jehad," implying that Hossain had written a receipt to himself for sending $2,000 to some terrorists.

On another occasion, Aref, during a conversation with Malik about the money received through the repayment of the loan, said, "You may send taxes." But the FBI transcribed it as "You may send terrorists." They kept insisting during the trial that that was exactly what Aref had said—namely, Aref suggested sending the money to terrorists. The tape was replayed a few times in court, and the jurors asked to listen to it again during their deliberations, and ultimately (and rightly) they rejected the FBI's version. Indeed, the FBI's version was contrary to their own logic. According to them, Aref was himself a terrorist and was proposing to Malik to send money to terrorists. But a real terrorist would never call a group with whom he sympathizes "terrorist." He would call it a "fighter" group or use an equivalently dignified word. "Terrorist" is an extremely derogatory word to Islamic extremists.

On the last day of the trial, the prosecutors played more than five hours of cherry-picked segments of the recorded tapes—some of them several times—to convince the jury of the criminal nature of the defendants' money dealings. But I observed some interesting paradoxes inside the court. Once I noticed that the prosecutors and the FBI agents were moving around with great enthusiasm, helping to present one surveillance clip after another, as if they were doing the most patriotic thing to prosecute the two Muslims—while on the back bench, three middle-aged, white, American, non-Muslim women were holding Aref's three lovely children on their laps as if they were trying to shield them from the powerful and arrogant agents who had decided to prosecute their father. Looking at me while clutching Aref's youngest son in her lap, one of the women said, "This is a persecution, not a prosecution." I looked back and forth between these two groups in the courtroom, and in my mind's eye I saw a similar paradox throughout the whole nation.

I was constantly trying to read the minds of the six men and six women of the jury by looking at the expressions on their faces as the trial progressed. I was not the only one doing this. Many reporters who had been attending the trial on a regular basis were also trying to read them that way. My impression was that they would let Aref go free, at least on the money laundering charges, but I was doubtful they would accept

LEFT TO RIGHT: Azzam and Salah Muhiddin, Yassin Aref's sons,
stand with Steve Downs, Aref's volunteer attorney,
in front of the Masjid As-Salam before the start of a march
and vigil organized in August 2007 by the Muslim Solidarity
Committee to mark the third anniversary of the arrests.

Photo by Katherine Hughes

Hossain's entrapment argument. During the recess, I asked two of the reporters with whom I had developed some frankness what they thought. I was surprised to learn that they had the same feeling. But when court was called back into session, the sky crashed down on us once more.

As the presentation of evidence was concluding, out of nowhere and for no apparent reason McAvoy said to the jury that "the FBI had good and valid reasons to target Aref. The FBI had certain valid suspicions," he said. I could not believe my ears. *My God,* I thought, *how can a presiding judge say that?* Members of the mosque in the back seats looked at each other in shock and disbelief. After the session was over, some mosque members said, "McAvoy sensed the jury would let Aref go free, so he rushed to rescue the FBI." I said to myself, *what member of a jury will dare let an accused "terrorist," whom the FBI has a good and valid reason to target, go free?*

Closing Arguments

Tuesday, October 3 was the day for closing arguments. In his ninety-minute argument, Pericak told the jury that the defendants were predisposed to terrorism, and that was why they willingly and knowingly participated in the sting. He indicated that Hossain's motive was monetary greed, while Aref's motive was ideological. He claimed to the jury that Hossain rushed gladly to his bank to get the cashier's checks to help Malik launder money and to promote his weapons business. Of course, in our judgment this was a blatant distortion of the truth. Hossain's actions were based on a contrary idea—that Malik was supporting and promoting Hossain's business of renovating properties by loaning him money to buy building materials. Naturally Hossain appreciated Malik's generosity and, according to the loan agreement, was repaying him gladly to fulfill his obligation.

Pericak told the jury that both defendants understood what the informant was proposing. The pair had decided to go ahead with the scheme even after the informant said his money came from the sale of ammunition, and even after he showed off a surface-to-air missile. Pointing on the screen to the familiar picture of Malik holding the SAM on his shoulder and Hossain, sitting on a chair in the same room, looking at it from a distance, Pericak declared, "This is a big elephant in the room."

Kindlon was very direct in his final arguments. His presentation was dramatic. Looking directly into the jurors' eyes, he said that the whole case was based on deception planned and executed in a post-9/11 climate of fear. He portrayed the prosecution as over-reacting to 9/11, and the government as unfair in its use of a desperate professional con artist to ensnare unwitting defendants. "The government wants you to think that Aref is a terrorist," he said. "He is the exact opposite. Ladies and gentlemen, what happened was 9/11. The world changed for all of us, and it really changed for people from the Middle East, and Aref was one of them. We did a lot of things right and a lot of things wrong. Our government made a lot of mistakes, and one of the mistakes was this sting operation."

He portrayed Aref as an Iraqi refugee from Saddam Hussein's tyranny, a scholar and cleric who came to this country in pursuit of the American dream only to fall into the trap of a misguided prosecution generated by a "low-life creep," referring to Malik. "Aref did not benefit a penny from the loan and never saw the weapon."

He compared the case to Harper Lee's masterpiece novel *To Kill a Mockingbird*, the story of the prosecution/persecution of an innocent black man accused and convicted of raping a white girl in the Depression-era south. "He [Tom Robinson, the defendant] was convicted not because of what he did, but because of prejudice and fear," Kindlon said. "Don't let that happen here."

Luibrand countered the prosecutors by saying that they cherry-picked portions from some fifty hours of tapes and used many comments wildly out of context to make the two men look guilty. He highlighted different segments of the FBI's surveillance tapes to give a different picture of the defendants, such as Hossain saying that the September 11 attacks on the World Trade Center were "bad" and that there was no need for Muslims to kill. He accused Malik of passing on wrong information to his FBI handlers regarding his discussions with Hossain in Urdu. Malik would depict Hossain as anti-American, while the actual translations that were done several months later showed that Hossain was actually espousing his respect for the United States and the American way of life and criticizing the terrorists who had attacked what he described as his country, the U.S. He highlighted portions of the transcripts that contained vague comments about arms dealing by the informant that supposedly referred to a legitimate business and business income. This was the trick Malik used to deceive Hossain into believing that he was dealing with a legitimate loan.

"What they're presenting to you was manipulated and deceptive," Luibrand said to the jurors. "Malik essentially persuaded my client to take part in the scheme." He said Hossain was a hard-working business owner who was leading an innocent life until the informant started working on him. "If Malik had not come into his life, Hossain would be making pizzas, tending to his family, and practicing his religion."

Lawyers from both sides urged the jury to look over the entire record when they began deliberating.

In a nutshell, the jurors' task was to decide if the defendants participated in the scheme because of their interest in promoting terrorism, or because they fell victim to a very tricky and elaborate FBI scheme. More technically, were they money launderers, or victims of government entrapment?

This cartoon by John deRosier appeared in the Albany *Times Union* on October 12, 2006, two days after the jury convicted Aref and Hossain.

Courtesy of John deRosier

CHAPTER 14

The Verdict

DELIBERATIONS

On October 4, McAvoy gave the jury two hours of instructions on the law, after which they went into a secluded room to deliberate. Journalists had a room in one area inside the courthouse to sit and wait for a verdict, and the defense attorneys had another room. Law enforcement authorities had the rest of the building. Hossain was with his attorney, while Aref was somewhere else in the building—in a windowless cell sitting on a stool, as he said later. Security inside and outside was extra-tight. I, along with two mosque members, sat in a car in the parking lot in front of the courthouse, watching the entrance. More than a dozen media cars and satellite trucks were parked on the opposite side of the street. We figured we would know about any developments because of the movements of the media people.

After approximately ninety minutes of deliberation, we heard that the jury was back. We had not expected a decision that fast, but of course, who knew? We rushed inside the courtroom after passing through the usual security checks. But the jury had only requested clarification of the wording in Count 29 of the indictment, regarding Aref lying to FBI agents about his membership in the IMK. They went back to deliberate after only a few minutes.

About two hours later, around 3:15 p.m., we saw everyone rush back to the courtroom once again. This time the jurors needed some further information: a read-back of the agent's testimony about Aref's interrogation regarding Mullah Krekar. After nearly five hours of deliberation, they could not reach a verdict that day, and about 5 p.m. they were excused and allowed to go home.

On Thursday, October 5, deliberations lasted the whole day. At one point the jurors wanted to review the tape of one of the earliest meetings between Malik and Hossain, because they wanted clarification as to whether Hossain asked for the loan or Malik made an offer of the money. Toward the end of the day, the jurors also asked to review the surveillance videotape of November 20, 2003, in which Malik displayed the missile on his shoulder while Hossain, sitting on a chair at a distance in the same room, was looking at him. No verdict seemed to be in sight as yet.

On Friday, October 6, the jurors asked to watch the FBI surveillance videotape of a meeting between Malik and Aref in January 2004, in which the words "legalize the money" and "send taxes" (the prosecution's version was "send terrorists") were mentioned. Also, toward the end of the day, the jury asked McAvoy to clarify two charges in the indictment. They wanted to know whether the charges, as written, required that the defendants knew the informant was making money from the illicit smuggling of any firearms, or specifically making money from the sale of the shoulder-fired missile that was used in the sting and was shown to jurors on the first day of the trial. The day passed without a verdict. The jury was excused and instructed to return on Tuesday morning, October 10.

THE VERDICT

On October 10, I sat for most of the day, as usual, with two other members of the mosque in a car in the parking lot facing the courthouse. At about 4 p.m. we saw some movement of the media people. We had become used to these movements over the past several days, but we went inside anyway, thinking that once again the jury probably wanted clarification on something. I speculated that if they had a verdict, they would not be announcing it at this time, because it was about time for them to go home. I saw McAvoy holding a small note in his hand, as usual. But he seemed to be waiting to read it as soon as the court was in session. "I have received this note from the jury," he said, looking at the note. "'We have a verdict.'" All of a sudden the atmosphere in the court changed; everyone became serious and attentive.

The jurors entered the courtroom and took their seats.

The female court clerk read Count 1 of the indictment and asked the foreman of the jury, "How do you find the defendant number 1, Aref?" "Guilty," he replied. She asked if the decision was unanimous. "Yes," was the answer. She verified it from the rest of the jury. She repeated Count 1 again and asked the foreman, "How do you find the defendant number 2, Hossain?" "Guilty," he answered. She asked if the decision was unanimous. "Yes," he answered. Again she verified it from the rest of the jury.

She moved to Count 2 and the response was "not guilty" for Aref, but "guilty" for Hossain. The procedure and the jury's responses remained the same until Count 9; then it started varying. Hossain was declared guilty on all twenty-seven counts for which he was charged. Count 1 was related to money laundering; Counts 2–11 were related to ten transactions between Hossain and Malik starting on January 2 and ending on August 3, 2004; Counts 12–19 were related to the plot involving the missile; and Counts 20–27 were related to providing material support to a foreign terrorist organization, JEM. The jury simply did not accept the entrapment defense for Hossain.

Aref was found guilty on ten counts: 1, 10, 11, 12, 18, 19, 20, 26, 27, and 30. Unlike Hossain, he was acquitted on all the counts of money laundering prior to June 10, 2004 because the jury apparently thought he had not understood the illegality of the transactions prior to that date. But they found him guilty on some of the counts for June 10, 2004, apparently based on their assumption that he did understand the illegality of the source of the money and the transactions after a conversation with Malik on that date, during which Aref and Malik had discussed a possible business partnership after buying Hossain's pizzeria. (See Appendix B, Sting Tapes 2004, June 10.)

In fact, Aref did not witness any transactions after June 10, but Hossain made two check payments to Malik of $2,000 each, one on July 1 and the other on August 3, 2004. (Even though the FBI claimed that Hossain gave a check to Malik in person on August 3, I did not find any evidence of it on the tape.)

Perhaps the surveillance tape of the discussion on June 10 convinced the jury that Aref understood Malik's illegal dealings with weapons. One juror later indicated anonymously to a *Times Union* reporter that he based his decision to convict Aref not on any recorded conversation, but on the understanding that there may have been conversations between the defendants that were not recorded. Either this same juror, or another one, persuaded his colleagues to believe that Aref was not as innocent or naïve about the transactions—particularly toward the end of the sting—as he claimed or as he appeared to be on the witness stand. In this juror's opinion, Aref was an extremely intelligent man and understood some of the illegalities of the loan arrangement.

The three additional counts, 28, 29, and 30, were for Aref alone. Count 28 was for making a false statement on an immigration form that was filled in for him on February 13, 2002, and Counts 29 and 30 were for making two false statements to FBI investigators on the night of his arrest: denying that he was a member of the IMK, and denying that he knew Mullah Krekar personally. Aref was acquitted on Counts 28 and 29, but was found guilty on Count 30.

McAvoy announced that the defendants would be sentenced separately in the same court on February 12, 2007.

For some reason, very few court observers or mosque members were present in the courtroom on October 10. We felt very disappointed and sad, but the defendants were very calm and composed. Aref smiled as he was taken out by the marshals.

The prosecutors asked McAvoy to revoke Hossain's bail and order him to be taken into custody, which he did immediately. As the marshals flanked Hossain, he became somewhat emotional. He took off his suit jacket, necktie, watch, and belt, removed his wallet and pocket papers, and handed everything over to Luibrand. Preparing to accompany the marshals, he looked at the people at the back of the courtroom and said loudly and emotionally, "Today is my victory. We are going to accept it peacefully." He raised his right hand and said, "Thank you very much, everyone. *As-Salaam Alaikum* (Peace be upon all of you)."

What did he mean by "today is my victory"? To my understanding, he meant it ironically: "Today is the day of my defeat and devastation, today I am sacrificed and destroyed." But both defendants had language deficiencies, and these deficiencies during the surveillance recordings gave the FBI good opportunities for exploitation. On November 20, 2003, after showing the SAM missile to Hossain, Malik asked if Hossain was interested in participating in Malik's weapon business. Hossain told Malik that "good money could be made, but it is not legal." The FBI exploited this statement many times by saying that Hossain was simply interested in making money, and that is why he said "good money could be made."

THE VERDICT • 165

But Hossain told me that he meant he was not interested in a business that was not legal, irrespective of how much money it could make.

Similarly, on another occasion Hossain had said to Malik, "Let us talk money, not philosophy." What he wanted was to talk about the simple loan that Malik had offered him earlier but was stalling on, and not about what Malik did, or how he made his money, or how many businesses he was involved with. But again the FBI exploited this, by claiming that Hossain was in a rush to launder money.

Hossain also made a statement, "kill or be killed," referring to a battlefield clash of opposing armies that he considered allowable, in contrast to a cowardly terrorist act that he considered forbidden, where innocents are killed without being aware of an attack and thus have no ability to defend themselves. The FBI made big propaganda out of this statement, claiming that he was willing to kill someone even at the risk of being killed. I felt great pity for both the defendants, whose excessive talking and poor communication skills gave the jury the wrong message. And the FBI's cunning twists and spins deprived the jury of its ability to properly analyze the real intent of their statements.

The prosecutors and FBI agents were very happy with the verdict, but they did not express their joy in demonstrative outbursts. I saw them congratulating each other quietly, keeping a low profile.

On the evening news, I heard statements from both the prosecution and the defense. Suddaby said to the media after the verdict: "We had a couple of individuals that were prone to support terrorism, and the FBI did what they had to do. This is what we should be doing and what we will continue to do in conjunction with the FBI."

Kindlon said, "We're profoundly disappointed, of course, but at the same time we are glad by the good news in the verdict that Aref was acquitted on the other twenty counts."

Luibrand was disappointed that the jury did not accept his entrapment defense. He expressed his outrage at the sting: "I believe the tactic of the government to target people who are not committing crimes, and if no one bothered them would never commit crimes, is wrong."

The next morning, I read in the *Times Union* part of my own statement to the media that had been widely circulated on TV and in the print media:

Shamshad Ahmad, President of the Central Avenue mosque, Masjid

As-Salam, where Aref and Hossain prayed, criticized the FBI's tactics in this case but said the mosque's community respects the jury's decision. "We are to respect the law of the land and the verdict of the court. We believe we had a fair chance of due process," Ahmad said. "We obviously feel saddened and disappointed with the verdict because the whole community feels they really did not do anything illegal or wrong. Somehow they were trapped based on deception, lies and cheating, and misstatements and distortions by the informant."

CHAPTER 15

Solidarity

FORMATION OF THE MUSLIM SOLIDARITY COMMITTEE (MSC)

The Muslim community was shaken by the guilty verdicts, even though we hadn't been very optimistic about the case from the beginning. We saw the FBI's resolve to obtain convictions, and the immense power and resources of the government in the post-9/11 era. We were disturbed by the "secret evidence" that the government claimed to have against Aref and Hossain. Nevertheless, we were thankful that at least an open trial had occurred. Everyone had heard about so many detainees held elsewhere in the U.S. who were dreaming of an open trial, or any kind of trial, or even to simply know the charges against them.

The majority of the general public believed that the defendants had been victimized and entrapped, and they were also not happy with the verdict. The media generally recognized the insufficient facts of the case, but in a milder tone. In an editorial on March 8, 2007, the *Times Union* stated:

> Federal sentencing guidelines allow, if not encourage, Judge McAvoy to send these men to prison for decades—if not the rest of their lives. But there are sound reasons for him to deviate from those guidelines, as the law also allows, and impose much shorter and more reasonable sentences. Justice will be served nonetheless if these men, who escaped countries where injustice is commonplace, and who previously lived honorable lives in the United States, are treated appropriately. Mr. Aref and Mr. Hossain are entitled to consideration of what kind of lives they might have continued to lead if they had never been lured into a sting operation.

On October 22, Fox 23 TV's "In Focus" broadcast an exclusive half-hour interview with me about the case. I discussed its impact on the Muslim community locally as well as nationwide, analyzed the verdict from various angles, and spoke about the legal plans for the future.

Even though a great deal of sympathy for the defendants was engendered by the verdict, the bottom line for everyone was that a fair trial had taken place and a decision had been made by the jury. It had deliberated long enough and had gone through its own difficulties in coming up with the verdict. Being able to critically interpret the many digressions that took place, and the developments of the sting operation, was not an easy task for an American, non-immigrant jury. We came to know that they had spent one full day going back and forth on whether Hossain's claim of entrapment was acceptable. It seems that one juror's strong opposition to it swayed the others. His argument was that, even if it were true that Malik was very cunning and deceptive, *what if* Hossain were a real terrorist? It was a typical play on the "fear factor" that was often used in terrorism-related trials.

A relatively small group of people consisting of intellectuals, humanitarians, and activists from the peace movement, labor and religious groups, and civil liberties and various legal organizations were furious with the outcome of the case. They were not willing to accept the verdict as the final word. They wanted to voice their concern with what they saw as a pattern of profiling, stereotyping, and discrimination against Arabs and Muslims. This was a national trend, but seeing it happen at home hit them hard. They were anxious to help the Muslim community cope with this tragedy.

On October 13, only a few days after the verdict, a formal meeting of about fifty activists and a few members of the mosque took place at the Friends Meeting House on Madison Avenue in Albany. Out of this meeting came an organization called the Muslim Solidarity Committee (MSC). Since then, this committee has literally assumed oversight of the welfare of the two defendants and their families. They have been steadfast in defending the Masjid As-Salam and its community, and have become a watchdog group to ensure that Muslims are no longer targeted by the government. I remember attending a small demonstration in front of the mosque on November 3, when a labor leader, Doug Bullock, who lived only a block away, stood up and declared (using his own bullhorn), "We will not let this government harass our Muslim brothers and neighbors!"

The next step seemed to be to wait for the sentencing in February

2007, and in the meantime do whatever was possible to minimize the prison terms of the defendants. So the MSC's first decision was to hold weekly vigils in front of the courthouse every Tuesday until sentencing day, in order to make the public aware of the case. I was opposed to this action, thinking it impractical, and I feared that after a few meetings the vigils would eventually collapse. I felt this was particularly true because of the bitter cold that was sure to come in the winter. I was positive no one would show up in that type of weather. But no one supported me in this, and in truth I was never proven more wrong!

The vigils continued, increasing to twice a week and with varying attendance of fifteen to thirty people, from November 2006 until the day of the sentencing in February 2007. Even with snow and ice and bone-shattering winds, we were there. The MSC also organized many meetings and public forums to talk about the trial and to make the public aware of the hidden dimensions of the case.

GETTING POLITICAL MILEAGE OUT OF THE STING OPERATION

There are clear indications that the Bush Administration used flawed and faked intelligence to justify its invasion of Iraq. This must have given ideas to the intelligence community and emboldened its leaders to follow the same trend. Many in Albany felt that the same politicians who had authorized the invasion of a foreign country also authorized the prosecution of Aref and Hossain, even if a mixture of faked, fictitious, and flawed evidence had to be used to justify it.

To my surprise, not many politicians tried to get political mileage out of the verdict, or at least they did not do so openly. This was contrary to what happened when the sting operation itself was made public in August 2004, when several politicians couldn't wait to get in front of the cameras. New York Governor George Pataki was in the lead, stating at a press conference in 2004 that "terrorists are living among us." At the time, he had a dream of seeking federal office in Washington, D.C. Politically he had no record to present to the public, but it was easy for him to fabricate an image as a "tough-on-terror" governor in order to attract attention, and he did not hesitate to trample on the backs of innocent Muslims to make that claim.

Vigilers outside the federal courthouse in Albany at the twice-weekly vigil for Aref and Hossain organized by the Muslim Solidarity Committee during the winter of 2006–2007.

Photo by Dave Capone

A Democratic member of the House of Representatives, Diane Watson, who represented part of Los Angeles County in California, jumped into the ring as well. She claimed in November 2004 that through the power of her "intelligence" contacts, she had discovered that a formidable terrorist plot was taking shape in Albany, New York—and she informed the Albany FBI about it. What a poor soul: she got the information about Albany's sting operation only three months after everyone else. Here is her claim: "In late 2003, I received information from an acquaintance regarding the planning of a terrorist plot in upstate New York. Like any good citizen, I passed the information along to the appropriate government authorities." She told the Associated Press that she had been tipped off by "a very close friend who worked in a temple in Albany" who called her and told her that "at the services they were planning an attack…I just passed on the information. Apparently based on that call [the FBI] investigated, and some months later people were arrested."

A terrorist plan of attack, as she understood it, was discussed during services that were normally attended by at least 300 Muslims in Albany. Wow! If there had been a real plot in 2003 known to 300 Muslims in Albany, wouldn't the FBI have been able to find enough real evidence of a crime so that a sting would not have been necessary? Not only that, but in a public meeting she insisted that "another attack on the United States of America is in 'the making.'" This intelligent politician further said, "I'm thoroughly convinced there's going to be another attack…I've got tips from my friends…from Egypt."

I'm not sure if her terrorist friends, who conveniently pass on such information to her, are only in Albany and Egypt, or in other places as well! Suddaby must have been beating his head against a wall, too, when he stated on behalf of the Albany FBI: "I don't know what she's referring to…I have no way to confirm when she called or whom she talked to."

The MSC considered Suddaby, though not a politician, one of those who sought to take advantage of this opportunity. He was interested in acquiring a "tough" record of his own by prosecuting Muslims as terrorists, whether rightly or wrongly. Should we blame him? First of all, he didn't want to join the club of nine U.S. Attorneys who were fired in 2006 for not prosecuting innocent people the way the Bush Administration wanted. Second, the temptation to make the case into an opportunity for him to climb the career ladder, and eventually to occupy a federal bench, was always there. The political winds of the season must have suggested to him the advantage of being known as "tough on Muslims."

But to me, the most surprising and shocking statement came from FBI Director Robert S. Mueller III when he visited the Albany field office on December 13, 2006. Referring to the sting operation, he praised the authorities for breaking up a terrorist cell in Albany. He said, "Terrorist cells can plan and finance an attack from anywhere in the United States." It forced me to wonder: if the head of the agency, who knew all the facts, had no problem branding Aref and Hossain as real terrorists, and Aref's home or Hossain's pizzeria as bases for a terrorist cell, then what credibility did any of their claims have?

Needless to say, the immediate beneficiary of this whole episode was the government informant, Malik, whose past crimes and conviction were erased as a reward for helping the sting succeed. On October 27, 2006, a federal judge, David Hurd, acting on the recommendation of the U.S. Attorney's office, set Malik free, and he walked away from the federal courthouse in Albany a free man under the watch of the FBI. While the Muslim community considers Malik as one of the lowest of God's creations on earth, he nevertheless must have felt pride in having served his bosses by cheating and deceiving two naïve individuals from his own community, destroying their families, and hurting the whole Muslim community.

LEGAL STEPS AFTER THE VERDICT

The fact of the matter is that the whole sting from start to finish was nothing but a game of distortion and deception mostly played by the cunning informant. We noted the same theme during the trial when the prosecutors presented their "evidence." While discussing this with the attorneys, I became convinced that the whole trial essentially revolved around a few points the prosecutors picked up that were based on either lies, gross distortions, or outright deceptions. A few such points follow.

1. The government's case depended on a very thin reed, especially with regard to Aref. According to the government's theory, Aref committed a crime when he performed an act (witnessing the loan), supposedly knowing all the while that the money for the loan came from the illegal sale of a missile and intending by his act to protect these illegal activities or assist the conspiracy. But how did Aref actually know that the money for the loan came from the illegal sale of a missile? The government pro-

vided as "evidence" only *one sentence* from the thousands of sentences exchanged over a ten-month period in a foreign language between Aref, Hossain, and Malik. That one sentence was uttered by Malik on January 2, 2004, when he first handed Aref a wad of money to count. While Aref was concentrating on counting, Malik pulled out the metal trigger handle of the missile and, showing it to Hossain, said, "This is $5,000, okay, I want you to count it, okay, here,…okay, and the $45,000 will be coming, like I have to give them something, you know, the instrument, and that will be coming like, in a, I would say probably couple of weeks from now, okay…*This is the part of the missile that I showed you.*" [italics mine]

But the whole conversation is as follows:

> Malik: Okay, let's do, do some business, okay, let us make some money, okay, okay. Uh, this is $5,000, okay, I want you to count it, okay, here Bismillah [Islamic term meaning to start something in the name of Allah].
>
> Hossain: Bismillah.
>
> M: Okay, and the $45,000 will be coming, like I have to give them something, you know, the instrument, and that will be coming like, in a, I would say probably couple of weeks from now, okay, cause you need money, then I have
>
> H: yeah
>
> M: to get that, you know.
>
> H: Insha-Allah.
>
> M: Because though, uh, because the last time I showed you, you know when I have to send this in, then they will give me $45,000, $50,000, okay. This is the part of the missile that I showed you.
>
> H: Oh, yeah [simultaneously with above]
>
> M: So as soon as it come, I'll give you, this is $5,000, so next couple of weeks, or less, I'll get you more money.
>
> H: Insha-Allah it's no problem, see, actually, I did not need all that, I just needed to keep going, just so I can, uh, pay the bills.
>
> M: Lets
>
> H: If insha-Allah give you insha-Allah guarantee.
>
> M: Yeah, it's $5,000?
>
> Aref: This fifty, yeah.

One should note that this conversation took place between Malik and Hossain while Aref was focusing on counting the money; Aref did not pay any attention to it at all, nor did he participate in it. Without hearing or understanding the context of the sentence, it is clear that there would have been no way for Aref to connect the illegal sale of the missile to the loan.

The prosecutors claimed that Malik showed Aref the trigger mechanism on this day, January 2, 2004, and talked to him about it (Government's Appendix Booklet, p. 543). But this was an outright lie. As it is described here (as well as in the transcript of the conversation, which can be found in Appendix B, Sting Tapes 2004, January 2), it is clear that Malik showed the trigger mechanism to *Hossain* and talked to *Hossain* about it, while Aref was busy counting the money. Aref had no chance, or desire, to pay any attention to it; bank tellers counting money are instructed to start the count over again from the beginning if they are interrupted for any reason. So why did Malik not show the trigger mechanism directly to Aref, or put it on the table in front of him, or talk about it when Aref was finished counting and could have seen it, listened to Malik's description of it, understood the description, and reacted to it?

2. The government claimed that on January 14, 2004, Malik discussed the missile twice with Aref. This is an even bigger lie. On the first occasion, while Aref was talking non-stop, Malik tried to cut him off by injecting, "I send the missile to…" (Government's Appendix Booklet, p. 247). It is absolutely clear from the tape that Aref never stopped talking, or slowed down his talking, or even paid any attention to these words that Malik uttered, who was unable to add any more words to complete his sentence.

3. The government claimed that Malik, during the same discussion, talked about a missile once again by saying, "—And that's why, the missile, that we sent it to New York City to teach Mu, uh, President Musharref, the lesson to not to fight with us" (Government's Appendix Booklet, p. 561). Here, Malik was asking Aref's opinion as an imam whether it was okay to support JEM in Kashmir financially in light of Islamic law. In the middle of this question, Malik jumped to another topic altogether to be able to insert the above sentence. Aref was focusing on the issue of Malik's previous long question about helping JEM, and gave his response in an equally long, non-stop lecture, essentially telling him that he (Aref) did not know if the leadership of this group was fighting in Kashmir for the sake of establishing Islamic laws, or for the sake of politics. Had Aref been listening

closely to Malik's long rambling speech, and then to the out-of-context reference to a missile in New York City, he would certainly have stopped and asked questions like, who was sending a missile? Why in New York City? Did President Musharref live in New York City? Who was going to use the missile, and how? To perform his counseling role properly, an imam cannot give an opinion unless he knows all these details. But Aref never heard Malik's reference to a missile, and had no clue about a missile being sent to New York City to shoot President Musharref; this was a fiction in the FBI's mind, and they carried this fiction into court.

4. The government also claimed that during the above discussion on January 14, 2004, Aref advised Malik to help JEM by saying, "I believe it is wise for you to help them if you can" (Government's Appendix Booklet, p. 563). This is not a lie, but it is outrageous, because it is taken totally out of context. Malik was seeking Aref's opinion as an imam regarding whether or not he should help JEM financially. Giving the whole background of such a situation in a lengthy lecture, Aref told him over and over again—at least ten times— that he did not know this group well, therefore he could not give a clear opinion as to whether Malik should or should not help them. He advised Malik in general terms, and then told him to help women and children, and advised him further that in case he decided to help the women and children, he should be careful that his help would not be interpreted as promoting terrorism. On the surveillance tape, that's the exact and undisputed context of the above sentence.

Another interesting point about this part of the conversation is worth noting. The FBI claimed that Aref supported terrorists because he advised Malik to help them. According to the FBI, Aref told Malik to help JEM by saying, "I believe it is *wise* for you to help them if you can." But the actual wording on the tape is, "I believe it is *wajib* for you to help them if you can." *Wajib* (prounounced w-aa-jib) is an Islamic religious term that means "a religious requirement a Muslim must perform." So with this statement, Aref was giving a religious, scholarly opinion as an imam that for a Muslim, it was required (*wajib*) to help the needy, women, children, orphans, and refugees among Muslims.

5. The government claimed that the meeting of February 12, 2004 that took place inside Aref's house was originally scheduled for the CW's (cooperating witness) office—where it would have been videotaped—but was moved to Aref's house instead because Aref had a dinner guest, an

Iraqi friend named Kassim Shaar (Government's Appendix Booklet, pp. 172, 182). This is both a lie and a fabrication. This meeting had been planned all along to take place at Hossain's pizzeria. Hossain had told Malik the previous day, when Malik had called him to schedule this meeting, that "[i]t is better if we meet at my place, I feel shy and ashamed that again and again so often [we meet at your place]." Malik said in response, "Okay, tomorrow at your place at 6:30 p.m." (This is what I heard on the tape when Malik called Hossain on February 11, 2004 at 5:30 p.m. Coll was monitoring the call.)

Around 6:30 p.m. on February 12, Malik did indeed go to Hossain's pizzeria, and Hossain called Aref to make sure he was coming. Aref then informed him that he had a guest at his house, but he had no problem if they came to his house. So Malik and Hossain went to Aref's house and completed the transaction in the presence of the guest, Kassim Shaar. Only the FBI could fictionalize in its imagination that Aref would be anxious to commit a crime in front of an invited guest. No one, especially not someone from the Middle East—and an imam to boot—would invite people to his house so that they could commit criminal acts in front of an unsuspecting guest and reveal a terrorist plot to them.

6. During this meeting, the government claimed that "Shaar moved aside during the transaction, but he overheard the CW warn Aref and Hossain, 'There is an attack coming to New York City, a MISSILE attack coming there'" (Government's Appendix Booklet, p. 173–174). This is a very big lie. First, Kassim Shaar had no place to move aside to. All four—Malik, Hossain, Aref, and Shaar—were together in the smaller-than-usual-size living room downstairs on the first floor; no additional space in Aref's house was available to move to. The entire first floor was rented to Aref's friend and tenant, and Aref was using the living room as "community property" because he had a guest for dinner and no additional space. The second floor was a small two-bedroom apartment used exclusively by the Aref family: husband, wife, and three children.

Second, in Muslim culture it is considered very humiliating to ask your guest to move aside, and it is very impolite to discuss something while hiding it from your guest. Muslims are not allowed to talk among themselves in a language that others present do not understand, unless there is a real linguistic problem.

Third, Shaar never testified in court that he had "overheard" anything—otherwise the defense could have discredited his testimony if the word "overheard" had been appended. He actually testified to the effect that the conversation in question took place in front of his eyes.

We have wondered again and again about this warning and its wording. Was it a forecast that the entire City of New York was going to be bombed by thousands of planes? "Do you think even a small child would consider a person sane who announces a sudden warning like this in these words?" observed a mosque member. Do co-conspirators in a criminal act really advise and warn each other in this manner?

7. The government claimed that "[a]lso at this meeting, the CW identified 'chaudhry' as the code word for missile when all three (the CW, Aref, and Hossain) were together." (Government's Appendix Booklet, pp. 237–38, 241). What a lie! If there were no physical opportunity or facility for the three to be alone and leave Shaar to an unknown imaginary space, why identify the code word "chaudhry" when the word "missile" had already been used by Malik in the same meeting?

The defense tended to think that something unfavorable to the FBI took place during this meeting, so the agents lied by saying that Malik's tape recorder fell off in the car and fabricated more lies as a cover, such as the "chaudhry" code word being identified at this meeting. Pericak claimed that Coll listened to the conversation from the street. But what happened to that recording?

Long after the trial was over, Shaar told me that the FBI had threatened to charge him for being an accomplice in the fictitious missile attack in New York City if he did not testify at trial against Aref the way they wanted him to testify. Shaar said they told him, "You were present at the meeting when Malik talked about the attack, and you never contacted us." The poor guest who had "overheard" had no choice but to testify against his dinner host.

8. In his testimony, Agent Coll said, "On numerous times, he [Aref] said, 'I understand you want to legalize your money and it is good for you and good for him, you should both have the benefit, it is part of the faith.'" But in the entire fifty hours of tape recordings, I found a discussion about legalizing money only once. Aref appreciated a (supposedly rich) Malik helping a needy fellow member of the community by loaning money. He also had the impression that Malik was claiming some kind of business tax credit by such transactions—the same way people giving

to charities get tax deductions. "I had no clue of any illegality of the loan arrangement," Aref told us. "How can I say money laundering is a part of our faith? Our faith forbids even interest." (Muslims do not pay interest, because it is forbidden by the Qur'an and the Prophet's teachings; this is why many Muslims give and receive loans among themselves, because no interest is appended.)

Unfortunately, this and other such points of Islamic culture were far beyond the capacity of the jury. The fear factor, the immense power of the judge and the FBI, combined with the lengthy, confusing, and contradictory discussions on the surveillance tapes, simply prevented them from sorting things out or challenging the prosecutors' version of the evidence. It was too much for them to pursue it further.

Many independent thinkers, when faced with the lies and distortions of the case, have wondered, "The jury saw and heard all these things. So why did they come up with a guilty verdict?" Well, this was not the only jury that got a case wrong. There are hundreds of cases in which a jury readily convicted someone accused of a serious crime, but years later it was found that the accused was not even remotely connected with that crime. What caused the jury to make a wrong decision in those cases? False evidence and over-zealous prosecution often accounted for these mistakes. Unfortunately in our case, even the role of the court was under suspicion, and we had very serious doubts about McAvoy's neutrality. The existence of the secret evidence must have also acted on both the judge and the jury in some unnamed—and unfavorable—way.

REQUEST FOR A NEW TRIAL

In early January 2007, Kindlon and Luibrand filed motions, based on Rule 29 and Rule 33, claiming that the verdicts were not supported by the evidence at trial and should be overturned. They requested either a new trial from Judge McAvoy or that the guilty verdicts be set aside and the case dismissed. Kindlon emphasized that Aref's discussion with Malik regarding his insistence to help JEM, as shown on the surveillance tape, did not prove that Aref supported terrorism. He said that the jury got it wrong and that language barriers and a manipulative informant prevented Aref from ever grasping what was taking place. According to him, Aref never understood that the loan was intended to launder money, or to "legalize the money," thus he never understood that witnessing the loan could in any way aid Malik in promoting terrorism or violating the law. "Aref never had any intent to aid JEM..." Kindlon wrote. "There is a complete lack of proof that he understood any connection between his witnessing the loan and discussions of helping JEM."

In response to the defense motions, the prosecutors submitted their brief, which essentially emphasized that the jury's interpretation of the case was correct. On February 22, 2007, McAvoy disappointed us again. In a sixty-one-page ruling, he refused the defense's requests for both a new trial and dismissal of the case. I was somewhat surprised with the language of this ruling. He selected phrases, sentences, and even entire paragraphs from the prosecution's memo and used them in support of his decision. I thought that his ruling should have been based on his own analysis and written in his own judicial language, and not simply a copy of the prosecution's arguments. On the same day, McAvoy also denied the motion filed by the New York Civil Liberties Union for public access to a classified document submitted by the government on March 10, 2006; he also denied the NYCLU's access to his own classified ruling on it.

Since we hadn't had high expectations for the motions anyway, we immediately began a campaign of writing letters to the court to emphasize other dimensions of the case. We wanted to bring to the court's attention the resentment the public had for the verdict, the community support that was being given to the defendants and their families, and the moral issues involved in the whole operation. We thought this would apply some pressure on McAvoy with regard to sentencing, or would at least help counterbalance the damage already done by the secret evidence. Kathy Manley, the assisting attorney from Kindlon's office, collected about fifty such letters and submitted them to the court, along with the sentencing memos. A similar number of letters were submitted by Luibrand with Hossain's sentencing memo. These letters were written by individuals from across the spectrum of society, as well as by community leaders and representative of various organizations, mosques, and churches. Aref's and Hossain's children also wrote letters to McAvoy to ask him to show mercy on them and on their fathers.

A common theme of these letters was to tell McAvoy that the defendants—though legally convicted—were not criminals and therefore deserved as much leniency as possible. Along with the letter-writing campaign, there was also a petition campaign for the same purpose, and the MSC collected the signatures of over 900 individuals and submitted them to the judge.

CARL STROCK'S DARING OPEN LETTER

A mong the local newspapers, the *Times Union* had the most regular and extensive coverage of the case, from beginning to end. Almost all the articles on the progression of the case were written by a staff reporter, Brendan Lyons. He always tried to balance the positions of the defense and the prosecution, which made it hard for the public to understand the reality of the case. On the other hand, the *TU*'s well-known columnist Fred LeBrun, who wrote occasionally about the case, was very clear that he thought it was a fictitious attempt by the FBI to set up and punish two Muslims. He openly branded the case an "injustice to American justice."

A much clearer and stronger position was taken by Carl Strock, a columnist at the *Daily Gazette* in Schenectady. From the early days of the case, he told the public in the strongest possible terms that he thought the case had no basis and was no more than a complex design to entrap the two defendants and ultimately convict them. He was right on the money. Several other reporters who disagreed with him in the beginning ultimately came to understand and agree with him in the end. After Aref's conviction and before his sentencing, Strock interviewed him in depth at the Rensselaer County Jail; at that time, Aref was writing a draft manuscript about his life, describing his experiences from childhood up until his arrival in the cell of that jail. It was ultimately published in March 2008 by the MSC as a memoir/autobiography, *Son of Mountains, My Life as a Kurd and a Terror Suspect.*

In his column on February 4, 2007, Strock essentially told readers that Aref was simply a human being: a foreigner, a Muslim, a victim, and of course innocent of the charges for which he was convicted. And on February 6, Strock wrote an open letter to Judge McAvoy about Aref's conviction and published it in his column. He reminded the judge to look into the motives of the FBI, and of the desperation of their slimeball informant to carry out the sting for his own benefit. Step by step, Strock walked McAvoy through each and every piece of evidence that he had observed throughout the trial, as well as the distortions and manipulations by the FBI and the prosecutor. He then wrote:

> Your Honor, I appeal to you as a human being:
>
> Can you possibly believe in the privacy of your heart that this is right?
>
> Can you possibly believe that these two men had it coming?
>
> Can you possibly believe the government was justified in marshalling its resources to trick these two men?
>
> Can you possibly believe the jury was justified in finding them guilty?
>
> This is not just a criminal case. It is an instance of how we responded and how we continue to respond to the horror that was inflicted on us on September 11, 2001. History will surely ask, what happened after those attacks? What did the United States do?
>
> Is it going to be said that one of the things we did was harass and persecute innocent Muslims? That we set them up and deceived them so we could send them to prison? Using secret evidence? Twisting reality to give us the desired result? Will it be said that we consistently and stubbornly applied massive force to the wrong people?
>
> This is now in your hands. To show these men leniency and impose sentences on them graciously less than the 30-years-to-life called for by federal guidelines will not even remotely give them justice, nor will it cloak you in the honor that your title calls for. Rather it will place you in the ranks of those now-nameless functionaries who sent Japanese-Americans to concentration camps in World War II and sent honest men and women to prison for refusing to answer the questions of Senator McCarthy.
>
> You have the opportunity in a small way to redeem the American justice system from the perversions into which it has strayed as a result of 9/11, and even, if I may so suggest, to redeem yourself.
>
> You can vacate the guilty verdicts, and you can send Yassin and Mohammed back to their families with an apology. I urge you to do so.

Abuhugifa Hossain, son of Mohammed Hossain, at the march and vigil organized by the Muslim Solidarity Committee to mark the third anniversary of the arrests.

Photo by Katherine Hughes

CHAPTER 16

"So Persevere with Patience"

SENTENCING DAY

After a postponement from the originally scheduled date of February 12, sentencing day was set for almost a month later, March 8, 2007. It was a very hard day for the defendants, their families, the Muslim community, the MSC, and many more from the community at large. We were hoping and praying for a minimal number of years in prison for both men, even though the prosecutors wanted both to be imprisoned for thirty years. I had prepared the mosque community to be ready to hear a term of five to ten years, based on my own assessment.

The court was not like a military zone that morning; it seemed instead to be a fortress. There were security guards on foot, on horses, on rooftops, in cars, next to cars, most of them keeping their fingers on the triggers of the weapons they were carrying. The building was filled with FBI agents and security guards. More than a hundred supporters of the defendants were lined up outside, carrying various banners and placards. As I passed by, I heard them praising the *Times Union* for their editorial of that morning and for publishing my op-ed piece about the case. Inside, the court hallway was filled with members of both the Muslim community and the MSC. We had pre-selected these members to be present in the courtroom because there was not enough room for everyone. Still, many could not get in.

The actual sentencing was to be done separately, with Aref first. A convict at his sentencing is given a chance to address the court, and Aref came to the dais without any written notes. Addressing Judge McAvoy in his shaky English, he said: "I know you, [your] Honor, and every single person and everybody, FBI, they check all my record, all my life, they interview thousands of the people…they knew never I did any violence, never I participate in any fighting, never I support any terrorist group…

everybody knew I did nothing to be one day in the jail for. And I did not come to this country to be in the jail. I came to be free. I did not come to this country to destroy [it]. I came to be my life. I [didn't] threaten any human being...I came for my children to be safe from terrorist...I believe what's done for me it is unfair and I believe, Honor, it is your duty to make sure that justice has been served."

Looking around the room, he then said, "I never had any intention to harm anyone in this country. And I don't know why I am guilty."

He alluded that the evidence used in his conviction was of the same nature as the satellite pictures, maps, and other "proofs" presented before the United Nations by former Secretary of State General Colin Powell, who sacrificed his credibility that day, February 5, 2003, by delivering a pack of falsehoods to tell the world that Iraq had weapons of mass destruction and therefore the U.S. attack on Iraq was justified. Aref also stated, "If you give me the death penalty, I will take it proudly. I will take it proudly, not because I am an arrogant or a proud person, but because they know and you know and everybody knows, I did nothing."

He made no secret of his troubled relationship with Kindlon and criticized him for not handling the defense arguments the way he had wanted. He said that Kindlon had been telling him all along that the prosecution had proven nothing, therefore there was no way the jury would find him guilty.

At the end he said, "I believe what's done for me it is unfair and I believe, Honor, it is your duty to make sure that justice has been served. If not, give me death penalty. Thank you for your time."

It was Judge McAvoy's turn. Following the tradition of sentencing, he asked the defense attorney, "All right. Any reason I should not sentence your client now?"

Kindlon replied, "No, sir, there's none."

"Mr. Aref, do you know any legal reason I shouldn't pass sentence on you?" the judge asked.

"I don't know. I'm villager, I don't know anything legal, Honor, please," replied Aref in a mild tone.

During the sentencing, McAvoy stated that any problems with the evidence used in the conviction should be a subject of the future appeals process. He recognized the community support for Aref. He pronounced a sentence of 180 months (fifteen years) in prison, with several sentences running concurrently; thirty-six months post-release supervision; and a fine of $110 per count of conviction.

We heard it all in silence and in helplessness. I remember looking at the MSC and the mosque members' faces, and their wet eyes made my eyes wetter. Aref's children had fallen asleep during the proceeding. His wife was confused and did not understand what it all meant.

After a recess, Hossain's sentencing took place. The court procedure was a repeat of the previous sentencing. Expressing himself as a fallen victim of deception, Hossain addressed the court with the help of a written note, saying, "When Malik first came into my life, he had everything I did not: he seemed smart and rich, I struggled every day." He said he did not know how to make a bomb. "I am a pizza man," he said. "I make good pizza."

Referring to the FBI's targeting of him, he said, "I do not know why it was me that was chosen. I was not a criminal. I was not even thinking of committing a crime."

He was given the same sentence—fifteen years. Luibrand had requested in a memo that Hossain be sent to a prison that had a medical facility, due to Hossain's high blood pressure and diabetes. In his sentencing, McAvoy added that he would make this recommendation to the Federal Bureau of Prisons.

MEDIA BARRAGE

I was the first one to face the barrage of about fifty reporters and cameramen after the sentencing. I gave a long post-sentencing statement on behalf of the Masjid As-Salam, the gist of which was as follows:

> The bottom line is that these two men are now sentenced to serve long prison terms, but the fact remains that they are not criminals, nor have they committed a crime. This trial occurred because of the immense power of the government and its resolve to punish these two men, and through them, to punish the Muslim community locally and nationally. I invite you to think: there are more than six million Muslims in this country, and almost six years have gone by since 9/11, yet not a single Muslim terrorist has ever been found here. We are not terrorists. We are part of this society, we share its concerns, and we want to share in its success and prosperity.

This cartoon by John deRosier appeared in the Albany *Times Union* on March 9, 2007, the day after Aref and Hossain were each sentenced to fifteen years in prison.

Courtesy of John deRosier

Cathy Callan, representing the Muslim Solidarity Committee and flanked by many of its members, read a long statement to the media, which stated in part: "We believe that the United States government has done and continues to do a grave disservice to the citizens of our country by targeting a specific group of people, expressly the Muslim community, and justifying its 'war on terror' by setting up elaborate operations to frame innocent Muslims, isolate the Muslim community within our country, and keep this community in a constant state of fear."

Suddaby and others, representing the government's side, repeated the same rhetoric: that Hossain was willing to help Malik promote his weapons business, and that Aref's diary and speeches proved he had terrorist connections. Suddaby said, "Obviously, after 9/11, the world changed drastically. Our obligation is to prevent the next one. That is what this case is all about." When reporters countered Suddaby and pushed him hard, he said, "What would you have us do? Sit on our hands?"

I believe that this was the most truthful statement made by law enforcement throughout the whole case, even though Suddaby probably didn't intend it that way. They wanted to do something, anything, to please the fear-mongering politicians and hard-right members of the public and make it seem as though they were increasing the safety of the country and its citizens—and there couldn't be an easier way to prove their authority and to secure a larger budget.

John Pikus, Special Agent in charge of the FBI's Albany Division, who had recently replaced William Chase, also gave a statement. He usually looked like a diplomat rather than an FBI agent, and he definitely talked like one. He said assertively that it was "[a] righteous case, a righteous investigation, a righteous prosecution." A little later the government's representatives came up with a somewhat unified statement about the sting, which they used to defend themselves against the doubting public: "It was a test, and the defendants failed."

The defense attorneys did not have much to say. They talked about appealing the case to the Second Circuit.

In its editorial the next day, the *Times Union* criticized McAvoy for making the controversial statement in front of the jury that "the FBI had good reason to target Aref." It considered the sentencing harsher than it should have been. Part of its editorial read as follows:

Mercy? No, 15 Years

If there was leniency in federal court in Albany on Thursday, it was leniency in name only. Compassion was rare too, almost as absent as the
fictitious terrorist attack upon which the federal government's prosecution of Yassin Aref and Mohammed Hossain was based. There
was Senior U.S. District Judge Thomas McAvoy, noting that Mr. Aref
and Mr. Hossain had no prior criminal records before being lured
into an FBI sting operation, were of otherwise sound character, and
enjoyed the widespread support of a community that hoped they'd
be spared harsh punishment. Yet for all that, the judge still sentenced
each of them to 15 years in prison for their convictions of charges of
conspiring to aid terrorism and money laundering.

A LETTER TO CONGRESS

On March 26, 2007, two members of the MSC, Steve Downs and
Michael Rice, finalized a draft of a very comprehensive petition to
be sent to Congress on behalf of the MSC. This petition was addressed
to Honorable Patrick Leahy, chairman of the Senate Judiciary Committee, and a copy was sent to six other senators: Arlen Specter, Charles E.
Schumer, Russ Feingold, Edward M. Kennedy, Hillary Rodham Clinton,
and Richard J. Durbin. The petition requested a Congressional investigation of the Department of Justice and the FBI, seeking to determine if
these agencies misused their power to investigate and convict innocent
individuals who posed no threat to our nation based primarily on their
religion—Islam—and their Islamic countries of origin. It included brief
information on several dozen cases nationwide where other Muslims had
been victimized in the same fashion as Aref and Hossain.

The petition highlighted the Albany sting in detail and presented it
as an example of injustice. The petition's supporting documentation included editorials and columns from several local newspapers that had
denounced the charges against and convictions of Aref and Hossain.
The petition also noted that their convictions were protested by more
than 900 people who had signed a petition to Judge McAvoy, and that
over 100 letters had been sent to the judge asking for dismissal or leniency. Writers of these letters (not to be confused with the writers of the

Congress letter) included the Albany Catholic Diocese, leaders of local Islamic communities, and the Council of Churches, as well as individual community members from all walks of life.

The petition requested that Congress not only investigate the policies and practices of the FBI and the Department of Justice, but also require that those agencies' policies and practices fully comply with the requirements of the law and the Constitution, and that any convictions, deportations, or other penalties that had been imposed unfairly, unlawfully, or were based on misrepresentations and deception by the government, be reversed.

Unfortunately we did not receive a response from any of the recipients of this petition, not even an acknowledgement of receipt, despite the fact that Downs followed up on this petition by writing reminders to each recipient.

THE FREEDOM OF INFORMATION ACT

During our discussions in the MSC, I mentioned to the members that many dozens of Muslims in the area had been contacted and interviewed over the past four years by FBI agents. We thought it would be interesting to know how many of them had actually gone through this process, so I proposed that we should make a request based on the federal Freedom of Information Act (FOIA) and the New York State Freedom of Information Law (FOIL) to find out about such investigations.

On April 2, 2007, on behalf of the MSC, one of its members, Maribeth (Mickie) Lynn, sent a request to Supervisory Special Agent Paul M. Holstein, chief division counsel and media relations coordinator of the Albany FBI, to obtain records or portions of them pertaining to contacts with Muslims initiated by the Albany field office of the FBI. She asked for the number of interviews, visits, letters or other written correspondence, phone calls and messages on answering machines, appearances at local businesses or places of work, invitations to share meals and conversations, and other forms of contact.

She also requested from them the number of interviews and other contacts with immigrants from specific countries of origin, including Iran, Iraq, Sudan, Syria, Afghanistan, Algeria, Bahrain, Eritrea, Lebanon, Morocco, Oman, Qatar, Somalia, Tunisia, United Arab Emirates,

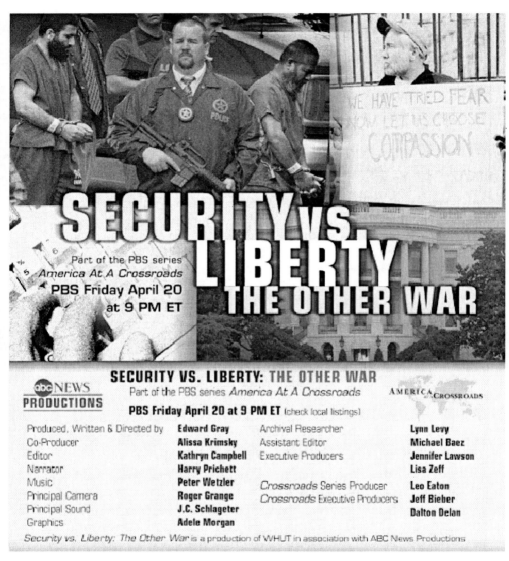

Ad for the segment of the PBS TV series *America at a Crossroads* that
featured the Aref-Hossain case and aired April 20, 2007.
Mailed (as a postcard) and e-mailed by the producers.

Yemen, Pakistan, Saudi Arabia, Bangladesh, Egypt, Indonesia, Jordan, and Kuwait.

She specifically sought numbers and dates of such contacts conducted by the Albany field office of the FBI and/or the Joint Terrorism Task Force in the tri-county area of Albany, Schenectady and Troy between September 12, 2001 and December 31, 2005.

She also requested the dates of such interviews and or contacts: "In addition, we ask you to provide us with data concerning numbers of repetitions and dates of repeated interviews/contacts with any given subject or family."

The Albany FBI forwarded this request to their federal office in Washington, D.C., which, after four weeks, replied: "This is in reference to your Freedom of Information Act (FOIA) request concerning miscellaneous documents. The FOIA does not require federal agencies to answer inquires, create records, conduct research, or draw conclusions concerning queried data. Rather the FOIA requires agencies to provide access to reasonably described, non-exempt records. Federal Bureau of Investigation records are indexed by the name of the subject or organization under investigation, not by the number of interviews and dates. Your request does not comply with the FOIA and its regulations."

SECURITY VERSUS LIBERTY

Producer Edward Gray of ABC News contacted me in early March and told me that he was producing a documentary for PBS entitled "Security Versus Liberty: The Other War." He wanted to highlight the Albany sting case, including filming at the mosque and conducting an interview with me. I gladly accepted the proposal.

Along with his crew, Gray made several trips to Albany for the filming of this documentary, and it was aired on PBS on April 20, 2007. While filming in a makeshift studio set up in a downtown Albany hotel, he asked me to respond to many arguments given by President Bush and his defenders that supported a compromise of liberty in favor of security to face the challenges of the time.

I responded, "These arguments are nothing but a twist and a distortion of facts to take away the privacy and liberty of the people. By its very nature, a government's appetite to empower itself at the expense of citizens' rights has no bounds. Usurping the people's rights and liberty under the pretext of making them secure is a dangerous and deceptive program. In fact, almost all examples of the claim that these new measures have prevented us from terrorist attacks are not even worth putting on the pages of comic books. The present administration has very cunningly exploited the fear of the people. We feel powerless to challenge the all-powerful tactics of the government." I quoted the famous words of Benjamin Franklin: "They who would give up an essential liberty to purchase a little temporary safety, deserve neither liberty nor safety."

"But they claim that there is a good deal of support in the public and the media for their new measures," Gray challenged me.

"Support?" I asked. "For sure there are plenty of cronies who will sing for Bush irrespective of reality, and for sure there are plenty of 'drive-by' media in the form of fear-mongering radio talk-show hosts whose only mission is to support Bush. They will go out of business if they have to talk of sensible things. Unfortunately, a cult has cropped up in this country, which, like a religious cult, is devoted to praise for its lord, the present administration."

I told him further that after demonizing Muslims and turning them into boogiemen, they had shifted their attention to marginalizing all Americans of conscience and intellect, branding them unpatriotic and sometimes even suggesting that such Americans should leave the country. The most polite phrases used for them, I said, were "soft on terrorism" or "naïve on security."

With respect to the entrapment and conviction of Aref and Hossain, Gray stated, "The FBI claims that this is their job and this is exactly what they should be doing," and he asked me to respond to that. "That's exactly what they should *not* be doing," I said. "The FBI is a very resourceful agency. They should be investigating real cases, not playing fiction and drama and punishing innocent individuals and torturing Muslim communities."

He asked me what I expected in terms of trends in the future. I said that the day was not too far off when Americans would wake up and say, "Bush has given this nation nothing, but taken away most of the things this nation was once known for." I quoted Thomas Jefferson, who once said, "The most sacred of the duties of a government is to do equal and impartial justice to all its citizens."

I was a little worried about being so forthright in a documentary, but I was moved to tell Gray, "Bloodshed, secret prisons, Guantanamo Bay, Abu Ghraib, torture, abuse of human rights, friendship with dictators, and violations of the U.S. Constitution—these will be the only legacy our president will depart his office with. I hope he will at least respect the Constitution and depart the White House when his term expires."

AN OPEN APPEAL TO LAW ENFORCEMENT

No doubt law enforcement agencies would like to take credit for making this country safe from terrorism. However, the truth of the matter is that it is American Muslims who are entitled to that credit. Anyone who is fair-minded and informed knows that the policies and actions of the Bush Administration have created more terrorists than they have gotten rid of. One should not forget that the individuals who carried out the unfortunate events of 9/11 in its various stages were from overseas. Not a single one of them was an American Muslim. Terrorism has no place in American mosques. The biggest concern of American Muslims, their intellectuals, imams, and mosque and community leaders, is an act of terrorism by a Muslim in this country. We see it as the biggest danger and the most damaging event that could happen to us and to our future. Such an act would be devastating to us. We would be disgraced and humiliated. We would be called murderers and traitors.

But an act of terrorism is not only against our religion. It is against basic common sense for those of us who wish to flourish in this country. We want to live with dignity and pride in this society and share in its prosperity. Thus it is almost impossible for terrorist tendencies to take root in the mainstream population of American Muslims. Immigrant Muslims are extremely wary of law enforcement agencies due to the corrupt and unjust policing they encountered in their home countries. The last thing they would expect is a similar situation here; they expect honesty and fairness from the government of this country.

Indigenous American Muslims, especially those coming from economically poor areas, may have deeper and more complex problems with law enforcement authorities. Some of those from the African American and Latino communities who have embraced Islam have had a previous brush with the law, and a good number of them owe the roots of their conversion to Islam to the prison system. So the targeting of Muslims through sting operations and other methods only intensifies their lack of trust in the authorities.

In recent years, every single Muslim in this country has been treated as a potential terrorist, and the government is distrustful of anyone who is Muslim. Targeting one of them and punishing him or her in violation of fairness and justice has been considered standard law enforcement practice. Muslims are considered guilty from the start, with no fair chance of proving their innocence. This has been the rule, rather than the exception. Such an attitude has led to establishment of laws, methods of investigation, and systems of policing that are unjust and are, in truth, wholly un-American. Law enforcement agencies have also manipulated the emotions of the public, exploited their fear, and used false propaganda to carry out this ill-conceived mission—and they enjoyed the blessings of the Bush Administration all the way to the top levels.

It is high time that some rational thinking takes place among law enforcement agencies and those who claim they are working to ensure the safety of our nation. Rather than wasting huge amounts of energy and resources on targeting innocent Muslims and their communities, they should focus on real intelligence and investigation in coordination with Muslim leaders, imams, intellectuals, and others. Once a relationship of honesty, trust, and confidence is built up, there will be no lack of cooperation from the Muslim leadership itself, and Muslims will be more than willing to open their communities, mosques, and institutions to law enforcement officials, reporters, and the non-Muslim public.

I beg the authorities, as well as the Muslim leadership in this country, to take concrete steps in removing the mutual distrust of each other that presently exists, and to develop a relationship of mutual trust and cooperation. Doing so will be a win-win game for everyone, in which there will be no losers.

To my non-Muslim colleagues, I say, let the struggle continue, let the standards of this nation be upheld, and let them not slide. And to my fellow Muslims, I say, "So persevere with patience, for the end success indeed belongs to those who are righteous." (Qur'an, Chapter 11, Verse 49)

May the Almighty guide us all to the right path.

POSTSCRIPT

I n August 2007, the attorneys for Yassin Aref and Mohammed Hossain filed appeals of their convictions with the U.S. Second Circuit Court of Appeals in Manhattan, and oral arguments were heard on March 24, 2008. On July 2, the court denied the appeals.

Attorney Steve Downs writes: "In a surprisingly cursory decision, considering the complexity of the case, the court ignored a number of key issues raised, mischaracterized others, and followed the prosecution's arguments on the remaining issues without significant analysis. Among its strangest holdings, the court held that Aref had not provided a 'colorable basis' (a legal term that means 'some reason to believe beyond mere speculation') to show that he had been subjected to illegal wiretapping and/or eavesdropping, even though on January 17, 2006 the *New York Times* quoted an administration official as saying that the NSA's warrantless (and illegal) wiretapping program had 'played a role in the arrest of an imam and another man in Albany in August 2004....' During the trial, FBI Special Agent Timothy Coll also implied under oath that Aref had been subjected to twenty-four-hour non-physical surveillance—suggesting that he had been wiretapped. If the printed admission of an administration official, and the implication of the agent central to the case, were not enough to raise a colorable basis to challenge the secret and illegal wiretapping, then it seems clear that virtually no basis would have been sufficient, and equally clear that the court was essentially covering up for the illegal activities of the Bush Administration. This impression was reinforced by the fact that after the main oral argument, but before court was concluded, a second, secret argument was presented to the court, during which only the prosecution was permitted to speak. The defense was excluded. The court's decision suggests that the judges were influenced by the secret information given to them by the prosecution, which the defense was not allowed to see or rebut. During the trial, the prosecution had introduced false and prejudicial information (including the notorious mistranslation of the Kurdish word *Kak* as 'commander' rather than as 'brother' or 'Mister,' its true meaning), and it is easy to wonder what inaccurate information they may have told the Second Circuit in secret, which influenced the judges' decision."

Aref and Hossain's appeal to the U.S. Supreme Court to hear the case was denied on March 6, 2009.

Both Aref and Hossain continue to serve their fifteen-year sentences. With time served and good behavior, Aref will probably serve ten more years, Hossain about twelve. What will happen during these years to Aref's wife, who is still traumatized from her ordeal, and to their four young and talented children? Or to Hossain's ailing wife and their six bright children, all under age fifteen?

From May 2007 to March 2009, Aref was at the Communication Management Unit of the federal prison in Terre Haute, Indiana, a unit designed to hold mostly Muslims of Middle Eastern descent with terror-related convictions. All communications, both incoming and outgoing, are monitored by the prison authorities. Inmates are allowed only one monitored fifteen-minute telephone call per week. Visitation rights are extremely limited; Aref's wife and children can visit him, but it has to be a non-contact visit conducted across a thick Plexiglas wall, with the visitors talking through a telephone. Before sentencing, Aref's defense attorneys, the community, and I requested that the judge add to the sentencing guidelines that because of Aref's family situation, he should be incarcerated close to Albany. The judge did this, but the Bureau of Prisons ignored his request. Given the 900 miles between Albany and Terre Haute, Aref's family was able to visit him only once a year.

On March 27, 2009, Aref was abruptly transferred to the Communication Management Unit of the federal prison in Marion, Illinois. Restrictions are the same as at Terre Haute. Aref is now over 1,000 miles from his family.

Hossain is at the medium-security federal prison in Fairton, New Jersey. Once again, despite the fact that the judge recommended to the Bureau of Prisons that Hossain be sent to a prison with a medical facility, he was not, and at Fairton he has been provided only minimal medical treatment for his diabetes, high blood pressure, and declining eyesight. His health has deteriorated markedly.

Glenn Suddaby, U.S. Attorney for the Northern District of New York, who aggressively pursued the successful convictions of several innocent Muslims under his watch, was nominated by President George Bush in 2007 for a federal judgeship on the U.S. District Court in the Northern District—a lifetime appointment—and was confirmed in July 2008.

MALIK STRIKES AGAIN

On May 20, 2009, another FBI sting operation, employing an operative (who was referred to as an "informant"), was announced in Newburgh, a small city about seventy-five miles south of Albany. This news galvanized the whole Hudson Valley area, as well as New York City. In this sting, four marginal Muslims, petty criminals who had converted to Islam in prison, were entrapped in a plot to shoot down military aircraft at the Air National Guard base in Newburgh and bomb two synagogues in New York City. As soon as we heard this explosive news, we began to notice many elements in common with the Albany sting operation, and because of details in the media we started wondering if the FBI had utilized Malik (Shahed Hussain) as an operative in this fictional plot. Within a few hours, we got confirmation that indeed it was Malik, who had used the fake name of "Maqsood" and had once again played the dirty game of entrapping Muslims in a scheme in which they appeared to be extremely dangerous terrorists with a plot of devastation that would reach far and wide.

The four men—James Cromitie, David Williams, Onta Williams (no relation), and Laguerre Payen—were described in the first media reports as members of the Masjid al-Ikhlas in Newburgh. But the four men were only occasional attendees at the masjid; three were paroled convicts who had met in prison; one was a cocaine addict; one had been raised as a Christian; and one, a Haitian immigrant, is mentally handicapped. "Maqsood" posed as a super-rich businessman, exploited the needs of these men and spent lavishly on them and their family members. and promised them large sums of money. It will be left to the defense lawyers (and to you, the reader) to determine how much of the plot was Maqsood's and the FBI's and in whose mind it originated; how much he was paid, as *agent provocateur*, to entrap these men so the government could once again claim they had preemptively protected America; and how much longer the FBI will continue to plant informants in mosques to spy on and disrupt Muslim communities, in the mistaken belief that real (as opposed to artificial) terrorists live there. Muslims are very frustrated with the FBI's cheap and dirty tactics of sending operatives into mosques.

We were a little surprised with this sting. We had presumed that these kinds of fictional entrapments were a thing of the past and that they had stopped with the departure of Mr. Bush. However, some of us gave him the benefit of the doubt, thinking that this sting was already underway when Mr. Bush was still occupying the White House.

According to some reports, the FBI used about 100 agents to make the yearlong sting operation succeed—so they could claim they were protecting the nation by uncovering this very dangerous terrorism plot. Many politicians and many in the media bought the FBI's reasoning enthusiastically and applauded the government for its efforts. On June 9, 2009, FBI Director Robert Mueller publicly defended the FBI's use of informants in mosques, despite complaints from all over the country that Muslim worshippers and clerics were being targeted—by the FBI, rather than by terrorists. Mueller's comments came in response to a Michigan Muslim organization that has asked the Justice Department to investigate complaints that the FBI is asking Muslim community members there to spy upon its leaders and mosque attendees. According to a news article, Mueller said there will be no change in the FBI's priorities in the Obama Administration: "I would not expect that we would in any way take our foot off the pedal of addressing counterterrorism." He also described relations with U.S. Muslims as "very good," but acknowledged disagreements.

All proceeds from the sale of this book will go directly to the Aref Education Fund, established by the author for the educational needs of Yassin Aref's four children. For more information about the fund, or to send additional donations, please write to:

Aref Education Fund
c/o Law Office of Stephen Downs
26 Dinmore Road
Selkirk, New York 12158

Some websites to visit for more information:

Muslim Solidarity Committee, **http://nepajac.org/Aref&Hossain.htm**
Updates on current efforts to help Yassin Aref and Mohammed Hossain and their families.

Yassin Aref's personal website, **http://www.yassinaref.com**
Excerpts from his book, *Son of Mountains, My Life as a Kurd and a Terror Suspect,* and new writing from prison, as well as some reports and news about the case.

Project SALAM (Support And Legal Advocacy for Muslims), **http://www.projectsalam.org**
A legal-based website with a substantial database devoted to researching and documenting the likelihood that the U.S. Justice Department's post-9/11 terrorism-related prosecutions and convictions have included a significant number of Muslims who are innocent of any crime. Other cases have been severely over-charged and/or over-sentenced. Project SALAM aims to examine these prosecutions and determine whether in each case there was substantial evidence of criminality, or simply evidence unfairly concocted and/or twisted to convict innocent Muslims. It also aims to examine the tactics and strategies of the prosecution to determine if the government, in its effort to obtain convictions against Muslims, has stretched legal concepts beyond the point where a fair trial is possible and has unfairly damaged communities.

Documentary film about the Aref-Hossain case, *Waiting for Mercy,* **http://www.waitingformercy.com**

Were Aref and Hossain, who had no prior criminal history, possible terrorists—or were they set up? Using some of the actual material recorded over many months by the FBI informant (a Pakistani and a convicted criminal) and featuring footage and interviews with defense lawyers, prosecutors, journalists, community advocates, and Muslim community members, *Waiting for Mercy* explores what director Ellie Bernstein calls the "broader issues" raised by the case, including warrantless wiretapping, secret evidence, entrapment, and the targeting of Muslims.

Thoughts on America in the Islamic World

HAJJ

In the winter of 2005, my daughter Huma and I decided to perform Hajj, a religious journey or pilgrimage to holy sites in Saudi Arabia that fulfills one of the five religious obligations of a Muslim and is one of the five pillars of Islam:

1. To declare belief in the Oneness of Allah, the Almighty God and His final Messenger and Prophet, Muhammad (Peace be upon him).

2. Pray five times a day and night at specific times.

3. Observe a fast from dawn to dusk during the Islamic month of Ramadan.

4. Pay *Zakaat* (charity) annually at a rate of 2.5% of a person's net surplus money, if it is above a certain amount and remains idle or unused over the entire year.

5. Perform Hajj once in one's lifetime, if one can afford to do so financially and physically after meeting certain other obligations.

Many Westerners and others think that Muslims go to the city of Mecca in Saudi Arabia to perform Hajj because the Prophet Muhammad (Peace be upon him) was born and lived there until he was fifty-three years old, when he was forced to migrate to Medina, a city about 200 miles north. He and his few dozens of followers were being persecuted in Mecca simply because he was calling the people to worship one God and to grant equality to all the people, and the idol-worshipping tribal leaders were not willing to accept any challenge to their forefathers' religion or to the existing order of society. As a result, the Prophet and many of his followers were not even allowed to leave Mecca; they had to flee to Medina under cover of night or in secrecy.

The Hajj actually goes back before the time of the Prophet to Prophet Abraham (in Arabic, Ibrahim, Peace be upon him), who was commanded by God to abandon his wife Hagar and their infant son Ishmael (in Arabic, Ismail) in a barren valley in present-day Saudi Arabia at a place that later became the city of Mecca. This was a test from God. When Hagar ran out of food and water, she left the baby Ismail in the valley and started running desperately between two nearby small hills, Safa and Marwah, which are roughly one-third of a mile apart, to look for any sign of food, water, or a passing caravan.

After completing seven runs between the hills and losing hope, she returned to Ismail and was utterly surprised to see water gushing out of the ground next to his heels. This was a miracle of God. She preserved the water in the form of a small pond that, in coming days, would become a precious source of water for birds, animals, and passing caravans. Water in a barren valley—what a blessing of God! That pond became an everlasting source of refreshment and a limitless water supply.

This well, called Zamzam, which still exists, is very precious and sacred for Muslims. When people go for Hajj, they drink from its water as often as possible. They also soak their clothes in it and bring it back home in bottles or containers to give as a gift to other Muslims. It is claimed that the water has certain minerals that help cure some diseases, and that one can survive for many days by consuming this water alone. Most likely Hagar and Ismail survived on it for many days, until they were helped by passing caravans.

Years later, God commanded Prophet Ibrahim (Peace be upon him) to return to the valley, build a house there for God's worship, invite people from faraway places to visit this house, and to worship God there on specific days of the year. Prophet Ibrahim and his son, Prophet Ismail (Peace be upon both of them) together built a structure out of stones, called Ka'bah. It consisted of only walls on a foundation roughly forty-three feet long and forty feet wide, and was built close to the Zamzam well. Upon their call, people flocked to Mecca, and the annual ritual of Hajj took root. The practice was strengthened in Islam with slight modifications on the original ritual.

Muslims consider the Ka'bah to be the first House of God built on earth for His worship, and when they pray, they face in its direction irrespective of where they are on earth. The Ka'bah has been built and rebuilt many times on the foundations of the original structure. At present, it stands about forty-five feet tall on its original foundation, and the whole structure is covered with precious black cloth containing gold and silver embroidery and writings. This cloth is changed annually, at a cost of about $5 million, in a solemn ceremony in the presence of Muslim dignitaries from around the world.

Surrounding the Ka'bah is the biggest mosque in the world, called Haram, where more than four million worshippers can pray together at one time. Haram is the holiest place on earth for a Muslim. In fact, the whole city of Mecca and its surrounding territories are sacred. No bloodshed, fighting, or hunting and killing of animals or even insects are allowed.

When Muslims go to perform Hajj, as part of the ritual they circumambulate the Ka'bah seven times in counterclockwise circles, and they also run and walk seven times between Safa and Marwah, the two hills, imitating the seven runs of Hagar when she was looking for help for herself and Ismail. Of course, there is no longer any sign of these two natural hills in a barren valley; everything is enclosed in a state-of-the-art modern structure with all the modern amenities.

Many times on American radio, I have heard talk-show hosts and their callers suggest that our president, as commander in chief, should order this holy site to be bombed and reduced to rubble. Had I not heard this again and again with my own ears, I would not believe that such ignorant and mean individuals live in the most advanced and civilized society in the world. These hatemongers must be mentally sick; they are nothing but a disgrace to mankind to display such hate for the peaceful religion of God that was sent through Ibrahim and Muhammad (Peace be upon them). How can we call terrorists "uncivilized" if such "civilized" people live among us?

ANOTHER COUNTRY

Huma was very anxious to go to Hajj and participate in all these rituals, and she insisted that I accompany her. I had performed my Hajj ten years earlier, so I was not as enthusiastic, but I agreed and made a plan to visit my relatives in India first, then my other daughter, Shazia, in Damascus, on the same trip. While overseas, I wanted to find out Muslims' opinions of the current situation in the U.S., but more interestingly, while in Damascus I wanted to take the opportunity to inquire firsthand about Aref's life when he had lived in Damascus.

At JFK in New York on December 15, 2005, we began to board a

Delta flight to Paris for the first leg of our trip. I tried to notice if we were treated differently than other passengers, since Huma was constantly whispering in my ear, "Watch, we'll be randomly selected, I bet you." She was absolutely right. While everyone else's carry-on bags were being checked by one person, we were surrounded by seven security personnel and asked to go to a different area. They put us in a corner and asked us not to move, dumped everything from our bags onto a large table, and performed visual and chemical tests by spraying some aerosol gas in the air. They did this repeatedly. It seemed that there was a false positive, because they called in a specialist to perform further tests. "It might be because of some of the medications you are carrying are testing positive," one of the security people said to me.

"Maybe. I am sorry, I am not a chemist," I told him. Huma was very irritated. "Let them do whatever they want," I told her, to calm her down. "Why bother yourself? It will not help."

Finally they let us go, we got on our plane, and the rest of the trip proceeded without incident. But when we reached New Delhi, two of our suitcases had not arrived. Knowing the Indian system very well, I was sure we would never receive them in India. It took us a couple of hours to report the missing bags at the airport. I called Faisal in Albany and asked him to request that Delta send the suitcases, once found, back to Albany. But to my surprise, the suitcases were delivered two weeks later to my house in India, just as we were preparing to leave for Saudi Arabia via the Dubai airport, where we were scheduled to meet a group of Hajj pilgrims arriving from the U.S.

We flew from Dubai to Jeddah with the U.S. group of pilgrims, and from there we were taken by bus to Mecca and placed in a nice hotel—an Italian chain called Sofitel—just next to the Haram. Men and women were placed in separate wings, but there was no separation in the dining room or in the waiting area.

Preparing for the Hajj is simple. A Hajj pilgrim, called a Hajji or Haajj, has to take a shower and put on a Hajj dress called an *Ihram*, a simple two-piece, white, unstitched garment. One part wraps around the lower part of the body from the waist down, and the other part covers the upper part of the body including the shoulders. Open shoes, sandals, or flip-flops are worn. Women are exempt from *Ihram* dress, but they wear simple and loose-fitting outfits.

The Hajj ritual begins with a prayer that expresses the intention to keep one's mind and body free from any sins, to seek forgiveness and repentance for past sins, to ask the Almighty for guidance, and to beg for the goodness of this world as well as of the world hereafter.

Huma and I left our luggage in our rooms and rushed to the Haram mosque to perform our first ritual. There is no segregation between males and females inside the Haram. We entered through one of the several dozen huge gates. Each gate is watched by several plainclothes unarmed security personnel, both male and female. Mostly they check individuals visually and do not allow any materials in, except for prayer rugs, books, and personal clothing. The security of millions of worshippers, as well as of the buildings, is a great concern for everyone. I have heard that there is an ongoing debate as to whether metal and explosives detectors should be installed on the gates.

Huma and I circled the Ka'bah seven times, along with a crowd of perhaps 25–30,000 others, while reciting portions of the Qur'an from memory and asking the Almighty for the forgiveness of our sins and to give us guidance and wisdom so that we would do only good in our lives and to all His creatures. Then we drank a lot of Zamzam and ran and walked seven times between Safa and Marwah. We drank Zamzam again and then came back to our hotel. The whole ritual probably took about two hours. The actual Hajj day was still a few days away, so this ritual was not really considered part of the Hajj. Such a ritual outside of the Hajj days is referred to as *Umrah*. I removed my *Ihram* dress and changed back to regular clothing.

The main ritual of the Hajj takes place on the ninth day of the month of Hajj on the plain (or valley, or mount) of Arafat, a place on the outskirts of Mecca. On the eighth day, pilgrims move to Mina, a place also on the outskirts of Mecca, and spend their nights in tents. We had the best site, with air-conditioned tents (the quality of the facilities depends upon the cost of the tour package). Hajj administrators are very sensitive to the living standards of pilgrims from Western countries; they allot the best sites for Americans, followed by the pilgrims from other Western countries. Our Hajj package—$4,500 per person for one week, including internal travel, accommodations, food, and return travel to JFK—was close to the best.

PROPHET MUHAMMAD'S LAST SERMON

On the ninth day of the month of Hajj, we moved to Arafat. We stood on the same plain where approximately 124,000 pilgrims had stood fourteen centuries ago when the Messenger of God, Muhammad (Peace be upon him), delivered his last sermon. Sitting on the back of his camel, he addressed the throng of pilgrims. His words were transmitted phrase by phrase, one after the other, by many in the audience so that even the person at the end of the sea of humanity could hear his message. It was 10 A.H. (After *Hijrah*, the year that the Prophet migrated from Mecca to Medina), or 632 A.D., and he was sixty-three years old.

After praising and thanking the Almighty, the Prophet said:

"O People! Lend me an attentive ear, for I know not whether after this year, I shall ever be amongst you again. Therefore listen to what I am saying to you very carefully and take these words to those who could not be present here today.

"O People! Just as you regard this month, this day, this city as sacred, so regard the life and property of every one of you as a sacred trust. Indeed you will meet your Lord and He will account for your actions. O Allah! Be my witness that I communicated the message.

"Return the goods entrusted to you to their rightful owners. Hurt no one so that no one may hurt you. Remember that you will indeed meet your Lord, and that He will indeed reckon your deeds. Allah has forbidden you the usury of the past, therefore any obligation based on that shall henceforth be waived. Your capital, however, is yours to keep. You will not transgress each other.

"Beware of Satan to safeguard your religion. He has lost all hope that he will ever be able to lead you astray in big things, so beware of following him in small things.

"O People! It is true that you have certain rights in regard to your women, but they also have rights over you. Remember that you have taken them as your wives, only under Allah's trust and with His permission. If they abide by your right then to them belongs the right to be fed and clothed in kindness. Do treat your women well and be kind to them, for they are your partners…O Almighty! Have I transmitted Your Message?

"O People! Listen to me in earnest, worship Allah, say your five daily prayers, fast during the month of Ramadan, and give your wealth in Zakat. Perform Hajj if you can afford to.

"O people! Indeed your Lord is One and your father is one. All of you are from Adam and Adam is from dust. The best of you is the one who is most pious in the sight of Allah. An Arab has no superiority over a non-Arab nor a non-Arab has any superiority over an Arab; also a white has no superiority over a black, nor a black has any superiority over a white—except by piety and good action…Have I communicated the message? O Allah! Be my witness.

"Remember, one day you will appear before Allah and answer for your deeds. So beware, do not stray from the path of righteousness after I am gone. People! no prophet or apostle will come after me and no new faith will be born. Reason well therefore, O people, and understand words which I convey to you. I leave behind me two things, the Qur'an and the Sunnah, and if you follow these, you will never go astray. All those who listen to me shall pass on my words to others and those to others again; and may the last ones understand my words better than those who listened to me directly. Be my witness, O Allah, that I have conveyed Your Message to Your people…And peace be upon you."

I had read this sermon in the past many times, but listening to it in its original atmosphere, and in the sea of humanity of about four million devotees, all standing and supplicating, was entirely a different thing. It shook me inside, and I saw that it shook others too. Our imam repeated this sermon after we finished the afternoon prayer outside of our tent in Arafat. We all cried. With a trembling heart and shaking body, I made a resolution and promised the Almighty that I would try my best to follow the Prophet's sermon in letter and spirit all my life.

I have violated his teachings since then very often. May Almighty forgive me.

In the evening, we started for Muzdalifa, another place on the outskirts of Mecca. We prayed and relaxed there, and after the morning prayer we returned to our tents in Mina. All these places are only a few miles away from each other, but because of the bumper-to-bumper traffic it took our bus several hours to cover these distances.

After awhile we walked to a nearby place called Jamaraat, where we threw seven pebbles apiece on two pillar-like structures representing

Satan. This was a symbolic gesture of hitting Satan to keep him at a distance, in imitation of the Prophet Ibrahim (Peace be upon him) who did the same thing at the same spot when Satan tried to tempt him to disobey God's command to sacrifice his son.

Then we went to the Haram, circled the Ka'bah seven times, and ran and walked between Safa and Marwah. It is difficult to describe the rush and the crowd. All four million pilgrims had to go through the same process on the same day. I got my hair trimmed—getting my head shaved would have been a preferred option. Women are required to clip only a little hair. That was also the end of *Ihram*, when I changed back into my normal dress.

We went back to Mina and stayed in our tents for two more days, during which we threw a specific number of pebbles on the two Satans again. And that was the end of our Hajj ritual. We returned to our hotel and packed our bags to go to Medina, the City of the Prophet, where he had settled after fleeing Mecca and spent the last ten years of his life teaching the religion, establishing a glorious society, and laying the foundation of an Islamic state. Visiting Medina is not part of the Hajj, but almost everyone going for Hajj visits it as a tribute of respect for the Prophet. Before departing, we went to the Haram and circled the Ka'bah seven times again, a practice called "farewell circling."

The Prophet's mosque in Medina, also called the "second Haram," is a huge structure, but smaller than the Haram in Mecca. At one end of the mosque is his grave. Next to his grave are the graves of his closest companions, Abu Bakr and Umar. Caliph Abu Bakr was elected the first ruler of the Muslims after the death of the Prophet. He died after less than three years of rule and then the second Caliph Umar, also known in history as Omer the Great, was elected to replace him. The three graves are enclosed in a room with screened windows on one side for visitors to see through. The graves are untouched over the centuries and they seem to be simple marks on the flat ground, originally the floor of the prophet's bedroom. He was buried in the same place he died. The area is under heavy guard and is opened at specific times for visitors to pass through a corridor and get a glance through the screened windows.

Mecca and Medina are modern cities, with Western-style high-rise buildings, hotels, shops, and shopping centers. We went to see several places outside of the cities that are historical sites where the Prophet went, stayed, conducted meetings, signed treaties, or had battles with attacking enemies. These sites are of great importance for Muslims, but they are unmarked, unprotected, and unpreserved. There are no guides and no signs. We had to struggle to coordinate the actual physical sites with what we had been reading about in books. The Saudi government, on the recommendation of religious scholars, does not want to preserve these sites, fearing that the Muslim masses, because of their immense love for the Prophet, will attach sentimental importance to such places and will mix them up with the actual sites that are part of the religious rituals.

OPINIONS OF AMERICAN POLITICS

During my various flights, I had to pass through the Dubai airport four times, with an average waiting period of eight hours each time. During this time, I met and talked to many people, particularly Muslims from European and Southeast Asian countries, and I became a self-declared journalist. Of course, I had also met and talked at length with dozens of people in India during my stay there. In Mecca and Medina, I saw and met Muslims of almost every nationality and ethnic group and talked to them at length. But I could hardly talk to Saudis. They are only in administrative and other high positions in the country, and are not very friendly to or communicative with foreigners. A foreigner cannot own property or a business in Saudi Arabia, and cannot become a citizen by naturalization. Foreigners can make agreements with Saudi businessmen to acquire a business, and can work there on wages, on commission, by contract, or in partnership, but I never saw a native Saudi present in any of the businesses. If I saw one elsewhere, I had to tell him that I was a university professor and lived in America before I would get a chance to exchange a few sentences. They seem to be very reserved people, although they regard Americans highly.

After having spoken with many dozen Muslims of so many different nationalities, I concluded that the overwhelming majority of Muslims thought that 9/11 was some sort of conspiracy, either purely American or involving the Israeli Mossad. They thought bin Laden had nothing to do with the event, that he knew about it only after it had taken place. Some thought that Bush had some idea about it beforehand. Even the highly educated suggested that it was a CIA conspiracy (involving al-Qaeda operatives) to make a big scene that included plane hijackings, but the operatives outsmarted the CIA and carried out their own plan of destruction. Almost all believed that the plane in Pennsylvania did not crash, that it was shot down by an F-16 fighter. Some suggested that the attack on the Pentagon was not by a plane, but rather was carried out by some sort of missile.

I was shocked to learn that many Middle Easterners knew much more about the U.S. Constitution and U.S. politics than I knew. I felt handicapped in discussing constitutional points with them.

Many said Bush was acting as though he were the greatest dictator on earth. He was doing things at will without regard for U.S. and international laws, the Constitution, or public or world opinion. They said, "It is very strange that with all these checks and balances in the U.S. system of democracy, and with Congress, the Senate, and the media, no one is able to stop him from this behavior." Some of them told me bizarre things: that Mr. Bush was a zealot Christian who was full of hate for Islam and Muslims and enjoyed seeing them killed. Or that he was behaving like a tribal leader who takes revenge on his enemies and punishes them collectively in any way possible. Or that he was getting enjoyment out of attacking Iraq to satisfy this feeling of revenge, which was also payback for his father's embarrassment at the hands of Saddam. Many people suggested that he would create another big conspiracy like 9/11 or an even bigger one to extend his office beyond his eight-year term, or that he might try to suspend elections due to the "war on terror."

They unequivocally ridiculed Bush and said that attacking, occupying, and bombing Iraq, killing thousands, and displacing millions of its people to establish democracy was a blatant lie that would not work even on children in their part of the world.

Some asked me if the present U.S. administration was going to transform the country into a state like the former Soviet Union. They suggested that Guantanamo Bay, Abu Ghraib, secret prisons, support for torture, and human rights violations were deliberately promoted by subordinates to please the highest levels of the administration. That this was happening in America was beyond belief to many of them.

I also heard their frustration about the lack of U.S. public outrage about the administration's policies. "Americans are good people," they commented. "They do not want their country to attack and occupy other countries, but they can never understand our pain and torture because America has no possibility of being occupied and its people being killed and their neighborhoods being bombed. They will understand us only if they imagine for a moment how they would feel if the Russians or Chinese attacked and occupied them and created a situation like Bush has created in Iraq."

Without exception, every Muslim talked about Palestine and the suffering of its people. They ridiculed Bush's talk about establishing democracy in the Middle East. "What is he doing to the Palestinians, who went through a fair democratic process of elections under the watch of the world?" they asked. "Now the Bush Administration is punishing them by imposing starvation on them." I heard these sentiments expressed frequently and loudly.

Most expressed hatred for terrorists and rejected their violence. They condemned suicide bombings and said it was evil for terrorists to kill innocents, including and especially their own people. But many made no secret of their belief that "had these few thousand kids not been fighting the American occupation, Americans would be roaming throughout Tehran and Damascus, kicking in doors and killing thousands of innocents there, just like they are doing in Baghdad."

Someone summed up the prevailing opinion in this phrase: "When Bush originally talked about the three axes of evil, what he meant was to attack and occupy the three countries, Iraq, Syria, and Iran, one after the other."

Several of them said that they wished and prayed that America would use its power and resources to establish justice in the world and help remove the suffering of the world's masses.

One mathematics professor took me for a Bush spokesperson and said to me angrily, "The world has seen Bush's proof of Iraqi WMD, uranium cakes, and the satellite pictures of WMD destruction sites. Have you seen the proof of Osama bin Laden's plan of 9/11? Why was Bush so much opposed to the 9/11 Commission?"

Several people asked me as a physicist to explain the "freefall" of the World Trade Center towers.

Frankly, I felt handicapped in trying to answer most of these and other questions.

One Lebanese teacher even asked me "about a mosque in New York that was raided and sealed by the FBI and whose two imams were arrested." I knew he meant Masjid As-Salam of Albany, but I did not tell him that I was from there. I only told him that no mosques had been sealed in America. One parking guard asked me if it were true that Muslims in

America were arrested only because of their long beards or long dresses. I was not sure how to respond. I knew that arrested or not, many have been targeted because of this.

When I told many of the pilgrims that there were plenty of non-Muslim Americans who were very upset with Bush's heavy-handed policies against Muslims, and that they were trying their utmost to support the rights of freedom and justice of American Muslims as envisioned in the U.S. Constitution, many of them expressed their happiness and appreciation toward them. But others looked at me skeptically, as if I were making this up.

IN DAMASCUS

Huma and I arrived in Damascus on January 15, 2006. It is an old city built on a mountainous site. Islamic and Roman civilizations met here in the early days of Islam, and it became one of the most important and advanced centers of learning for Muslims. Even today the city is filled with Islamic schools, institutions, and printing houses. There is no shortage of top religious scholars. People are extremely nice, well mannered, and religious. Wherever I went, I found the mosques filled with worshippers. In one mosque, I saw a gathering of more than 3,000 people where a famous local scholar was presenting his lecture. I was told it was a weekly routine.

Unfortunately, Syria is ruled by an anti-religious, nationalist dictatorship. People have the freedom to practice their religion only so far as it does not challenge dictatorial rule. Every citizen understands very well that even a slight suspicion of anti-government activity will lead to dire consequences for him or her. However, I have seen that many American Muslims are more afraid of the FBI than Syrian citizens are of their dictatorial government's agencies.

We stayed in Shazia's apartment that was very close to Abu Noor University, from which Aref had graduated. I prayed in its mosque many times during my stay. I became interested in locating the IMK (Islamic Movement of Kurdistan) office where Aref had worked for several months before coming to Albany. I wanted to take a picture of this place and talk to people there about Aref's past, but I did not have any clue as to where to look for it; I didn't even know if the IMK or its office was still in existence. It seemed that nobody had ever heard of it. I did not dig any deeper, thinking that if the IMK office was still in existence, and if Syrian intelligence had a clue that the FBI ever considered it a dangerous place, they might become interested in me. Syrians are tremendously scared of government informants; they think that every other person is an informant. I tend to think that the FBI used Malik after learning the tactics of the Syrians. But after seeing the role of the FBI and their informant in the Albany sting case, I think the Syrian government might like to hire Malik to train their informants!

I was also nervous because at that time Syrian and American relations were at a dangerously poor level. The Syrians were bracing for an American attack any day.

I could not enjoy my stay in Damascus. It was very cold, windy, and rainy for all five days that I stayed there. I spent three days looking for a two-family house to buy for Faisal and Shazia, who wanted to live in Damascus for a few more years to finish their studies. But there were no houses in Damascus, only apartments. I did not like most of them, and the ones I did like were very expensive—more expensive than in Albany. I dropped the idea of buying and decided to let them keep renting.

Huma was planning to stay in Damascus with Shazia for several weeks. Meanwhile, Faisal had decided to return to Damascus, and by coincidence his flight from JFK was the same day as my flight back. We must have passed each other in the air somewhere over the ocean or over Europe.

I found very good and cheap Arabic books in Damascus and bought about twenty of them without realizing that all together they were very heavy. At the Damascus airport they refused to allow any overweight luggage. They wanted to charge me $25 a pound for my extra twenty pounds of books. "No way," I said. So I overfilled my backpack and managed to fill two plastic bags with the rest of them. I knew that if they did not allow three carry-on items, I would be in trouble. But I took a chance. It was not easy for me to walk with those three bags.

COMING HOME

In the Middle East as well as in India, the only security measure was to pass through metal detectors. But I expected that there would be heavy security at Gatwick Airport in London. Every passenger was being interviewed; a passenger ahead of me was interviewed for a long time. I was prepared for an even longer one, but the interviewer looked at the data on the computer screen, did not notice anything against my name, and handed over my passport to his colleague very quickly. He asked me why I had gone to Damascus, and when I had packed my luggage, and then let me go ahead right away. It was a relief.

After awhile I entered a bathroom, placed my carry-on luggage on the floor in a corner, and started washing my face. After a few minutes, two security guards showed up in the bathroom. "Is this stuff yours?" one of them asked. "Yes," I replied, wiping my face. "No problem," he said, and both left in a hurry. I thought that either they must have seen my stuff via a secret camera, or someone might have reported it. I did not see any camera in the bathroom.

My Continental flight on January 19, 2006 from London to Newark was only half-full. As soon as the plane parked, an announcement was made: "Passengers should exit with their passports in their hands. Immigration authorities are already outside the plane." It sounded a little odd to me: Immigration has its own rows of desks and computers in one area of the airport, so why should they be outside the plane? But I did not pay much attention to the announcement, and just pulled out my passport and started walking along with the others. I saw two young Customs officers, one black and the other white, standing on both sides of the row of walking passengers taking passports, glancing at them, and quickly returning them.

I handed my passport to the black officer. He looked at it quickly and, holding it in his hand, started walking along with other passengers, without saying a word to me. I had no choice but to follow him. I guessed he was waiting for me and was taking me to an office for some sort of interview. A minute later I saw the white officer join his colleague. He took the passport from the black officer and told me, "You were selected for checking because your name came up for frequent travel overseas."

"That sounds funny," I told him. "This is my first trip overseas in eight years."

"Maybe it's someone with a similar name," he said.

It was apparent to me that he was making it up. I followed him. It was a very long walk, especially with my three heavy carry-on bags, and I was already exhausted from the trip. He got my passport stamped ahead of passengers waiting in very long lines. I noticed people staring at me, perhaps wondering why I was being accompanied by two officers. I was sure they did not consider me to be a VIP, even though I did not have to wait in long lines like they did. At the same time, perhaps they did not think I was a captured "terrorist," either, because I was cool, composed, and a normal-looking guy.

The Customs officers took me to the luggage collection area and told me to wait there until my two suitcases arrived. They wanted to check all my stuff. I waited, and they watched me from a distance. After awhile, I noticed an elderly lady close to me trying again and again to put her suitcase on a cart, with no success. I walked over to her and put the suitcase luggage on the cart. The two officers immediately rushed toward me, thinking that I was bypassing my luggage through that lady. But they did not say anything, realizing perhaps that it was not the case, and went back to their places.

My suitcases eventually arrived, and I wheeled them to the Customs clearance area with the two officers following me. By this time, all the other passengers had been cleared. About a dozen officers were gathered around a table, gossiping and laughing. The white officer told them that he wanted to search my luggage. Some of them smiled at him and they moved to a distant table. He asked me to put my suitcases on a table. I did so with great difficulty because the table was waist high and the suitcases were heavy. Then both officers started the search item by item, including my medication bottles, wallet, and carry-on bags. The white officer, while searching the items, kept asking me who I was, where I lived, what I did for a living, how many languages I knew, why and where I traveled, where I stayed, etc.

It had been almost two hours since my flight had arrived, and more than an hour since all passengers from the flight had gone. I was concerned that my friend who had come to pick me up might think that I had missed the flight and would decide to leave. I asked the officer again and again to permit me to just go to the arrival area to indicate to my friend that I had arrived. I told him, "You have my passport and my luggage, I cannot disappear. Let me walk there, or let someone walk with me. It wouldn't take more than two minutes." But each time I asked, he responded, "You have to wait, it won't take too long."

By observing their search, I figured out that they were looking for documents. I had none. I had been very careful when I packed my stuff. I had heard a story about a young Muslim who was held for several days because he had wrapped his shoes, before putting them in his suitcase, in a newspaper that was published by an organization critical of Bush. As the search was nearing its end, I noticed visible disappointment on their faces. Finally, the white officer said, "Everything's fine. I'm going to photocopy your passport and your Hajj itinerary. I'll be back soon and then you may leave." Both of them left together. The other officer had not spoken a single word to me since he met me.

But the officer was taking too long to return. I thought I would walk toward the exit hoping to see my friend and at least wave to him. A woman officer from a distant table immediately warned me not to leave. Finally the white officer came back, handed me my passport, and walked away without saying a word.

As I came out into the arrival area, I was happy to see Faisal's father-in-law, Azmat Sharif, who lived in Poughkeepsie, a town halfway down the Hudson River between Albany and New York City, still waiting for me. I felt relieved. He drove me to Albany. As soon as I saw my house, I smiled. "No place is better than home," I said. Finally I was home after more than two months of being tossed around the world.

Except for Faisal, I did not tell anyone about my airport "reception"—until now. I thought that anyone hearing about it would feel bad; a Muslim especially might feel even more scared. Had they found any paper in my luggage that they considered suspicious, I probably would not be home yet.

APPENDIX A

Sting Tapes, 2003

The following samples are taken from the government's transcripts, or from surveillance recordings from selected sections of the sting tapes.

AUGUST 7

Hossain meets Malik in his office at 892 Troy-Schenectady Road (Route 7) in Latham. This office has been set up by the FBI to convince Aref and Hossain that Malik is a genuine businessman who has a place of business. The surveillance video shows a room with a desk, three chairs, and a large empty rack. Coll has installed a camera inside a clock in the office and is monitoring the meeting from a disguised vehicle parked nearby. Malik can control the camera through a button in his desk. Malik and Hossain sit down across the desk, facing each other.

Malik offers to arrange a driver's permit for Hossain's brother and pushes Hossain to accept the offer. Hossain refuses and resists, explaining that his brother is mentally deficient and will never be able to drive. Malik tries to convince him to go for it because he (Malik) will be able to do it in five minutes while he is working at DMV. All Hossain's brother has to do is to accompany Malik there. Malik offers to pick him up from Hossain's pizzeria (and he does so a few days later). The permit will be valid for ten years, and hopefully someday the brother will be cured and will be able to drive. Malik shows Hossain a document with his picture on it as proof that he (Malik) works for DMV.

Then they talk about Hossain's pizza store, with Malik as a prospective buyer. They discuss various amounts of income and expenses for the store. Hossain tells him the final asking price is $75,000. Malik tells him he will look into the figures and get back to him later.

They pray the sunset prayer together in the office after laying a cloth sheet on the floor. Hossain is just about to leave when Malik asks Hossain to teach him some religious knowledge for five minutes or so. Hossain feels very excited and sits down on the chair once again.

"All this is happening against Muslims these days, why?" asks Malik, posing as an extremist.

"All this is happening to Muslims because they neglect the Sunnah, the teaching of the Prophet. From morning till evening, how many teaching of the Prophet do we follow? This is the reason why Muslims are taking the beating everywhere," explains Hossain.

Malik then asks about suicide bombing and about bin Laden. Hossain explains that the truth about bin Laden is not known—perhaps it is all propaganda about him, but according to the Qur'an, suicide is *haraam* (a sinful act totally forbidden).

M: What the Saudis did with the World Trade Center? In your opinion, was it good or bad?

H: This—of course, this was bad. This was bad. Do you understand that? It was bad because—I'll tell you. You are in possession of something good.

M: Right.

H: You want to sell this to me, understand? If you want to sell to me, how will you treat me?

M: Right.

H: You'll shake hands with me, visit, offer a cup of tea—because you'll be getting money from me, right? In other words, when you sell this thing, you want to profit. If we are true Muslims, and want to spread our Islam throughout the world, we can't frighten others like this. Now people say, "Look, it's a Muslim!" "Oh, this is a Muslim! He's very cruel—he'll kill us!" "Oh, watch out—it's a Muslim!" So before we even say what we wanted to, you'll run away. Understand? Just as if I came here and after greeting you, began abusing you. You'll say, "Man, what are you doing?" If I say, "It's prayer time, it's time for this or that," etcetera, you'll say, "Get out from here!" So, how will you sell your product? You'll have frightened me away. No! You should invite me politely, have me sit down, offer me some tea, and then say, "Look, I have this excellent product." Understand? We should have a good relationship with the unbelievers. Then, because of our goodness, Islam will spread, and continue spreading.

M: That's correct.

H: Now, I don't rightly know whether BIN LADEN did this or someone else did it, for whatever reason. God the Master knows this.

M: God IS the Master.

Hossain then does a lot of explaining to conclude that he does not know who was really responsible for 9/11.

M: But don't you think that has come bad name for the whole Muslim society?

Hossain becomes very emotional and stands up and starts shaking his body and hands.

H: Indeed, indeed. Certainly it did, it took me/him two hours to—USAMA BIN LADEN. I am a true citizen of this country, I am one of the best citizen in this country. I am teaching my children behave. I am a businessman, I am house owner, I have nothing to do with the anything else. And this is my country, other, why I'm doing all of these things? Am I right or wrong? I am paying tax. I am praying. I never harming anybody. People like me. Society get benefit.

(The government excluded the translation of the following discussion in its script; the reader may figure out why.)

About 9/11, Hossain mentions that he has heard that the White House had its knowledge beforehand, and that perhaps the hijackers who died in the plane were regular passengers traveling on a normal business trip. He gives several examples from the Prophet's life and emphasizes that Muslims should follow only his teachings. "It will be very much wrong to harm regular people," he says.

"What about Muslim world against Christian world, what do you…?" asks Malik.

"Muslims should not go against the Qur'an and Sunnah, Qur'an never allows somebody to kill themselves. Why Allah created you and then you suicide yourself? No," Hossain explains. "Yes you are allowed to go to war, like battle with the Romans. This is not a fight that you go and kill someone. This never happened. In the history of Islam there is no evidence that the Prophet and Sahaabaas [Prophet's companions] ever did thing like this."

"What about Palestine, whatever is going on…?" Malik asks.

"It is totally wrong, there is no right to suicide oneself. Why suicide? Why Allah made you? Suicide kills you," explains Hossain.

"Why they say they are martyrs, they will go to Paradise?" asks Malik.

"I don't know why they say so, according to the Qur'an if someone suicide, committed Haraam. If someone commits Haraam cannot enter Paradise. OK, I have to leave." Hossain starts heading toward the door.

"OK, I will take your brother," says Malik.

Hossain asks, "What is the fee for that?"

"Seventy-five dollars including everything," replies Malik.

"Insha-Allah, you will take him with you if I am not there," says Hossain.

They exit together and talk briefly outside. Malik returns inside and after closing the door calls Coll: "He is leaving, now."

AUGUST 13

Malik comes to Hossain's pizzeria to take Hossain's brother, Qayyum, to the DMV to get the driver's permit. Malik mentions to Hossain that normally he charges $500 for a service like this, but since Hossain is so truthful, sincere, and honest, he is going to charge him only $75. He collects various documents and drives Qayyum to the DMV. During the test, Malik communicates with him in Urdu (Qayyum's language is Bengali, which Malik does not speak). Qayyum knows very little Urdu, but is able to write down the multiple-choice answers provided by Malik. Malik brings him back to the pizzeria, with his learner's permit, about two hours later.

SEPTEMBER 30

Malik is sent to meet Hossain in his pizzeria. There have been several meetings between them since August 13, during which no information of any relevance is provided by the government. Malik tells Hossain that he (Malik) is not able to sleep due to his guilt over not doing anything good to deserve Paradise, and he is determined to do jihad to achieve that. He asks Hossain what jihad is.

Hossain explains, "Jihad is seeking knowledge, just like you have come to me to learn about the religion. Get up early in the morning while the sleep is overwhelming you, do brush, wash up and go to the morning prayer."

Malik insists that he is interested in the jihad of fighting, but Hossain emphasizes again that one has to carry out inner jihad first before thinking of a fighting jihad, like defending the boundaries of a Muslim country: "You cannot do that kind of jihad until you purify yourself and make yourself prepared. It is just like you cannot read a text until you learn the alphabet, or you cannot throw yourself in the ocean until you have learned swimming." Hossain gives a very lengthy description of the virtue of daily prayers and advises Malik to start from there.

"Infidels are killing Muslims left and right," says Malik. "I want to fight with them and teach them a lesson."

"Muslims are suffering because they are not following the religion, the teaching of the Prophet," explains Hossain. "Even if some Muslims are killed by infidels, while they are righteous Muslims, they will go to Paradise."

During this meeting, more than ten times Malik asks, declares, or claims to go to violent jihad to please Allah or to answer His call. Each time Hossain emphasizes, "You should do first things first. There are so many preliminaries that are required to please Allah. Allah will ask whether you were good, did right things, invited others to do good things, sir, there are too many evil things around here."

Malik leaves the meeting by making the statement, "Prayer will not open the gate of the Paradise, maybe it will help but will not open. Jihad will open it."

OCTOBER 20

Malik is sent to Hossain's pizzeria. He prays the afternoon prayer with Hossain and his children. Afterwards, Malik continues his earlier discussion about jihad and about seeking religious knowledge from Hossain. Hossain has to deliver pizza, so Malik goes with him to keep the discussion going.

M: If I do a sin in the name of Allah, is it still a sin?

H: To tell you the truth, a sin is a sin.

M: If I do a sin and earn some money in the name of Allah, is it still a sin?

H: Sure, but if you earn money like I am delivering pizza to take care of my father, my children, it is accepted by Allah.

M: What about committing jihad in the name of Allah?

H: You do jihad of your money, jihad of your self, our jihad is to live a righteous life and help guide so many Muslims to the right path, stop the wrong actions, to come to the prayer. This is jihad.

M: What about if money is earned through jihad in the name of Allah?

H: Jihad is for the sake of Allah, not for making money, just like you pray and fast. You don't make money that way.

M: Is it a sin to make money in the name of Allah?

H: You may buy and sell Islamic dress, koofi [Islamic hats], dates during the month of Ramadan. Maybe help build a masjid. I have to pick up a brother from the mosque who is to fix up the heating in one of the buildings and still I have to do one more delivery. That's my jihad.

M: [laughs loudly] You are my teacher you know. After a week or two, I will come and ask your opinion about making money through jihad in the name of Allah.

Anyone, after hearing these conversations, would conclude that a person like Hossain, who presents a passionate argument like this, cannot be a terrorist and cannot support terrorism. I would have thought that after hearing these conversations, the FBI would have dropped Hossain from further efforts to entrap him, but they did not—either because they were totally lacking any other targets, or because Malik gave them the wrong information, because the translation of the discussion was done several months later. In fact, Malik had a much bigger stake in continuing the sting than the FBI.

NOVEMBER 20

Hossain goes to Malik's office. I have not been able to figure out the background of this meeting—what was its purpose, when was it planned, etc. Most likely Malik had invited Hossain to discuss some sort of business venture in which Hossain could participate. The meeting is videotaped. The entire discussion is in English. This is the meeting in which Malik shows Hossain a shoulder-fired missile (a SAM)—the picture that was widely circulated in the media.

Malik hugs Hossain as soon as he enters the office. They sit down at the desk facing each other. Malik tells him that he imports his merchandise from China and he also imports weapons "such as this." Malik uncovers a SAM gun barrel that is on the floor covered with a tarp and puts it on his shoulder. He describes to Hossain that he supplies SAMs to some *mujahideen* in New York City and makes good money on it. Hossain seems to be in deep thought, emotionless but concerned. Malik invites Hossain to join him and participate in this business. Hossain shows no interest and rejects the offer, saying that the business is illegal. Malik laughs loudly and ridicules his statement.

M: …Did you like this business? So this is one of my other businesses.

H: Hmm. Good money could be made from this—

M: A lot.

H: —but it is not legal.

M: What is legal in this world? [laughs very loudly] What is legal in this world? What is legal? Huh? Tell me what is legal in the world? Huh?

Malik goes on to explain that by doing this business, he achieves two objectives at the same time: first, making good money, and second, helping his friends to fight non-Muslims. Hossain explains to him at great length that creating violence here or there is neither the solution nor the practice of the Prophet. A Muslim's mission should be to follow the practices of the Prophet. He explains the famous teaching of the Prophet: try to prevent the evil in society by force if possible, but if not possible then by verbal preaching and teaching of people, and if that is not possible then finally hate that evil in your heart. He advises Malik to stay away from the people he has been working with.

Malik insists that attacking non-Muslims and killing them are his way to please Allah and go to Paradise. Hossain becomes very angry and says, "You have your own ways but Allah will not allow you in a billion years to kill yourself or someone else. Establish the five daily prayers, that's the way to begin with." He says that he would begin with fighting with Muslims first because they are involved with a lot of evils. He recites two verses from the Qur'an and quotes them to support his argument that unless and until Muslims follow the practices of the Prophet, they will never succeed. "Allah has created every single human being in love, He has created non-Muslims and given extra blessings to Muslims. If the non-Muslims really know what Islam is all about, they will die and cry to accept Islam," Hossain says, very emotionally.

"But what is your mission?" asks Malik, interrupting him.

"My mission is I am going to take care of myself and my family, my brotherhood as well, like Allah's Messenger said. And that's how we will establish," answers Hossain. "You do your family, I do my family, and that's how the other follow. Muslims feel ashamed to follow the Prophet. See the Palestinian people fighting and dying. Look at them and their leaders, none of them are following the Prophet. How the victory will come?"

Then they talk about 9/11 and al-Qaeda. Malik pretends to be supporting al-Qaeda.

"I don't know if they are doing it or not, whoever doing this are not following the Prophet," comments Hossain.

After fifty-one minutes, Hossain is ready to leave. He and Malik hug each other. Hossain seems to be a little tense. "Think about what I said," says Hossain, heading toward the door.

"You think whatever I said," says Malik in response.

After Hossain exits, Malik closes the door, presses a button in his cellphone, which is hanging on his pants belt, and informs Coll, "He is leaving."

The FBI has provided a transcript that contains only the first one-third of the discussion in this meeting. Perhaps their mission was completed when the camera recorded the picture of Malik holding the SAM on his shoulder, with Hossain looking at it. Very few will bother to investigate what actually went on during the rest of this meeting. Any honest soul will feel sorry for a person who expressed his views as Hossain did, and who was subsequently entrapped and convicted for promoting terrorism.

After this meeting, it seems that the FBI concluded that Hossain would never become involved with any sort of terrorism activity—such as participating in Malik's weapons business, or transporting, storing, or doing anything with weapons—or with anything that was illegal. Therefore they decided to entrap him with a tricky and deceptive scheme. They focused on a plan in which Malik, as a supposedly super-rich Muslim businessman, would give Hossain a loan under very attractive terms and ask Hossain to repay the loan on an installment basis by means of checks. The tricky and deceptive conversations would help the FBI fill in the gaps and claim it was money-laundering activity to promote terrorism. But this could be achieved only by Malik developing a strong friendship with and trust in Hossain, and by Malik taking Hossain into his confidence.

NOVEMBER 26

Malik meets Hossain in one of Hossain's buildings where he is doing some repair work. After having talked about the repair work and the expected monthly rental income, etc., Hossain engages in discussion with Malik. The following conversation is all in English:

H: Whatever you said the other day, I thought about it and came to the conclusion that a good thing is a good thing and a bad thing is a bad thing, everyone should...

M: Everyone does in the name of Allah. I have earned so much money. The question is what I have done. I have done everything in the name of Allah. Everything you do is for yourself. You don't do for your neighbor, or for your father. I do for my own sake.

H: That's true, but because we are friends, I am saying that everything has its final stage and you cannot reach there without going through step by step. The final step is the step of the Prophet.

M: I have heard Prophet Moses said you never know what Allah likes from you.

H: That's true, but obligatory things are obligatory.

M: I was born as a Muslim child.

H: Look, the famous Islamic scholar Maudoodi said, "Anyone born in a Hindu family is a Hindu, anyone born in a Jewish family is a Jew, but anyone born in a Muslim family is not a Muslim unless he follows Allah and the Prophet and practices Islam." Believe me, Islam is practicing.

M: You talked about the other day that suiciding is not from the Qur'an, I understand that, but fighting a non-believer is not a sin.

H: It is.

M: Fighting a non-believer is a sin?

H: YES, it is.

M: How?

H: You cannot fight. If that's so, there was an old [Jewish] lady that used to make trouble to the Prophet day and night but they [the Prophet and his followers] did nothing.

M: OK, suppose a non-believer fights us, kills us, what should we do?

H: In order to protect yourself, you fight back. If someone slaps you, you slap back only as much as you are slapped. If you cannot do slapping, Islam says you forgive them.

Then Hossain's telephone rings. "Brother," he says to Malik, "I have a delivery to make." They laugh loudly and exit the building, but Malik pushes the conversation.

M: I know it is a long theory, but let us talk.

H: I know it's a long theory, but

M: When I wake up see so many killed, what should I do?

H: Nothing, you practice Islam.

M: When I wake up and see in the TV so many Muslims are killed, what should I do?

H: What will I do? By God, read the Qur'an with its meaning and all the teachings of the Prophet in my language, and practice according to it.

M: Are you practicing according to Islam?

H: Some cases not.

M: What will you do if you hear that a Muslim is killed?

H: Well, I have to identify myself.

M: How will you identify yourself?

H: I have to identify them also if such a person is killed, what was the cause. And then you cannot fight by yourself, one over here, one over there, and losing your strength. That's not so. In the [battle of] Badr, the Prophet called everyone under one umbrella. "Come under my command." Go and kill, no. All have to join.

M: How can we join?

At this point, Hossain loses his temper and becomes extremely angry and shouts at Malik. They argue back and forth. Hossain argues that a Muslim has to have patience and wait until a declaration to fight is made by a legitimate Islamic government, under the banner of the Prophet and according to the rules and regulations of the Qur'an. If the leader of such a country commands a person to go and fight against a country that is committing oppression, then you can go and fight alongside other Muslims. This will be an individual responsibility of the person. In that situation, the fight is under the watch of God and His blessings will accrue to that effort, with Allah watching the leadership.

"This is the thing," Hossain says. "I cannot do this individually, I will damage everything. You see some people were trying to establish an Islamic government in Afghanistan and doing good thing and then all of sudden the bomb exploded. They killed 2,800 people, and then United States retaliated by attacking with bombs killing 10–15,000 people and destroying everything."

M: Who was responsible for the killing of 2,800 people?

H: [becomes very angry and starts shouting] Responsible for that, ignorant people who do not have enough brain cells!

M: How can you justify killing of Afghani kids and Iraqi kids? I think the proper way has to come, until it comes we have to survive.

H: Practice Islam, follow Sunnah, wake up early morning for the prayer, read the Qur'an. Look at the history, twenty-three years I have been in this city and I see people same way, same dress. Allah is the creator of our heart, brain, and soul. If I am not mad enough to practice my creed according to my Prophet why…

M: How are we going to keep the war alive? How are we going to say that we are Muslim and we are fighting?

H: We don't fight. We have to practice Islam.

M: You will be killed. I will be killed.

H: That's OK. As long as I am practicing Islam according to the Prophet who said if you kill one person like you kill whole world, you save one person like you save whole earth. If you have a leadership, you follow. If you don't follow the Prophet…

M: Will you join my leadership? I have a lot of experience.

H: Oh! [laughs] I have my own experience. I have to teach my children according to the Qur'an and Sunnah, feed them, educate them, my children, my family and then prepare them to teach others the same way. I have to practice Islam as the Prophet did.

M: What are you teaching your kids?

H: I am teaching my kids to be one of the best, kind, and proper Muslims as they should be. Yesterday I fed non-Muslims in my house, lot of non-Muslims in my house. We talk with them, sit with them, eat, and they had a dinner. I talked with them.

M: When you wake up and open the newspaper to see 200 Muslims are killed in the Middle East—

H: I wouldn't care for them.

M: Then I have a problem with that.

H: All those people they are dying themselves. They look like Muslims, but I don't know if there is Islam, if they are Muslim or not. They don't practice Islam. They are finished. According to the scholar Maudoodi, if you don't practice Islam according to everything what is haraam [forbidden] as haraam and what is halaal [allowed, lawful] as halaal, if you don't do that you are not a Muslim. If these people are dying, who cares who they are? If somebody died practicing Islam, according to Islam, according to Sunnah…

M: What do you think about bin Laden? I think he is a good man.

H: I don't know who he is. I don't know he did or didn't. I have never seen him. Only God knows better.

M: I think he is a good man.

H: I don't know.

M: I think he is a good man.

H: Everybody is good until proven guilty. I didn't see any action any reaction. I don't know who is bin Laden. I haven't seen him. I didn't sit in his gathering, I couldn't talk to him. I don't know who he is. I have seen him in pictures, I know he has a beard, follows Sunnah looks like, but I don't know his attitude. Whether he was involved with all these things, I don't know.

M: We have to discuss.

H: A lot of talk, Brother. A lot of talk, by God.

Then someone else arrives and greets Hossain. He starts talking to him. Malik leaves, saying, "Insha-Allah, we will talk about."

DECEMBER 2

Malik is sent to meet Hossain in his pizzeria. Hossain reminds him about his (Hossain's) loan request for $2,000 or $3,000. Malik tells him that he has been thinking about it ever since he asked for it, and says that in the whole of Albany he trusts Hossain only, and he feels comfortable sharing secrets with him about the kind of work he is doing. "You showed me a way of truth. When I listen what you say, it makes me happy to be with you and it is my duty to you as my elder," says Malik.

"I love you," says Hossain. "I must have appeared to be a good man in your eyes, otherwise why would you share your secrets with me, but at the same time you should remember the old saying that 'walls have ears.'" Then Hossain scolds Malik for wearing a golden chain around his neck: "I have been advising you from the first time we met that gold jewelry is forbidden for Muslim men, but still you have that chain around your neck." Malik says it was a gift from his deceased mother. "She should not have given you

this in the first place," Hossain says. "…We are spending so much time together, perhaps your time is more valuable than mine. I am doing this only
hoping that you will follow Sunnah, do prayers, follow the teaching of the
Prophet. September 11 was very wrong, it was contrary to Sunnah."

Finally it seems that Hossain gets tired of this long talk, and says,
"OK, let us not talk useless things, I need the loan, for three or four
months, and the day you ask, I will return on that day, Insha-Allah." He
explains to Malik that according to the Prophet's teaching, he will need a
document prepared for the loan transactions between the two in front of
a witness. Hossain emphasizes that this is very important for him because
the Prophet had advised a Muslim to do so while arranging a loan agreement. Hossain insists that he is not prepared to compromise with the
Prophet's teaching in this case.

Malik asks Hossain to wait for three more days; after that Malik will
be able to come up with whatever money Hossain needs—ten or twenty
thousand dollars.

As Malik is about to leave, Hossain reminds him not to share these
discussions with anybody, telling him that it may circulate. "So many innocent Muslims have been arrested because of suspicions only, you know."

DECEMBER 3

The next day, Malik calls Hossain to tell him that he is coming to his
pizzeria to talk with him. Coll had coached Malik to propose a money-
laundering scheme to Hossain in a very subtle way. When Malik arrives,
it is time for the noon prayer. Hossain invites Malik to join him in the
prayer. They pray together, then start talking in their usual style.

M: I think you have to open with some person to take into confidence,
and in the whole world I found only you because I see you the way you
walk, the way you talk. You are the person, if I trust someone, it is you. A
human becomes a human through another human, not through an animal.
You and I will transform together, I alone cannot become anything.

H: Look, sir, Satan involves a human being in the affairs of greed.

M: I don't think you are a greedy man. I see your children, your wife,
I see in you the character of the Prophet. I will kill myself to become like
you. That's what it is. You have a simple way of living, if I do not trust
you, I cannot trust anyone in the world. Okay—ah— yesterday, you—you

asked me for some money, right? Five thousand rupees.

H: Whatever you can afford.

M: You know, I may—I may—I get some of the ammunition out of China, okay? That's what I do, okay? I make a lot of money, okay? I do it for—in the name of Allah and I do it in the name of Islam to satisfy my inner soul, therefore I do it. That's the only reason to satisfy my inner soul, and I make a lot of money. I—I—I was doing this because I get all these Chinese products from here, you know, all of it, to store owners, you know? It's all Chinese products, all from China, all Chinese—99-cent stores China—all Chinese products. You understand that, right? So, I make lot of money, and I have a lot of money, okay? I get a lot of money from other resources to do that. Now, what should I do with this money? What should I do with that money? Okay? And the only way I used to do it by—I used to go in Chinatown, give the money and buy the merchandise and use up my money. But now because China—have you read in the newspapers? They have been raiding Chinatown, I couldn't do. I'll give you fifty thousand dollars, okay? Fifty thousand, I'll give you. Five thousand you keep it to yourself. You don't have to give me back. That's my gift to you, okay?

H: [laughs]

M: Brother, what I'm saying to you is, you can—whatever you want to do with it, I don't even care. I will give it to you.

H: Please say everything openly [unintelligible].

M: You—fifty thousand rupees, right? I—I will give you fifty thousand, right? You do this—give me a check of $2,000 every month. Forty-five thousand—forty-five thousand dollars. Five thousand is yours, give me checks for $2,000. In two years, I'll get the money in the form of checks. What do you think?

H: It sounds very good, but you are making such a big sacrifice? You'll give me so much money and then afterwards—

M: Yes. Where are you going? Where can you go? [laughs] You're a brother like me, okay? You've earned through hard work. You're not going to run away from me! What's wrong with you? I trust you, buddy.

H: That's God's blessing. May God reward you.

M: I wanted to give you—to you—to you—I—I trust you so much that I talk to you openly.

H: No, no, no.

M: You're the only person in this world I can open up and talk to.

H: That's quite right—that's quite right. May God bless you with success in both worldly and religious matters. Still, I—I will wish you well.

M: I—look—listen to this: whatever I do, I do it.

H: Right.

M: You understand? Whatever you do, you do. Have I ever asked you what you do?

H: You know that very well.

M: No—[they laugh] Huh? I—I never ask you, "What do you do?"

H: No, you—you—this is your—

M: Whatever I do, I do. Whether I sin or do what is right, go to Paradise or to hell, that's my life. But I do this to please God. The person who does everything to please God pleases everyone. Methods are different. Your method is different, your method is different. That's why God created differences among human beings, because you have to live in different ways. If He had created all men the same, with the same face, the same habits—then—God's enjoyment of human beings would have ended. Then there would have been no need for prophets.

H: Whatever our dealings—whatever we do, will be documented accordingly. I never do anything contrary to the practice of the Prophet.

M: Me—look, listen to me. I will not charge any interest.

H: Right.

M: I won't take any interest. I won't take any interest from you, okay? I won't take any interest and I will do things according to the practice of the Prophet. Do you understand?

H: Yes, definitely, according to the practice of the Prophet.

M: I will do it as you want it done.

H: We'll draw up a document—

M: Yes, yes. Have a person as a witness—a person as a witness. We'll put up somebody a witness in there, and no document. I don't need any paper. Just a witness is good enough for me. Put up one person witness—that's good enough. No paper—I don't like paper. One who—one who—one who does not intend to return the money will not return it anyway, paper or no paper.

H: By God, it was the Prophet's practice.

They argue about the witness and document for awhile, and all of sudden Malik injects the following:

M: I have—we—I do—look—listen. All the missiles which come go for the jihadis, okay? They all go for jihadis, okay? What they want to do it, it's up to them—they don't tell me, okay? They don't—I don't want to know that. What's their program, I don't even know that. They come for jihad, okay? I'm doing it for jihad too. Making money is—it's—it's—it's a business too.

H: Sir, I actually—from my heart, I'm surprised that you opened yourself to me.

M: I think in this world you have to open to one person to take into confidence. I think in the whole world I have to take you in confidence because I have seen the way you talk and…[the recording dies at this point. Why?]

After the gap in the recording, the transcript begins again as follows:

H: I am telling you the truth. At the moment, I need five to ten thousand dollars—

M: Brother—

H: I can fix up that house.

M: You can do it, right?

H: Because after two to four months, I will have five or six thousand every month, insha-Allah.

M: It doesn't matter. So utilize this money, I don't care. Give me a check for $2,000 each month. I'll give you a receipt that I—you—I worked for you.

H: I'll give you the checks.

M: Yes, do that.

H: Or I can do that.

M: It's all right. Done, it's done. Right?

H: It's all right, insha-Allah. Even then, witness—we still need a witness.

M: Yes, we'll do that, we'll do it. We'll do it. So, how will you show where you got this fifty thousand, forty-five thousand dollars, fifty thousand rupees—where it came from, etcetera? How you gonna—uh—justify it IRS, etcetera?

H: IRS—I have lot of—I have lot of expenses.

Then they discuss the IRS, taxes, expenses, charitable donations, earnings. After another brief gap in the tape and the transcript, Hossain seems to sense some problem with Malik's offer of a large sum of money for the loan. The conversation starts again:

H: I'll meet with you, although I don't actually need this much. Do you understand what I'm saying?

M: God!

H: You—you think about it.

M: No, no I have thought. I—because I have the money, see. I have a lot—you can't imagine, see. God Has blessed me so much.

H: I—there's another—

M: You understand, right?

H: Another—

M: I don't want—I don't want my money to be taken by these wicked infidels.

H: That's right.

M: Why would I pay these people? Why? Why can't I pay poor people? Why can't I pay you? You need money. Why can't I pay anybody else? Why do I have to pay these taxes? What do you think? After—after September eleven, you—you can't even send—send money to Pakistan. They control you. So I have to justify somewhere, so why not justify it to you? I will—I'll give you a receipt. You give me—I'll give you a receipt for the services rendered. I do my work. I got my own company. Huh? You understand?

H: [unintelligible] Because I—I—I borrowed money from you and then—er—I don't—er—justify to—er—.

At this point Hossain seems to realize that all the talk about justifying the big money is about something other than a loan, because one does not have to justify anything about a loan. And Malik, realizing Hossain's confusion, does not let him complete his sentence and cuts him off:

M: You are a landlord, I am a trucker, you know.

H: We are like policeman of the world. People can attack and finish a policeman because they do not like him or do not like his religion or he looks ugly. We are policeman. Anyone can transgress upon us as much wants, but we cannot break the law because we are law enforcer.

M: Only law is Allah's law. That's the only law. [both laugh loudly]

Malik starts to leave.

"Please eat something before you go," says Hossain.

"I ate just now and I am a diabetic patient, you know," says Malik, and leaves quickly.

DECEMBER 5

Malik meets Hossain in his pizzeria. By this time, Malik has been coached by Coll to go for a bigger fish, Aref. His task is somehow to involve Aref in Hossain's loan deal. It seems that at this stage, the FBI concluded that they would be able to implicate Hossain in the loan trap anytime they wanted. Therefore they shifted their attention to Aref, in whom they had a much bigger interest. Later they claimed that Aref was their ultimate target.

According to their plan, they wanted Malik to get closer to Aref and develop a relationship of friendship and confidence with him in the same way he had done with Hossain, and then to engage him in talking. The FBI had already noted Aref's close friendship with Hossain and his trust in him. They knew Aref would be very willing to help Hossain in his loan arrangement with Malik. Therefore he would be willing to come closer to Malik without getting suspicious. The FBI's long-term plan was to use Malik to get Aref to talk (and talk and talk). By doing so, they had two purposes in mind: first, to probe Aref's past activities overseas, and second, to record any "useful" conversations to be used later for court or media purposes.

Hossain begins the meeting by giving some religious lessons to Malik. Hossain explains that on a Friday, a Muslim should take a shower, put on nice clothes, recite from specific chapters of the Qur'an, and prepare to go early to the mosque for the Friday prayer. Then Hossain talks about Special Agent Timothy Coll, and about the FBI's resourcefulness and their in-depth information about things. He mentions the FBI's interview with him about Ali Yaghi when they were investigating Yaghi in 2001, and their questions about the imam of the Albany mosque, Yassin Aref. Hossain and Malik express confidence in their mutual friendship and they promise to protect each other.

"In whole Albany, rather whole world, I only trust you," claims Malik. "I know you will never betray me." Hossain promises to protect and defend Malik as a Muslim brother deserves from another brother. "You love God in a different way, I love in another way. There are so many ways," says Malik.

"That's your idea, mine is different. I don't believe in your method, that's why I don't take that path," Hossain responds.

"Okay, what I do, I do. What you do, you do. You are responsible for what you do. I am responsible for what I do," Malik says.

As usual, once again Hossain emphasizes the peaceful path shown by the Prophet. He gives an example from the Prophet's life when he went to a town called Taif, some distance from Mecca, to invite its people to Islam. The evil residents there became very upset with his invitation. They were not willing to tolerate any message that wanted to take them away from their forefathers' religion of idol worship. They sent rowdy kids after the Prophet; the kids bombarded him with stones until he fell down, injured, his body, clothes, and shoes soaked with blood. But he never thought of revenge. He prayed to Allah to forgive them and change their ignorance into rightful guidance. The same people later accepted and defended Islam. "What we are doing today is simply due to our ignorance. We should invite non-Muslims the same way the Prophet did," explains Hossain. "If not, and we get involved in politics, we will get the beating as well as they will get the beating." He expresses frustration: "Our character is so low that even the devil will stay away from us."

"I came here to follow up our last discussion concerning the witness," says Malik. "I don't want any Pakistani or Bangladeshi or Indian to be the witness. If you know somebody else it is fine."

Hossain proposes the name of Imam Aref of the Albany mosque. Malik becomes very pleased and repeats, in appreciation, "wonderful" five times in a row. Hossain describes Aref to be "a very trustworthy Brother who speaks the truth, always keeps his word. He is not afraid of anything. He is only afraid of God."

With this discussion, it seems Malik succeeded very well in executing the FBI's plan to entrap Aref.

DECEMBER 9

Malik informs Hossain that he is going to receive a payment of $40,000 or $50,000 soon. More payments will follow, implying that he wants to hand over the promised loan money to Hossain fast.

Hossain again reiterates he does not need that much money. But Malik boasts, "From my side the money is there. I can't utilize it, nor can my daughter, nor my son. Any one of us cannot use it in any way, so who do I care? Do you understand? My business is such that if you are eating two pieces of bread, and even if someone gives you four pieces of bread, you will still eat only two. What will you do with the other two pieces of bread? What will you do with them? Either you will throw them out or you will ask some brother to eat. You will say, 'Big brother, sit and eat two pieces of bread with me.' Right or wrong?"

"You're right," Hossain replies.

Malik suggests that he, Yassin Aref, and Hossain all sit down together and discuss the loan arrangement. Hossain agrees to such a meeting for the next day at 12:15 pm.

Malik asks Hossain once again if the mosque is in need of some money. Hossain tells him that the mosque has sufficient money.

It appears that the FBI was interested in somehow getting the mosque involved in these transactions, or at least in a similar separate transaction. But since I was the one who was handling the mosque's finances, they were very cautious when moving in that direction. They were concerned that I should not be tricked into the scheme, or else I might destroy their whole plan. In one of the phone conversations, Malik suggested that Hossain might want to pass on some of the money to the mosque. But as soon as Hossain suggested that Malik should talk to me, the FBI cut the connection with a click.

In Verse 282 of the second chapter of the Qur'an ("The Cow"), the Almighty commands Muslims that when they transact a loan, they should write the contract and get it witnessed. The translation reads: "O you who believe! when you deal with each other in contracting a debt for a fixed time, then write it down; and let a scribe write it down between you with fairness; and the scribe should not refuse to write as Allah has taught him, so he should write; and let him who owes the debt dictate, and he should be careful of [his duty to] Allah, his Lord, and not diminish anything from it; but if he who owes the debt is unsound in understanding, or weak, or [if] he is not able to dictate himself, let his guardian dictate with fairness; and call in to witness from among your men two witnesses..."

Aref, being an honest gentleman and the imam of the mosque, had been doing this kind of loan witnessing among the community members on a regular basis. So when Hossain approached him in the mosque and told him that a very rich brother named Malik was willing to loan him some money so that he could fix his properties, Aref accepted Hossain's request to witness the loan. There is never any fee or commission involved in such witnessing.

The FBI knew that Aref and Hossain's mutual friendship and trust were very deep. They also knew that Aref would be willing to go to any trouble to help Hossain, particularly in witnessing or assisting the loan arrangement.

DECEMBER 10

At 12:20 p.m., Coll activates Malik's body recorder and sends him to talk to Aref and Hossain together. Malik calls Hossain and finds out that Aref has gone to Ravena (fifteen miles south of Albany), presumably for his part-time job of driving an ambulette to transport medical patients, and is expected back by 2 p.m. Malik calls Coll and informs him of this. Coll recalls Malik and sends him back again at 2 p.m. after resetting the recorder.

Aref, Abdulbarr Shuaib, Hossain, and Malik meet in Hossain's pizzeria. (Shuaib is a senior member of the mosque who was the third person arrested when Aref and Hossain were arrested on the night of August 5, 2004. Presumably he accompanied Aref from the mosque to participate in discussions about the loan arrangement. All three knew each other very well and were very good friends. This is the meeting about which the prosecutors questioned Shuaib in court after Aref and Hossain's arrests and during their indictment).

Malik introduces himself to Aref and tells him that because of his success in his business ventures, many call him Malik ul-Muluk (king of the kings) or, in short, Malik. Hossain explains that he needs a loan from Malik on the order of $5,000 to $10,000: "But because of his generosity, he offered me $50K and asked me to return him at the rate of $2K a month. It is good to talk about this in the presence of our imam and Brother Abdulbarr, whom I have known for some time."

Malik describes his business—importing merchandise from China and distributing to local merchants. He tells them that he makes a lot of money and wants to help the brother by giving a loan of $50K and asking back only $45K, in installments. He talks about a side business he also does—importing ammunition—and mentions that he is not sure if it violates American laws. He states that he cares about Allah's laws only.

Aref states that loans are not against American law: "I don't believe it is against the law."

Malik says, "Because I do not pay taxes, I do not keep in the bank, I do not show it in that, it's the money which I make it with my brother mujahideen and uh, that's how I, I do it, as Mosharref knows…" Malik keeps on talking about his gas station business and providing help to 500 to 600 immigrants with their official papers, mentioning the names of many individuals whom he has helped.

Since Malik states that he might be violating American laws and then mentions that he is not paying taxes, it seems that Aref might sense that Malik has some tax advantages by giving a large loan to Hossain.

Regarding the loan, Malik proposes to make a document so that in case he dies, the $2K per month that Hossain will pay back should go to his (Malik's) wife. Aref suggests making a document that may achieve three things: compliance with Sunnah, a record of the dates of the transactions, and a proof of the loan. He suggests making two copies, one for each party (or for each one's wife, as if it were a will), and placing it in a special box or at a special place to be taken care of in case of death of one of the two men. Also Aref suggests including a default policy, in case Hossain is not able to pay for some months. "Hossain is like my real brother, helping him is my jihad," proclaims Malik.

This is the usual way in which Muslims meet, discuss, and work out a loan arrangement. In no way does it give any indication that an arrangement of some sort of illegal money-laundering scheme is being worked out. Moreover, why would Hossain bring Abdulbarr to the meeting if in his mind something sinister would be discussed? Why would Malik discuss an illegal scheme in Abdulbarr's presence, anyway?

Malik asks about Abdulbarr—who introduces himself and tells Malik that he is from "here," meaning born and raised in America. Soon after that Abdulbarr leaves the meeting to pick up his son from school.

After the meeting, when Malik goes to his car, Coll calls him and asks about the "other person" at the meeting. "He is an African American," Malik says, and informs Coll that "[t]hey are traveling in Hossain's white van and turning left on the next light."

It seems that Coll is very concerned about Abdulbarr's presence at this meeting. This is not in their scheme, and may potentially even damage their plan.

DECEMBER 11

Malik is instructed to call Hossain on his cellphone. Special Agent Christopher Bean is monitoring the phone and asks Malik to proceed.

M: Assalamualaikum, Brother how are you?

H: Blessings of Allah.

M: I wanted to talk to you about something.

H: Sure.

M: The person who came with Yassin yesterday, who is this guy?

H: He is a Muslim since the last twenty, twenty-five years. He is quite trustworthy.

M: Can I trust him, he will not talk about here or there?

H: No, no. You can trust him. He is very humble brother. He is the best brother to me.

M: I was being troubled because of him, not knowing who he is.

H: No, no. He is such a brother that if there is something good, he will do, nothing wrong. Did you understand? I have known him since twenty, twenty-two years, OK.

M: But when I do something like that, I do not tell anybody. The kind of work I do, I hide everything. Brother Yassin, I can trust him, but I do not know who Abdul Jabbar was. [Apparently Malik confuses Abdulbarr's name with, perhaps, a very famous name]. I was troubled when I saw him.

H: His worship and devotion are very fine. He comes to the mosque every day. He fasts every alternate day. He is a good person. He is no nonsense just like we have among our Pakistanis or Bangladeshis or Indians.

M: Since I don't know him, I thought I will ask the brother who he is.

H: He is very fine individual. He lives on Benson Street. [Apparently Hossain is confused; Abdulbarr lives on a different street.]

M: I had to ask you another thing. I mean, I will give the money after the next week. The money is dispatched from there, but I was thinking this much money, you...

H: I have to fix the property. I will fix up the store, as well.

M: OK, you have to do fixing up, why don't you pass on some money to the mosque?

H: If the mosque needs, it could be passed on there. If there is no need in the mosque, there is no benefit to...

M: Is there no need of any kind in the mosque?

H: In our mosque there are already $35, $40K [this is an exaggeration on Hossain's part] surplus lying around. In order to invest in the mosque, in the council of our mosque, Mr. Shamshad is its president, I don't know…

All of sudden the call is disconnected with a click, apparently by Agent Bean. After a brief pause, Bean asks Malik to proceed again.

H: Hello, Assalamualaikum.

M: Yes brother I had lost you.

H: OK, are you in Albany or somewhere else?

M: No dear I am in Latham. When I get out of here, when I come with my truck tomorrow, I will sit down with you and we will talk.

H: No, no, he is a very fine brother.

M: Rest is OK with you? OK, will meet you next time.

H: OK, insha-Allah.

DECEMBER 31

On the instructions of Coll, Malik calls Hossain and asks to meet with him on January 2, 2004 at his office in Latham. He asks Hossain to bring his checkbook and to bring Aref along with him in order to witness the transaction.

Hossain seems to be very happy with the appointment. "Should I bring the other brother [he means Abdulbarr] too?" asks Hossain.

"No, I don't think so," replies Malik. "Just bring Yassin only. I trust him, he will not talk to anyone else. OK, see you then in my office at three o'clock."

It seems that Hossain interprets Malik's concern as fear of gossip in the community about who is giving a loan, to whom, and how much. He does not sense anything illegal in the arrangement.

Sting Tapes, 2004

January 2

At 3:07 p.m., Malik calls Hossain to check if he is coming (the meeting was arranged on December 31, 2003; Hossain will meet Malik at Malik's office in Latham). Coll is monitoring the call. Hossain confirms that he is coming with Aref, and they will arrive in fifteen or twenty minutes. Malik receives them in his office at 3:30 pm. Hossain and Aref sit down on plastic chairs across from Malik, Aref facing Malik and Hossain on Aref's right side, and start talking. The whole discussion is in English, the only common language between the three.

Hossain initiates the discussion by mentioning that Imam Aref's salary is very low compared with those of other area imams, whose salaries are about three times higher than Aref's. Malik mentions that the ICCD (Islamic Center of the Capital District) mosque has millions of dollars in its account. It has big donors like Dr. Bhatti, who donates about $100K every year. Hossain mentions that Dr. Chaudhry, when he was alive, used to donate a lot as well (Dr. Ashraf Chaudhry, who had passed away about ten years earlier, was a very active and generous member of the ICCD). They keep chatting on several other topics.

Malik pulls out, from the front pocket of his shirt, a wad of money in $100 bills and extends his hand to give it to Hossain, saying, "Okay, and the $45,000 will be coming like, I have to give them something, you know the instrument, and that will be coming like, in a, I would say probably couple of weeks from now..." Hossain asks him to give the money to Aref for counting, which Malik does.

Aref starts counting, keeping his eyes fixed on the bills, and continues to count. By the time he reaches the count of eighteen, Malik, while talking non-stop, pulls out from a shelf next to him a shoe-size black metallic object and—keeping it parallel to the table's surface—moves it toward Hossain. It appears that Malik is expecting Hossain to take this item in his hand and look at it while holding it. But Hossain is not interested in this item; he glances at it while Malik is moving it toward him but quickly removes his glance, indicating that he has no interest in it.

Malik continues to talk very fast, saying, "Then they will give me $45,000, $50,000, okay, this is the part of the missile that I showed you, so as soon as it come, I'll give you, this is $5,000, so next couple of weeks or less, I will get you more money." Simultaneously, Aref finishes the count of the money and gives it to Hossain, saying, "It is fifty." At about the same time, Malik places the metallic piece on the table at the far end from Aref. Aref does not look at this metallic item, or pay any attention to it, nor does he show any reaction or emotion, suggesting that he has neither seen the metal item nor heard anything about it because he has been too busy concentrating on counting the money. Malik uses the word "missile" in a suppressed tone and pronounces it "mee-zaael," as it is pronounced in Urdu. Aref, who does not know Urdu, might not have recognized this word even if he had been paying attention to Malik's chatter.

This was one of the trickiest games of the FBI's plot: to set Aref up for a photograph with the missile trigger handle. They knew all along that if Aref sensed anything beyond a simple loan between the two Muslim friends, he would walk away and destroy the whole plot. So the metallic item was to be photographed in his presence in a way that Aref would not be aware of it. Aref was not paying any attention to the metal item due to Malik's diverting fast talk about money, and because Aref was busy counting the cash. The metal item would later be declared in court to be a triggering device for a shoulder-fired missile, such as the one Malik had shown to Hossain seven weeks earlier in the same office.

The FBI made good propaganda of the photograph, declaring that "the informant had shown both of them (Hossain and Aref) weapons and talked with them about them."

After Hossain takes the money, it is time to record the transaction. Aref tells them that he does not know how to write in English, and therefore Hossain writes a receipt on a piece of paper. Aref signs it as a witness. When Aref is almost finished signing the paper, his eyes fixed on it, Malik picks up the metal item from the end of the table and puts it back on the shelf. Aref again fails to pay any attention to this process. Why doesn't Malik show this piece to Hossain when Aref is free from any distraction, so he can pay attention to it? Why doesn't Malik put it on the table in front of Aref, or somewhere closer to him?

Malik asks Hossain to give him two checks for $2K as agreed earlier. Hossain agrees to do this after he puts the money in the bank. But Malik asks for the checks now, even undated or post-dated. Hossain has not brought his checkbook with him, so Malik makes arrangements with Aref to pick the checks up from him (Aref) in the evening. (Malik had been instructed by Coll to collect two checks on the spot: one will be for the regular monthly payback, as agreed, but the other one will be interpreted as being part of the money-laundering scheme. This way, the FBI can presumably claim later that this transaction was money laundering, not a simple loan).

Hossain comments that it is good that the transaction has been done according to *Sunnah*. Malik responds by saying that he wants to do everything according to Islamic laws, he does not want to break any Islamic laws. Hossain calculates and totals the monthly rents that will come from his various properties, about $5-6K, and assures Malik he will repay him fast. Malik tells Hossain that there is no need to be in a rush. He says that he is very happy to give him his money that Allah blessed him with. He says that Hossain is going to put it to good use and will not use it in wasteful ways. Malik then instructs Hossain to write the checks in Hossain's business name, Hay's Distribution.

Aref asks Malik if it is necessary that Hossain pay off the loan by checks, and Malik answers, "The check, you know, just write the check, you know I don't have to call Brother Mosharref [Hossain] and Brother Mosharref really need the money, you know, I don't do it, I will never do that, you know. If he gives me check, it's fine with me, you know. Just write on this name, okay, okay, that's my business." Malik talks too fast and says too many things about the repayment and the checks, so that Hossain seems to be confused. Hossain asks again, "Two $2,000 every month so…" Malik cuts him off and says, "Two thousand dollars every, every thing, you know. This is a trial basis, you know. This is just a small trial basis, okay."

Malik takes Aref's telephone number in order to contact him later directly so he can collect the checks. He hugs both of them before leading them to the exit door. The meeting ends after about thirty-one minutes. Then, looking outside through a window, he calls Coll and informs him,

"They are leaving, just taking right turn."

By evening, the FBI was very concerned about not having a check from Hossain in their hands. Their plan was to claim that the cash was given with one hand and a check was taken by the other—which meant nothing but money laundering. They needed at least one, and possibly two, checks to claim a money-laundering case; in the absence of those check(s), it would appear to be a regular loan transaction. However, Aref was also puzzled as to why Malik was interested in receiving a check on the spot. Malik had shown every sign of trusting Hossain, and had claimed to be a very rich businessman—then why was Malik so impatient to collect a check so much in advance?

At 7:50 p.m. on the same evening, the FBI instructs Malik to call Aref and find out if Hossain has given him the check(s):

A: Yes, he gave me one check. I have a copy [of the transaction] for you.

M: Okay, he gave you one check or two checks?

A: One.

M: He was supposed to give you two checks.

A: No, I asked him. He said no, monthly one check.

M: But I told him ten, 20th, okay. Where are you Brother?

A: I, in home.

M: You want to meet me at Dunkin Donuts on Central Avenue?

A: Yeh, what time?

M: What about 8:15, 8:30?

A: Yes 8:30 is good, 8:35, which place?

M: You know Dunkin Donuts by Home Depot? [about two miles up Central Avenue from the mosque]

A: Top Quality, you said, no? [a store next to the mosque] Which shop you said?

M: Dunkin Donuts, coffee shop by the Home Depot on the Central Avenue.

A: Why don't you come to the Top Quality, beside the mosque?

M: Yeh, the Top Quality? [Malik hesitates, lingers with some inaudible words. He seems to wait for Coll to give him a signal]

A: Yeh.

M: I want to buy coffee. I want to buy coffee too for you.

A: May Allah reward you. Thank you very much. Night time coffee no...

M: I drink coffee. Night time is good for the health, you know. I want to meet you at Dunkin Donuts, coffee shop, on Central Avenue.

A: Then give me quarter to nine. I have left everything in the mosque…

M: No problem, I meet you then at 8:45, okay. Insha-Allah, Brother.

At the Dunkin Donuts, Aref expresses concern about loaning so much money to Hossain, as well as about asking for a second check. Malik keeps on talking, mixing up various things and not giving Aref a chance to get his concerns clarified. Malik emphasizes that Hossain has approached him for financial help, so he feels obligated to help him, but it also helps Malik to legalize his money, which comes from the black market, by showing it comes from some business activity. Aref seems to understand that by getting the repayment in business checks, Malik obtains some tax credit or some similar business benefit. Aref gives him the check for $2,000 (post-dated to January 10) and suggests to Malik that he get his next payment on the tenth of the next month, when the next monthly installment of $2,000 will be due. Malik agrees and ends the meeting, while praising Aref's car. He has already talked about Aref's car three times, at the beginning of the meeting. It seems that he wants to make sure it is Aref's car. Maybe the FBI had a plan to bug that car.

JANUARY 12

At 3:27 p.m., Malik calls Hossain to inform him that he is going to deposit the check he's received from Aref. He tells Hossain that he will meet him next time and pass on some more money to him. Hossain thanks him for the money.

It appears that after the completion of the exchange of money, the FBI's focus shifted totally from Hossain to Aref. The FBI had known from the beginning that Aref was a very intelligent man, and even a slight suspicion on his part of something unusual might derail the whole scheme. Therefore they wanted to proceed slowly and with a lot of caution. They had marked two clear weaknesses in Aref: religious zeal, and non-stop, open-ended talking with no boundaries and no reservations. So Malik has been instructed to take Aref into his confidence and to engage him in exhaustive discussions. Malik tries to approach Aref humbly, as an extremist Muslim with no knowledge of religion, who wants to learn about

Islam from a highly qualified and knowledgeable imam such as Aref. The FBI's aim is to record hours and hours of discussion between them so that something "useful" can be picked out of it.

JANUARY 14

Malik calls Aref and makes arrangements to pick him up at the mosque after the night prayer to have a discussion with him. After arriving at the mosque, Malik calls Coll to let him know that Aref is not picking up the phone, should he go inside? Coll instructs him not to. After awhile he calls Aref again, who invites him inside the mosque. Malik tells him that he wants to buy coffee and persuades Aref to ride with him. When Aref joins him in his car, Malik tells him that he has to keep his car warm, otherwise the battery will die and the car will not start again. They drive toward the Dunkin Donuts on Central Avenue. Malik tells Aref that he needs some spiritual advice from him, being his imam and the spiritual leader; he has developed a great confidence in Aref and appreciates and values Aref's concern for him, which he noticed from the earlier discussions; and he feels very comfortable with him and sincerely wants to learn about Islam from him. For the next hour and forty minutes, they remain engaged in discussion inside Malik's car, and it is Aref who is doing almost all of the talking.

Malik tells Aref that he picked up the check from Hossain and wanted to give him $50K, but Hossain asked him to discuss the matter with Aref. After talking for almost ten minutes non-stop, Aref suggests that the kind of arrangement for a loan and its repayment that Malik has made with Hossain should be abandoned, because Hossain is not comfortable with it and he does not want that much money. He suggests that Malik should give Hossain some money as a help, and leave it to him to return it according to his ability. He also suggests that if Malik is interested in exchanging some cash for a check from Hossain for business credit or tax purposes, they should be able to do so as friends and helpers of each other. "I believe this is part of our faith to help each other," Aref says. "And I believe you take the reward, even if you loan them, the people the money." Aref talks in detail about the virtues of giving loans to needy people.

With reference to Malik deriving tax benefit or business credit from his loan to Hossain, Aref says, "…maybe that way it is helping you a little bit for your business, too, to, like you say, legally [legalize] your money or anything. That's Alhamdulillah [praise and thanks to Allah] if you have some benefit and he have some benefit, and Alhamdulillah, that's the duniya [worldly, materialistic matter], as they should."

Aref also advises Malik to be truthful and honest, because the Prophet was well known among his people for being truthful and honest. "So this is part of our faith, is part of our religion, is part of our personality," Aref explains. "We are Muslim and we should to try all of our life to have these two quality and character for ourself."

All of sudden Malik jumps to an irrelevant topic: he asks Aref about his opinion of, and advice for him to help, a group called Jaish-e-Mohammed (JEM) that has been fighting India for the independence of Kashmir. Talking about the current leader of JEM, Malik says: "He is in Pakistan right now, and he is trying to liberate Kashmir from India. And, uh, he has been fighting the Holy War for almost now, so many years and we are trying to help them in that war. And this President Musharref, the president of Pakistan is, uh, is against him and, uh, against the Holy War because he is helping the mushrik [polytheists], uh, and, uh, we are fighting him, too. Uh, that's why, the missile, that we sent it to New York City to teach Mu, uh, President Musharref, the lesson to not to fight with us. And I don't know how, how I do look at in Allah's way. What do you think about that? I mean, I want to make my mind clear with God about JEM."

The FBI had coached Malik to say something like this to Aref so they could claim later that "Malik had discussed the missile with Aref," and also that Aref understood that "Malik [was] supplying shoulder-fired missile(s), which he imported from China, to JEM in New York City, to shoot down an airplane in which the Pakistani ambassador to the United Nations was traveling." The fact of the matter is that only the FBI could have understood it that way; anyone hearing Malik's statements for the first time would have understood nothing. Aref only understood that Malik wanted to know Aref's religious opinion about Malik helping JEM in Kashmir.

Aref replies: "Look Brother, especial, I am not talking about that group and that organization, especially, because what I know I hear the couple times from the TV, which is they are the group they call Jaish-e-Mohammed in the Kashmir."

Then, in a lengthy, non-stop lecture of about twenty minutes, Aref tells Malik that he may help them if they are religious people fighting for Allah and fighting for their independence, just like Palestinian and Kurdish people are fighting for their statehood. He advises Malik to help the needy, women, children, orphans, and refugees among them. He emphasizes that his advice is general. Aref mentions to Malik that JEM is classified as a terrorist organization by the U.S.; therefore he should be careful not to be targeted as a suspected terrorist because of providing help in Kashmir. He states: "But with that, with that you should be very, very careful about this point. I don't say don't help, and I don't say stop your help. I say it is Allah, was duty for every Muslim anywhere he can help any Muslim, especially they are needy for help, especially in their situation like Palestine and Kashmir it is danger."

Elaborating further, Aref explains to Malik that a Muslim is required to help others, and this help must be based on the right intention and on the guidance provided by the Prophet. He also advises Malik to be very careful if he decides to help, because the atmosphere in the country after 9/11 has changed tremendously, and anyone sending money overseas, even if it is a charity for the needy and destitute, becomes a suspect in supporting terrorism, and many times donors are punished unnecessarily based on mere suspicion. "Many Muslim businessmen and religious people have been victimized this way and Muslims have stopped sending their charities overseas due to this reason," Aref explains.

As noted earlier in this book, an interesting point in the FBI's transcript is also worth noting here. The FBI claims that Aref supported terrorists because he advised Malik to help them. According to the FBI, Aref told Malik to help JEM by saying, "I believe it is *wise* for you to help if you can." But the actual wording on the tape is, "I believe it is *wajib* for you to help if you can." *Wajib* (pronounced w-aa-jib) is an Islamic term that means "a religious requirement a Muslim must perform." So by this statement, Aref gives a religious, scholarly opinion as an imam that for a Muslim, it is required (*wajib*) to help the needy, women, children, orphans, and refugees among Muslims.

Then Aref talks about the history of the Muslim world, colonialism, the policies of the West toward Muslim countries, present-day developments and politics, dictatorship, non-Islamic trends, violence, infighting in Muslim societies, etc., non-stop for the next half-hour. At one point, as Aref keeps on talking, Malik all of sudden tries to inject, "I send the missile to…" into the conversation, but Aref keeps on talking without paying any attention to this incomplete sentence. Malik attempts to inject the same question many times regarding the propriety of him helping JEM, and Aref repeats the same answers and keeps on talking.

"What does—what do you say about the—suicidal bomber in Palestine?" asks Malik.

Aref explains that killing oneself is totally forbidden in Islam. Allah has given someone a life to do something good with it, rather than destroy it in a suicide. He elaborates on this point for the next fifteen minutes. Malik also asks such questions as, "Which law is important—American or Islamic?" and "How should we teach a lesson to non-Muslims?" Aref tells him to follow the teachings of the Prophet, and explains and repeats the same things he has already been talking about. Aref says that when immigrating Muslims come to this country, they promise to obey American laws, and emphasizes several times how important it is for Muslims to keep their promises.

After roughly one and a half hours of discussion, Malik receives a call, apparently from Coll, who instructs him to ask something else.

"Wasn't bin Laden a leader?" Malik asks suddenly.

"For some people," answers Aref. "How many people? In Saudi Arabia there are fourteen million people. Out of them, how many followed bin Laden? 400. A Muslim leader is the one whom every Muslim follows." Aref continues to talk, but Malik seems to have heard enough, and interrupts, "I have learnt a great deal from you, you are very learned man. You are a true spiritual leader."

But Aref continues to make his "final point," which lasts for another ten minutes. Malik finally drops him off saying, "Someday I will come and sit down with you again."

Then he calls Coll and says, "He is gone. You should have given me some Tylenol, I have headache now."

JANUARY 20

At 3:30 p.m., Malik calls Hossain and asks him to come to his office, along with Aref, at 7:30 p.m. the next evening.

JANUARY 21

Aref, Hossain, and Hossain's ten-year-old son Abu Hamzah go to Malik's office in Latham. Hossain explains to Malik that he was doing pizza delivery and his son was with him, and that's why Abu Hamzah is here. Hossain proposes to discuss with Malik some internal politics that have developed among different ethnic groups at the ICCD and the An Nur Islamic school (Hossain's and Aref's children attend the An Nur school).

They discuss this topic for a long time. I am not able to figure out why Hossain introduced this topic, and the discussion appeared to conclude without any point or resolution being arrived at.

Then Malik hands over $10,000 to Hossain. Aref counts it twice and confirms that it is $10,000.

Malik informs Hossain that he has cashed his prior check without any problem. Hossain tells Malik that his properties are being rented and he will be able to repay more money on top of the agreed-upon $2K per month. Malik tells Hossain again that he will give him $50K, that he can keep $5K, and that he will not have to repay it, but the remaining $45,000 will have to be paid back with checks.

Hossain writes a receipt for the cash: "I, Mosharref Hossain, received $10,000 from Shahed Hussain." Aref signs it as a witness.

It seems Aref and Hossain are preparing to leave. All of sudden, Malik, posing as a radical Muslim, begins with his previous style of questioning. "Tell me one thing Brother, like Saddam, Yassir Arafat and [General] Musharraf say, 'Follow us first, Islam later.' What do you say about it?" Malik directs this question to Aref.

Aref explains, giving lengthy explanations (as usual) and examples of how a Muslim should follow the Prophet. Malik asks again and again, implying that he wants to punish these people and non-believers by staging violent acts against them, but Aref emphasizes that they should be left alone and that Muslims should work together to follow the example of the Prophet, acquire collective strength, and then try to solve problems. Malik tries to engage Aref in further discussion, but Aref stands up abruptly, laughingly looks around the table, and says, "I hope there is no recorder around here, you looking danger." [meaning dangerous]

Aref used to say similar things in the mosque, too, when one of his friends would comment against the government in a tough manner. Muslims very often gossip among themselves, using heavy criticism against the government, and then laughingly say, "Let us hope no one is recording." But here, ten-year-old Abu Hamzah Hossain, who is present at the meeting, really does search for a recording device everywhere, concentrating on Malik's desk, moving from one end of the desk to the other at a snail's pace, carefully inspecting it. Malik becomes alarmed and asks him to sit down quietly on a chair.

Hossain gives Malik a check for $2,000 post-dated to February 1. But Malik asks for another check, too, and Hossain seems to be confused as to why. Malik talks quickly to trick Hossain into giving him another check, but ultimately Malik has to be satisfied with the one post-dated check. He then expresses his concern about Abdulbarr, who had attended the first meeting between the three men. "Is he trustworthy? Will he talk to other people about this money going in?" asks Malik. "He don't know, he don't know anything," says Hossain. "He was just in the first meeting," comments Aref.

Once they leave, Malik calls Coll. "They are leaving...hold on, turning right toward Latham, okay."

After a few minutes, Coll comes in with another agent. He asks Malik, "How did it go?" "He is very intelligent," replies Malik. "At one point he said 'I hope there is not a recorder on.'" "Did he say that?" says Coll. "I like that." Coll pulls out the videotape, puts a label on it, packs it in a small cardboard box, and carries it out. The other agent follows him.

JANUARY 26

Malik goes to Hossain's pizzeria. Hossain discusses with Malik immigration problems for his mother-in-law and her children. Then they express their innermost trust and confidence in each other. Malik boasts of making many hundreds of thousands of dollars in the past and that he is looking forward to making business deals to earn big money. Hossain expresses his concern about the displeasure of Almighty God if the business is not *halaal* (permitted, lawful). Malik claims that he is earning money by doing business—by supplying merchandise and getting money for that. "Why should there be Allah's displeasure? Prophet had done the business too?"

JANUARY 28

Malik calls Aref to arrange to pick up the receipt of the transaction on January 21. Aref makes an appointment to give it to him the next evening.

JANUARY 29

Malik calls Aref in the morning and leaves a recorded message for him. He calls a second time and says he will pick up the receipt from Aref around noon in front of the mosque. Aref makes a photocopy of the receipt in a store three buildings down from the mosque. Malik is instructed by Coll to remain in his car. Aref gives him the original and walks to the mosque with the copy.

FEBRUARY 2

Hossain calls Malik to invite him, his wife, and his children to Hossain's house to celebrate Eid-al-Adha. (Muslims celebrate two Eids: the first, called Eid-al-Fitr, celebrates the end of the month of Ramadan, the month of fasting, during which adult Muslims fast from dawn to dusk. The second, Eid-al-Adha, is two months and ten days after the first one and commemorates the historical sacrifice by Prophet Abraham of his son.)

Malik calls Hossain in the afternoon, accepts his invitation, and talks about the checks. Hossain tells him that he has already deposited the money into the bank and Malik should cash the check. Hossain also tells him that the last check was cashed, but the bank did not send him the cancelled check along with the monthly statement. Malik says that he has no idea why the bank did not send the cancelled check along with the statement.

FEBRUARY 3

Malik meets Hossain at his 329 Clinton Avenue property, where Hossain has been doing some repair work. Malik says that he has come in person to offer his excuse for not being able to come to Hossain's house this evening to celebrate Eid. After some discussion, and expressing a lot of praise for Hossain's repair work, Malik offers to give him $10,000 next week. Hossain says that he feels embarrassed to take Aref to Malik's office to witness the loan. Malik repeats three times, "I will come to you, buddy." Then he asks, "In your opinion, how many times can you give me the check, once in a month, twice, three times?"

Hossain replies, "Two or three times, because I have expenses. I have lots of expenses for my pizza shop."

Malik says, "I will give you $10,000 next week. So, one thing can be done, why don't you get me a cashier's check in the amount of $6K, $5K, $6K?"

"I will make cashier's check," says Hossain.

They agree to meet in the evening on Wednesday, February 11, when Malik will give him $10,000 so that Hossain can deposit it in the bank on the following morning and give Malik a check for $5K in return. "Everything is supposed to be according to the Prophet's practice," says Hossain. "By God, when you divert even a little from the practice of the Prophet, there will be problems."

Then Malik proposes to Hossain a code word, "chaudhry," to be used for the "missiles and stuff." They talk about Pakistan and its politics. Malik uses hateful and dirty words for General Musharref and his policies, and claims that in order to take revenge on him, Malik's associates are going to shoot down the Pakistani ambassador's airplane in New York City the following week. Malik asks Hossain if he has heard of a group called Jaish-e-Mohammad (JEM). Hossain says he is not familiar with JEM, and speculates that it might be a musical group. Malik describes JEM as a militant group that has been fighting for the independence of Kashmir from India. Malik claims that his association with JEM is a secret, known only to Aref and Hossain. Hossain says he wonders how Aref knows about it. Malik tells him, "No, he knows. I have talked to him."

"You have talked to him?" asks Hossain, very surprised.

"Yes. He knows," says Malik. Then Malik offers a lot of praise for Hossain's character, truthfulness and trustworthiness. He claims to have gained a lot of knowledge from him. Then he condemns General Musharraf and talks about politics and violent jihad.

After leaving Hossain, Malik calls Coll (or another agent) and suggests that he meet the agent at the OTB (Off-Track Betting) building rather than at Home Depot, because he suspects that Hossain might be going there for some purchases.

FEBRUARY 11

At 5:30 p.m., Malik calls Hossain and makes an appointment to see him and Aref at Hossain's pizzeria the next day at 6:30 p.m. to give him some more money.

FEBRUARY 12

Malik meets Hossain at the pizzeria. Aref does not come because he has a guest at his house, but offers to let them come to his house for the meeting. Malik asks Hossain to bring his checkbook along, and the two drive separately to Aref's house. Another FBI agent follows them secretly and remains in his car, parked near Aref's house, while Malik and Hossain go inside and complete the transaction in the presence of the guest, Kassim Shaar, an Iraqi friend of Aref's.

Suddenly, out of the blue, Malik tells Aref—in front of Shaar—that he should not go to New York City next week because there will be an attack of some sort. Nobody knows what to say in response to this odd statement, and it passes without further comment. The discussion inside Aref's house is not recorded, and so it is not clear exactly what Malik said. Malik later tells the FBI that his body recorder fell off inside his car and he went inside the house without the device on him.

FEBRUARY 13

Hossain gives Malik a check for $6,000. They start arguing about the last transaction that took place in Aref's house in front of Kassim Shaar. Malik says he thinks it was unwise to do the transaction there because Shaar must have become curious to know about Malik and the loan. Malik says that if Hossain wanted $100,000 in the middle of the night, he would come and give to him, but he does not like the idea of other people knowing about it because he is doing something illegal and wants it to be kept secret.

Hossain assures him that it will not happen again, and mentions that Malik's statement of the night before, warning people "not to go to New York City the following week," was very dangerous. Statements like that could be heard by law enforcement agencies, Hossain says, and then they would start suspecting the imam. Hossain mentions that the FBI has come to Aref's house five times already, and that they have come twice to his own house, and he has had to go to their office twice to answer questions.

Malik assures Hossain, "It is between me and you. There is no involvement of FBI or CIA in this case." Malik says, "This dealing will go no matter what, it won't stop. When I have given you $50,000, keep $5,000 as yours."

Hossain tells him that he will send that $5,000 as a charity donation to a religious school for children in Bangladesh that has been opened by Jamaat-e-Islami, a famous religious organization. "I have told Brother Yassin, too." Hossain says that he belongs to the Jamaat-e-Islami of Maudoodi. (Maudoodi, who died in 1980, is one of the most famous religious scholars of the Indian subcontinent. Jamaat-e-Islami is the most popular Islamic organization or group in Pakistan, India, and Bangladesh. It is a political party as well in Pakistan and Bangladesh, contesting national elections and having elected members in the regional and national parliaments).

The transcript provided by the government of the above discussion contains only two-thirds of the actual contents of the tape. Many statements are simply dropped. The translation is also very troubling: "transaction of money," for example, is translated as "money laundering."

FEBRUARY 19

Malik calls Aref and makes an appointment to pick up the receipt of the transaction of February 13. Around 4 p.m., Malik drives to the mosque. It appears that Coll is nearby, communicating with Malik. Malik calls Aref, who is at Central Avenue and North Allen Street, about a mile from the mosque. Malik drives there, and Aref gives him the receipt.

FEBRUARY 24

In the afternoon, Malik calls Aref's number six times before he makes contact with him. He asks Aref if he would be willing to perform a *Nikaah* (wedding) for one of Malik's relatives. Aref agrees, provided the couple can obtain marriage papers from the city authorities. Malik wants to meet Aref to discuss things, but Aref tells him that he is too busy that day.

(In New York State, a marriage license is issued only by the city government. Religious institutions solemnize the marriage. Normally a Muslim couple gets the license from the city and then goes to a mosque or an Islamic center to have the marriage solemnized, which Muslims commonly refer to as a *Nikaah* ceremony, or Islamic marriage. It is conducted according to Islamic laws. In Islam, marriage—also referred to as the "marriage contract"—is a contract between the wife and the husband. Islamic laws of marriage are very simple. The bride, with the consent of her guardian, presents herself (or her guardian presents the bride with her consent) to the groom for marriage in front of two witnesses, and the groom declares that he is ready to accept her in marriage. The groom must offer his bride a mutually agreed-upon "marriage gift." The marriage has to be public; it cannot be a secret wedding.)

FEBRUARY 25

At 5:55 p.m., Malik calls Hossain and tells him that he is doing a delivery in Albany and would like to sit down with him in his pizzeria and have a cup of tea with him. Hossain agrees gladly. Malik informs Hossain that the attack on the Pakistani ambassador's plane did not take place because he (the ambassador) did not show up. He tells Hossain that he has to transport a missile to Kingston (a town forty miles south of Albany). This will bring him $10,000, which he is willing to split with Hossain if he can help him or can arrange for someone to help him, since the missile requires two people to transport it. Hossain refuses to be part of it.

Malik asks Hossain why he does not hire Aref to work for him in his pizzeria. Hossain informs him that Aref used to work for him, but after 9/11 he was attacked, and since then Aref has refused to work in a pizza place.

Then they talk about Jamaat-e-Islami (JEI), its branches, and its local and overseas members. Malik informs him about two other Muslims in the area whom he knows to be members of the JEI of Pakistan. Then they talk about Presidents Bush and Clinton—Malik branding Bush as a "bastard" and Clinton as a good president. Malik states that bin Laden is a good man and a true *mujahid*. Hossain states that he believes that bin Laden did not do the 9/11 event.

When Malik starts to leave, he asks Hossain to find two or three people who can help him transport the missile to Kingston. Hossain laughs loudly, turns around, and walks away to attend to some business.

The government has provided two transcripts of this meeting. One has only one-third of the contents of the second. The shorter one is full of serious errors. Many statements are mistakenly associated with wrong speakers. For example, a statement is made by Malik, but the script says it is said by Hossain. The longer one has also dropped many sentences and phrases that are present on the tape.

MARCH 1

Malik calls Aref and makes an appointment to pick him up in front of the mosque the next day around 4 p.m. after the afternoon prayer. Malik says that he is eager to sit down with Aref and learn some more about Islam.

MARCH 2

Malik arrives at the mosque late; Aref has gone back to his house. Malik informs Coll, who asks him to go to Aref's house, which Malik does. Malik sits down with Aref and has a long discussion regarding his transactions with Hossain and what happened a few weeks ago in the presence of Kassim Shaar.

Aref then talks to him for a long time about various aspects of Islam and the situation of Muslims all around the world. He mentions that these days, there are a lot of suspicions about Muslims, and they should be careful not to give law enforcement authorities a chance to victimize them based on suspicions, or a chance to give them a hard time. Aref says that he suspects that he, the mosque, and the members of the mosque are under surveillance, but he is not worried because nothing wrong is going on around there. Muslims should follow their faith and stay strong.

Malik praises Aref a great deal, saying that he is a truly knowledgeable and caring imam, that he has the greatest respect for him, and that he would like someday to sit with him again to learn more from him.

MARCH 22

At 11 a.m., Malik calls Hossain to get Abdulbarr's telephone number. Hossain tells him that he does not have the number but will be able to get it when he sees Abdulbarr in the mosque later. Malik also informs Hossain that he has opened a store at 142 Central Avenue (just one long block up from Hossain's pizzeria, and a block down from the mosque).

The new store was a fake wholesale store set up by the FBI to make Malik's business activities look realistic and to help trick Hossain and Aref into becoming further involved in the plot from this location without any suspicion. Being close to the mosque, Malik could meet Aref more easily and videotape him more frequently. The FBI did not want Malik to meet Aref in the mosque, out of fear that exposing Malik to other members of the mosque might cause them to suspect him.

At 4:50 p.m., Malik calls Hossain again and gets Abdulbarr's home telephone number from him. Hossain assures Malik that he has known Abdulbarr for the past fifteen years and that he is a very nice guy, not a "chaudhry" kind of person. Both laugh loudly at the use of the code word. This code was introduced earlier by Malik to refer to a missile. What Hossain perhaps meant here was that Abdulbarr posed no danger with regard to exposing their money dealings to anyone.

MARCH 31

In the evening, in his new "store," Malik greets Aref, Hossain, Hossain's six-year-old son, and Mohammad Gobial (a student friend of Aref's who came with him), apparently to bless the opening of his store at its new location. (Traditionally, when Muslims open a new business they invite their friends and some religious people to have a little ceremony and a prayer to bless the business).

They all chat about business, Middle Eastern politics, religion, the nuclear programs of Israel, India, and Pakistan, etc. Aref advises Malik to replace the animated pictures on the walls with pictures of natural scenery. He tells him that the angels of blessing do not enter a place where pictures of animated creatures are displayed. Then he advises him to put his trust in Allah for the business, only engage in trade that is *halaal* (permitted, lawful), and to avoid anything that is *haraam* (prohibited). Then he offers a prayer: "May Allah bless you, your family, and your business." Others say, "Aameen" (amen). How could Aref have known that this person, whose fake business set up by the FBI that he was blessing as an imam, was soon going to ruin his life and destroy his family?

Malik states that now that his location is very close to Aref's and Hossain's, he will be able to interact with them easily and more frequently. Aref and Hossain suggest that since he is very close to the mosque, he should join them in daily prayers in the mosque without any excuse.

At the end of the visit, Hossain gives Malik a check for $2,000. They discuss the money transactions that have taken place so far: $25,000 paid in total by Malik; $6,000 paid back by Hossain by cashier's check, plus four checks for $2,000 each month, making a total of $14,000. Thus there is a balance of $11,000 to be paid.

After everybody leaves, Malik calls Coll, who gives him further instructions.

APRIL 14

Malik calls Hossain and asks him to come to his new store with Aref the next day to receive some more money. He warns Hossain not to bring anyone else.

APRIL 15

The three men meet and, as usual, have a long chat covering business, the population of Muslims in the local area, religion, etc. Malik hands over $10,000 to Hossain, and Hossain gives Malik a check for $2,000 to cover the next monthly payment. Malik asks him for $5,000 instead. Hossain shows some resistance to this demand, because he needs money to buy materials. But Malik insists that Hossain keep $5,000 (out of the $10,000 he has received just now) and just bring a cashier's check for $5,000 the next day. He explains that next time he will give Hossain another $15,000, to make the total payment $50,000, and then Hossain will return only $10,000 (out of $15,000), thus keeping $5,000 as a gift, according to the promise made in the beginning.

Malik tells Aref that next month he is going to Pakistan. He invites Aref to join him in his travel. Aref says that he cannot travel because he does not have a passport; he is a United Nations refugee. He says that if he had travel documents, he would have gone to visit his own country.

Then Hossain talks in detail about his mosque school (*madrasa*) in Bangladesh, to which he will donate the $5,000 of the "gift" money. Hossain praises this school by describing what a useful educational contribution it is making in the lives of forty to sixty poor students ranging in age from three to fifteen years. He writes a receipt: "I received $10,000 from Hay's Distribution," and gives it to Aref to witness. Aref and Hossain remind Malik again to come to the mosque whenever possible for prayers. When they leave, Malik calls Coll. "Yes sir…Yes sir…I did," he says.

APRIL 16

Malik calls Hossain, who says that the check is ready; it is in the cash register of his pizzeria, and Malik will be able to pick it up at his convenience.

APRIL 30

At 10:55 a.m., Malik calls Hossain and tells him that he will pick up the check from the pizzeria on May 4.

MAY 4

Malik comes to Hossain's pizzeria and picks up the check. Malik, Hossain, and Hossain's wife discuss various transactions and bank statements. Malik takes some of the statements, promising to return them later after making photocopies.

JUNE 1

Malik comes to Hossain's pizzeria, returns Hossain's bank statements, and tries to talk about fighting against non-believers. Hossain again talks about prayers and doing good deeds instead. Malik says that he wants to send his two boys to Madrasa Dar-ul-Uloom in Buffalo to study Islam. Hossain praises Malik for helping him financially and says that he prays for him. He tries to convince Malik to buy his pizzeria. Malik suggests that Hossain involve Aref as a partner in his pizza business.

After the meeting, Malik calls the FBI agent who is monitoring him and goes to meet him at Malik's "store" at 142 Central Avenue.

JUNE 9

In the evening, Malik, Hossain, and Aref meet in Malik's office inside his "store." This appointment was made two days earlier. Coll monitors the meeting from the street. Malik hands over $5,000 to Hossain to make his total payment $40,000, and tells Hossain he will give him another $10,000 next time to complete the $50,000, then Hossain can keep $5,000 of it for himself. After some discussion, they finally agree that at this point Hossain has to return $17K, after taking into account all of the previous payments.

Aref informs Malik that he is going to buy Hossain's pizzeria for $60,000, and together with Farouk (Aref's neighbor), they will run the place. A friend of Aref's from England, who has lived in Albany in the past, will pay $30,000 as a silent partner, making it a three-way partnership. The remaining $30,000 will be paid from the business on an installment basis. They discuss various details about operating this new business, and they chat about other topics. Aref invites Malik to become a partner in this new business to replace his friend from England. Malik asks for time to think about it.

JUNE 10

Aref and Farouk and another man from the mosque, Moosa, come to Malik's store. After an introduction, Farouk and Moosa wait in another room while Aref and Malik sit down at a desk in his office in the store and discuss a possible partnership of Aref's proposed business. Praising Aref, Malik states that an imam has an extremely honored place in his heart and it will be his pleasure to finance Aref's business. As usual, Malik talks fast, mixing up topics and confusing things: "If I could give Mosharref fifty thousand, I can certainly give you fifty thousand dollars, too, you know, I can, that is, that is not even a problem because my business comes from selling ammunitions, you know, chaudhrys, we do that, that's where the business money comes from…" He pronounces "ammunition" as "ammution" and pronounces "chaudhry" very fast, in a low voice. But Aref has never been told that the word "chaudhry" is a code word for missile, and so this conversation must be meaningless to him. He is not focusing on what Malik is selling (selling ammunition is legal regardless), but rather on whether he can get a loan from Malik to finance his business.

This was, of course, the FBI's ploy, because they feared that if Aref really understood that Malik was dealing with missiles, he would walk away and the sting operation would collapse. On the other hand, a recorded statement of this sort would give them enough material to manipulate and play with.

Malik continues in the same breath, "I, I import them, I sell them, and they give me money…" While saying this, he looks all around, so that Aref would get the impression that Malik is referring to the merchandise inside his store.

Of course, after transcribing the tape recording as a written transcript, the FBI would be able to claim that Malik was referring to ammunition and "chaudhrys." Thus they could also claim that Malik had discussed his weapons business with Aref, and that Aref understood what Malik's source of income was.

Malik says that his money could take up to forty-five days to come to him. Then they talk about various options for a possible partnership for the pizza business. Aref is about to rise from his chair to leave, when suddenly Malik jumps to another topic: "Remember that, uh, you remember that, uh, it was a month ago we wanted to, that chaudhry was going to New York to make that money, but it didn't use. So I, I, I, this, when it happens, I have to leave this country for two months, and then, you know, I'll just go away."

Malik had already mentioned to Aref on April 15 that he was planning to visit Pakistan. He had invited Aref to join him in that trip. It appears that the FBI had planned such statements quite a bit in advance, so that Aref's mind would go back to that earlier statement.

For this reason, Aref is not surprised by Malik's statement that he is going to leave the country. Aref seems to be tired of the long discussion and anxious to leave.

A: No problem, no problem, that's no problem.

M: So, and then, two month I, I have to go, because if they use the chaudhry on 142, then I have got a problem. And there is one more thing I wanted, because I, you told me one time that the FBI looks here, with you in front of the house and was there. But when I spoke with you never, we will have, get a problem, I'm thinking, you know.

A: In that case, I believe you are danger. [he means more dangerous in the sight of the FBI]

M: (laughs) What do you mean that?

A: (laughing) Because, because you look like danger, you know.

Aref stands up to leave.

M: No, I, I have to hide myself, you know.

A: Hiding yourself?

M: Because you said they come down here, they come down there, you know.

A: Told me they know me, you know, then they know I am doing nothing, I am just eating and drinking and talking about, nothing more. So I have not a problem.

M: Okay, okay. Then as long as, because...

Aref opens the door and enters the other room where Farouk and Moosa have been waiting. Malik follows him.

A: I have no problem.

M: ...I don't want to be a part of any of this because I do, I do a lot of...

A: I don't have any problem.

All four talk in the room for some time. The conversation on the tape is not audible.

JULY 1

Malik meets Hossain, who gives him a check for the month of July. They talk a great deal about a feature article a few months earlier in the local newspaper, the *Times Union*, about Hossain's life and his business. Hossain expresses his love for America and his appreciation of the success America has offered him. But Malik ridicules him for having this attitude. Posing once again as a violent jihadist and an anti-American supporter of terrorism, Malik criticizes Hossain and argues with him. Hossain fights back emotionally and shouts at Malik, saying that he is not bin Laden, he came to America because he saw some good in this land. Again and again Hossain emphasizes that Muslims must be nice to people and to the society for their own good and for the good of their religion. And again and again, Malik ridicules him and pushes him to hate non-believers.

Hossain tells Malik that he has informed the *madrasa* management in Bangladesh that somebody is going to donate $5,000 to the *madrasa*, and that upon hearing this their happiness had no bounds.

JULY 6

Malik and Hossain chat about the sale of his pizzeria. Hossain tells him that Aref has lost interest in buying it, and so far he has not found another buyer.

JULY 20

Malik calls Aref to inquire whether he can conduct a *Nikaah* (wedding) ceremony for his cousin, who may come to Albany with his bride from New York City for that purpose. (Malik talked about this wedding for the first time on February 24.) They discuss Aref's possible dates of availability for the ceremony. Aref tells Malik that he is thinking about making a short trip to Florida in the coming week. (The FBI had devised the whole fake wedding ceremony possibility just to find out if Aref was planning to remain in Albany or travel somewhere, because they were planning to break the case in the coming days.)

JULY 21

Malik is instructed to call Hossain and ask to meet with him in his store. Malik mentions to Hossain that he has heard that Aref will be traveling to Texas or California. He asks Hossain if he has heard about it. Hossain tells him he has no knowledge of it. He informs Malik that he has finished fixing up all his properties. He asks Malik to give him the $5,000 gift money so he can send it to the *madrasa* in Bangladesh with his mother-in-law, who is leaving on August 7. Hossain explains, "This will avoid any problem of transferring money through any banking channels. Transferring money by a Muslim is a big problem these days, you know."

JULY 22

Malik is instructed to invite Aref to his store, where they talk again about Malik's cousin's wedding, as well as several other topics. Malik offers to arrange a $99 ticket for Aref if and when he decides to travel to Florida.

JULY 27

Coll instructs Malik to meet Aref in his store and discuss a few topics. It seems that the FBI was exploring the possibility of involving Aref in yet another money-laundering scheme.

Mujib, a Muslim who knew Hossain and who was originally from Bangladesh but had British citizenship, had arrived in Albany two years before from London with his British wife and child. Mujib lived in Albany for several months. He wanted to take the bar exam and perhaps work in the field of law. At an auction, he bought, for $10,000, a rundown two-family house at 450 First Street in Albany to renovate and use as an investment property. In the end, he could not handle the renovation and decided to donate this property to As-Salam mosque. Because of the property's very poor condition and the bad neighborhood, the mosque was not interested in accepting the property. However, an arrangement was worked out, according to which Hossain would renovate the property and keep the net rental income for the first five years, and the mosque would pay for the repair materials. After five years, the mosque would keep 50% of the net rental income and the remainder would be donated to a religious charity in Bangladesh designated by Mujib. During his discussions with Malik, Hossain had mentioned that he was going to fix up this property next. Somehow it drew the attention of the FBI, and they became interested in Mujib and in the background of this house.

Malik asked Aref several questions about the whole situation during their discussions. It was the same Mujib who had recently sent Aref a check for $11,000, with a promise to send some more to help Aref buy a house in partnership with him. Since Aref could not find a suitable house to buy, he decided to invest Mujib's money in buying Hossain's pizzeria with another partner, Farouk. But that did not work out. Then Aref wanted to return part of the money to Mujib and keep part of it as a loan to himself. Unfortunately, Aref, who grew up with little understanding of modern banking and financial transactions, did not know how to do that. So he approached Malik as an experienced business tycoon to cash this check and send part of the money to Mujib.

Clearly the FBI thought: why not utilize this opportunity to entrap Aref in another money-laundering scheme?

The quality of the tape is extremely poor, and it is very difficult to hear, but what I figured out was this: Malik wants to transfer the money through *Hiwala* (an illegal underground money transfer method), at a commission of 4%, and justify the money as payment for some imaginary merchandise that Malik has bought from Aref and/or Mujib. And Malik will write a receipt for the purchase. Aref says, "No problem." But it is very clear that he is totally confused and does not understand what is going on. Malik, whose tongue normally works like scissors and who is capable of speaking many sentences in one breath (as he does during the main entrapment scheme), is somehow not able to talk much during this one. His words are lingering, and he speaks only in half-sentences.

For some reason, the FBI did not pursue this scheme any further; perhaps they were running out of time.

Aref mentions to Malik that he, along with his wife and children, are interested in visiting his wife's cousin's family in Seattle in a week or so, and he is trying hard to get some cheap tickets. Malik promises to look for some cheap online tickets.

JULY 28

Aref and Malik meet again in Malik's store and talk further about the money transfer to England and tickets to Seattle, among other things.

JULY 29

Malik calls Hossain and says that he will give him money on Sunday, August 1. He asks about the travel plans of Hossain's mother-in-law, who is planning to return to Bangladesh accompanied by two of Hossain's children. Hossain tells him that still nothing is finalized because her passport has to be renewed and tickets have to be purchased through an office in New York City. Malik offers to pick up her papers from there next week. Hossain tells him that someone else is already handling that.

JULY 31

Malik goes to Aref's house and informs him that he has not been able to arrange for the tickets to Seattle. He expresses his regret for this.

AUGUST 3

Malik comes to Hossain's pizzeria. Hossain tells him that he has not seen him for a few days and has been concerned because his (Malik's) telephone is also not working. Malik asks Hossain to meet him on August 5 with Aref to receive the last payment of $10,000 to complete the transaction. Hossain informs Malik that his mother-in-law, along with his two children, will be leaving for Bangladesh on August 7, and perhaps he and his wife will also go there after two months. He hopes his business will be sold by that time. If not, he will close it for couple of months.

AUGUST 5

During the night of August 4 and 5, the mosque is raided, Aref and Hossain are arrested, their houses are searched, and the sting operation becomes public.

Shamshad Ahmad, Ph.D., is founder and president of the Masjid As-Salam mosque. He was born in India, educated in Australia, and came to the U.S. in 1979. Since then, he has taught physics at the University at Albany/SUNY. During the Aref-Hossain trial and its aftermath, when many local Muslims were understandably too afraid to speak publicly, Dr. Ahmad worked with the Muslim Solidarity Committee (MSC) and others to bring out the truth of the case. In 2007, he received the Jim Perry Progressive Leadership Award from Citizen Action of the Capital District.